THE
CHINESE
PAKUA

THE CHINESE PAKUA

AN EXPOSÉ

Ong Hean-Tatt

Pelanduk
Publications

Published by
Pelanduk Publications (M) Sdn. Bhd.,
24 Jalan 20/16A, 46300 Petaling Jaya,
Selangor Darul Ehsan, Malaysia.

All correspondence to:
Pelanduk Publications (M) Sdn. Bhd.,
P.O. Box 8265, 46785 Kelana Jaya,
Selangor Darul Ehsan, Malaysia.

All rights reserved.
Copyright © 1991 Dr Ong Hean Tatt.
Cover design © 1991 Pelanduk Publications (M) Sdn. Bhd.
No part of this book may be reproduced in any form or by any
means without prior permission from the Publisher.

ISBN 967-978-371-5

1st printing 1991
2nd printing 1994
3rd printing 1996

Printed by
Eagle Trading Sdn. Bhd.

Dedicated to ... my ancestors who sought or worshipped the One True God through the ages ...

Table Of Contents

Preface *xiii*

PART A
The Auspiciousness Of The Pakua

1 Origins Of Pakua In Ancient China
- Pakua As The Symbol Of Chinese Culture — 3
- The Binary Secret Of Pakua — 7
- Evolution Of The Pakua Or I Ching — 10
- Purposes Of The I Ching — 14
- Emperor Wu-Wang Consulted The Great Plan Of Pakua — 16

2 Magic Square Of Pakua - alias Sigil Of Saturn
- The Lo-shu And Hou-T'u Magic Squares — 20
- Lo-Shu And Middle East Kabalic Sigil Of Saturn — 24
- Lo-Shu's Nine Numbers And Pakua's Eight — 26
- Common Origin Of Chinese-Hebrew Kabalic Magic Squares — 29

3 Mystery Of The Pakua In The Ganzhi System
- Introduction — 32
- The Celestial Stems And Terrestrial Branches — 32
- The Twenty Eight Constellations — 38
- Four Heraldic Animals Of The Ten Celestial Stems — 41
- The Twelve Zodiac Animals — 46
- Ganzhi Link Between Chinese And Hebrew Languages
  - And True Origin Of Alphabetic Language — 47
- The Ganzhi System Of Twenty-two Symbols Is The Same As
  The Hebrew Kabalic Twenty-two Letters — 48

4 The Four Heraldic Animals Of The Pakua
- The Four Heraldic Animals Of The Pakua — 50

	Four Heraldic Animals As Four Spirit Beings	52
	Four Heraldic Animals Are Biblical Angelic Four Beasts	54
	Kabalic Four Directions And Angelic Beasts	58
	The Pakua Is A Universal Gammadion	59
5	**Pakua As Recorder Of Environmental Change**	
	Family Of Eight Persons Represented In Pakua	61
	Changes In Sequences In I Ching Caused By Climatic Factors	64
	Order Of Mutual Production Changed To Mutual Conquest	65
	Relationship Of Later Heaven Array To Phases Of Solar Year	68
	"Li" For Fire Moved From East To South	68
	Memory Of Climatic Changes Caused By Flood	69
6	**The Esoteric Thunder Magic Of Pakua**	
	Five Elements As Basis Of Pakua Magic	70
	Demon Fighting And Black Magic	72
	The Pakua Thunder Magic	74
	Memorial Of Lao Chun's Ancient Battle Against Evil	77
	Link Of Lao Chun's Battle To Dragon Boat Festival	79
	Ancient Festival To Bring Rains	84
	The Five Poisonous Animals Pakua Exorcism Of Demons	88
	5th Day Of 5th Moon Is A Universal Festival	90
7	**The Five Emperors Pakua Talisman**	
	The Way Of The Talisman	91
	The "Five Emperors" Pakua	92
	Fortune Telling With Song Of The Four Emperors	95
	Talismans Of The "Five Emperors"	96

Part B
Role Of Pakua In The Development Of The History And Language Of Ancient China

8	**Debate Over Beginnings Of Ancient Chinese History**	
	Reliability Of Ancient Chinese History	107

Where Were The Hsia And Earlier Emperors?	111
Problems Of Personification And Euhemerisation	113
Historical Reality Of Hsia And Legendary Emperors	116
Evidence Of Ancestral Lineages And Details	118
Overlooking Evidence Of Migration Of Chinese Civilisation From Middle East	120

9 The Five Emperors And Three Dynasties

Dawn Of Ancient Chinese History	121
Theories Of Migration Of Chinese From Mesopotamia	121
The Legendary Emperors	125
The Legendary Hsia Dynasty (BC 2205-1740)	128
The Shang Dynasty (BC 1794 - 1120) And Chou Dynasty (BC156 1150-249)	130
The Three Sages	131
Historical Significance Of The Five Emperors Pakua	133

10 First World Emperor Fu-Hsi, Originator Of Pakua Alias "Lung" At The East

The First World Emperor, Fu-Hsi	138
The Works Of Fu-Hsi	139
The Identity Of Emperor Fu-Hsi, The First Man	143
Emperor Fu-Hsi The Azure "Lung" At The East	148
Shen-Nung The Divine Husbandman	152

11 Basis Of The Chinese Ideograms

Tradition Of Pakua As Origin Of Writings	155
Alphabetic Languages Arose After Pictorial-Ideographic Languages	157
Similarities In Structures Of Chinese And Sumerian-Egyptian Characters	158
Ideographs As Memorials Of Ancient Events	161
Similarities Of Sumerian And Chinese Words	162

12 Middle East Legends In Chinese Ideograms

Middle East Legends In Chinese Ideograms?	166

The Creation Ideograms	167
The Fall Of Man Ideograms	171
Original And Future States Of Man	172
The Flood Ideograms	175
Tower Of Babel Ideograms	182

13 The Gammadion-Pakua Ideograms

What Is The Gammadion?	185
Chinese Words Have The Gammadion	186
Pakua Has Roles In The Origin Of Languages	191
Path Of Righteousness In Chinese Ideograms	191

Part C
Role Of Pakua In Religion Of Ancient China

14 Pakua Is Original Ancient Religion Of China

Original Chinese Worship Had Very Few Gods	201
True Nature Of Original Ancestor Worships	204
Proliferation Of Deities During Eastern Chou Era	207
The Mother Goddess	209
Original Ancient Chinese Religion Is Just Pakua	211

15 The Worship Of Shang-Ti, The Supreme God

Shang-Ti And Tien	213
Ancient China Worship Only Shang-Ti	214
Initial Corruption Of The Shang-Ti Worship Extend To The Four Heraldic Animals	216
Worship Of Shang-Ti At Sacred Mountains	218
What Confucius Said About Gods	218
Lao-tzu Version Of Shang-Ti	222
Historical Evidence Of Chinkang Corruption Of Shang-Ti Worship	223
Conclusion: Return To Sole Worship Of Shang-Ti	224

16 Circumpolar Star System Of The Pakua

Circumpolar Chinese Astrology	225
Emphasis On Some Stars	227
God's Throne In Northern Heavens	231
Circumpolar Nature Of Chinese And Jewish Astrology And Their Old Babylonian Origin	233
The Link Between The Sphinx And The Pakua	235
The Abraham Factor	236
Under Whose Influence?	239

17 Pakua-Sigil Formations In Nine Emperor Gods

Introduction	240
The Nine Emperor Gods	241
Planetary Equivalent Of Nine Emperors God	243
The Three Stars-Emperor Gods	245
Pakua-Sigil Formations In The Nine Emperor Gods	247
Origins Of The Nine Emperor Gods	249
Tabernacle System Of The Temple Of Nine Emperor Gods	251

18 Chinese "Lung" At The East

Chinese "Lung" Is The Symbol Of China	256
The Chinese "Lung" Symbol	258
What Is Really The Biblical Dragon?	261
The Character For Chinese "Lung"	263
Original Western Version Of "Dragon"	265
"Lung" Different From "She" Serpent In Four Major Angelic Beasts	266
"Lung" As A Biblical Seraphim	268
Association Of Dragons With Chinese Emperors	271

Part D
A Synthesis

19 Pakua Link To Tower Of Babel

Attempt To Destroy Secrets Of God At Babel	277
Tower Of Babel Was A Perverted Astronomical Tower	278
New Testament Testify Of Evil At Tower Of Babel	282
Attack On God's Language Structure	283
Attack On God's Astrology Structure	284
Tower Of Babel, Alias Dragon Boat Festival, Was A Major Ancient Middle East War	285

20 Pakua As Essence Of Ancient Chinese Culture

Pakua, The Device Of Time And Direction	289
Major Historical Epochs Symbolised By The Pakua	290
Major Pakua Culture Links Between China And Middle East	292
Chinese Preserved Worship Of The One True God	297
Reference	299

PREFACE

This book is about the meanings of the enigmatic Chinese Pakua. It is written for both the laymen and scholars who seek to understand the Pakua. Many traditions about the Pakua would be described. But the book is a new and fresh journey where many secrets of the Pakua would be re-discovered.

The mystic Pakua, hanging over Chinese house-hold doors, has been a fascinating challenge to both Oriental and Western thinkers. In truth, the Pakua's mysterious multiple layers of significance would be better understood if studied in relation to the origins of the ancient history of China because the variants of the Pakua are intimately linked to the development of ancient Chinese history and culture.

There are universal similarities in the ancient religions, cultures and histories of Egypt, Assyria-Babylon, Greece, Rome and Teutonic lores. Many of these similarities are difficult to explain through mere chance. They indicate close communication links, diffusion of cultural symbolism and artifacts, that the similar roots of these ancient nations arise from the same basic sources. They support theories that the cradle of human civilisations may be in Mesopotamia, in agreement with the Middle East-Biblical legend of the Flood.

Are there evidence of similar diffusion of cultural symbolism and artifacts from the Middle East into China?

Although the recorded history of Chinese civilisation went back as far as 2943BC, archaeological evidence shows that the Chinese urban civilisation appeared quite suddenly in China around 1400BC The Chinese civilisation is comparatively newer to the older urban cultures of the Indus Valley (2350-1750BC) and the oldest urban Mesopotamia (3000-2300BC). Where were the civilised Chinese people before 1400BC? Some historians speculate that the Chinese originally came from Akkadia in Mesopotamia and reached China by passing through Khotan in Central Asia.

The Chinese culture stands out as one with the longest recorded historical continuity, dating back from modern times to the claimed 2943BC (the Biblical Flood occurred around 2348BC). Unless the Chinese ancient figures were figments of pure imagination there must be some connections between the ancient Chinese figures and events and ancient Middle East – Biblical or even western figures and events.

The book examines the problems of personification and euhemerisation in ancient Chinese history and takes the stand of anthromorphism. That is, legends are based on original historical figures.

The first section of this book, covering the initial seven chapters, highlights several auspicious aspects of the Pakua and presents a number of new revelations about the Pakua. The implications of some striking Pakua aspects on the development of the ancient Chinese civilisation should be noted, viz:

1 Why is the magic square sign of the Chinese mystic Pakua, including that of the Nine Emperor Gods version, so similar to the Hebrew Kabalic talismatic sign of the Sigil Of Saturn?

2 The 22 alphabets of the Hebrew script are alike to the 22 symbols of the Ganzhi system, composing of the Ten Celestial Stems and Twelve Terrestrial Branches.

This may be evidence of how alphabetic languages arose from pictorial languages.

3 The Four Heraldic Animals of the Pakua have universal parallels in other ancient Middle East cultures. They are also the same as the Biblical four angelic beasts around the throne of God.

One of the most striking revelations from the study is that the sacred Chinese "Lung" often misleadingly called the "dragon" is not the Biblical "serpent" symbolising Satan the Devil but rather is the holy winged-limbed "seraphim" of the Bible.

4 The Pakua's eight trigrams represent a eight members family; this is the eight members family of Noah.

Why is it the Chinese word for "boat" contains sub-characters depicting eight persons and a boat, reflecting the eight persons of Noah's family in the ark-boat which brought Noah and his family safely through the Biblical Deluge?

Several other Chinese ideograms describe other ancient Middle East-Biblical legends from Creation to the Flood and to the Tower of Babel!

The change of the Pakua array from the Early Heaven to Later Heaven reflects changes in climatic conditions. The changes include an indication that the Chinese people were originally in a place where the sun shines in from the East.

5 The Chinese Pakua's astrology differs from Western elliptical astrology in being circumpolar which also characterises the Hebrew-Biblical stars system.

6 The Pakua is a memory of the Chinese Imperial worship of the imageless Supreme God, Shang-Ti. The Chinese historical records show that Shang-Ti was

the only deity worshipped from ancient times until 500BC. This is very different from the Sun God Earth-Mother-Goddess worships of other nations. The Chinese preserve a monotheistic worship more akin with the monotheism of the Hebrews.

Many of these symbolism of the Chinese Pakua thus find close kinship with the Middle East, especially Hebrew culture.

The Pakua and the Ganzhi system are Chinese devices to divide and categorise time and direction. Analysis of major features of ancient Chinese history, religion and culture, in two sections of Chapters 8 to 18, reveal that many forms of the Pakua symbolism are actually time devices to record major epochs in the ancient history of China!

Several aspects of the Pakua are references of Middle East – Biblical legends of Noah's family as well as the nine antediluvian patriarchs from Adam to Lamech the father of Noah. The ancient Chinese knew who Adam and Noah were and gave them prominent places in the ancient Chinese history as the first and second world emperors Fu-Hsi and Shen-Nung. The "Five Emperors" Pakua symbol is a memorial of the time when Emperor Huang-Ti separated the races to the Four Directions.

Apparently, the legendary Nimrod tried to destroy the original God's inspired astrology and pictorial language with a perverted zodiac-astrology and introduction of the alphabetic language. But the Chinese left Mesopotamia to escape the Babylonian idolatry, preserving the ancient astrology, pictorial language and the worship of Shang-Ti the One True God. The Chinese preserved this Tower of Babel legend in the Dragon Boat Festival, a memorial of how "Golden Lung" Emperor Huang-Ti acted against the Serpent Chih You (the

Chinese memory of Nimrod) to release water to the people.

Significant cultural aspects did diffuse, through the migration of the Chinese people from the West, from ancient Middle East into China.

The Pakua symbolism indicates that the ancient Chinese, like the ancient Hebrews, had a monotheistic religion. The Chinese worshipped the One True God as Shang-Ti the Supreme God until around 500BC when political motivations introduced deviant polytheism. The Pakua is a memorial that the original religion of mankind involves only the worship of the One True God, who is surrounded by His four major angels.

This book "The Chinese Pakua" should help to encourage Chinese to reexamine their Chinese culture, for there is much therein, which, being from the True God, are good and pure.

❂ PART A ❂
THE AUSPICIOUSNESS OF THE PAKUA

This first section describes the many fascinating significance of the Pakua Or Eight Diagrams throughout the Chinese culture. It is linked to the Ganzhi system, The Chinese device to categorise cyclic changes in time and direction. The Pakua is represented by the Four Heraldic Animals of the Four Cardinal Points. It permeates the philosophy and arts of the I Ching, Feng-Shui, Lo-Pan, and the Chinese Almanac, the Tong-Shu.

The talismatic and mystical uses of the Pakua take several forms. These range from the magic squares of the Lo-Shu, Hou-T'u to the talismans of the Five Elements and the esoteric Taoist Thunder Magic.

You will find that these many auspiciousness of the Pakua have universal significance in other ancient cultures, reinforcing the Chinese tradition of the immense importance of the Pakua.

1. Origins Of Pakua In Ancient China
2. Magic Square Of Pakua - Alias Sigil Of Saturn
3. Mystery Of The Pakua In The Ganzhi System
4. The Four Heraldic Animals Of The Pakua
5. Pakua As Recorder Of Environmental Change
6. The Esoteric Thunder Magic Of Pakua
7. The Five Emperors Pakua Talisman

1

ORIGINS OF PAKUA IN ANCIENT CHINA

... the abstruse work known as the "Canon of Changes", the most venerated and least understood of the Chinese classics... (William, 1931 p.121-123)

■ Pakua As Symbol Of Chinese Culture

Despite a long tradition of intensive research and studies, including by the great sage Confucius, the Pakua remains an intriguing mystery. Confucius wished that he had another fifty years to study the secrets of the Pakua of the I Ching.

The Pakua is the powerful symbol of Chinese culture and magic. Significant sectors of the Chinese culture, astrology-divination, and philosophy-religion are infused with the unique symbol of the Eight Diagrams or Pakua (Figure 1.1). The circular eight-sided diagram, often with a central mirror (or Yin-yang symbol) and the figure of Taoist Pope Chang Tao-Ling riding a tiger, is commonly hung over the household main door by the Chinese to ward off evil (Figure 1.2). "Pa" means "eight" and "kua" means "diagram," the later being a trigram of three lines which may or may not be broken – hence, Pakua means "Eight Diagrams" or "eight sets of trigrams."

The Pakua is a cyclic symbol with several layers of significance. It is most associated with the eight trigrams arranged to the four cardinal points as well as the four corners, thereby covering the eight points of the compass

4 THE CHINESE PAKUA

Figure 1.1 The Pakua — *Auspicious symbol of good fortune, happiness and longevity.*

Figure 1.2   Pakua Charm with Chang Tao-Ling riding the Tiger.

6 THE CHINESE PAKUA

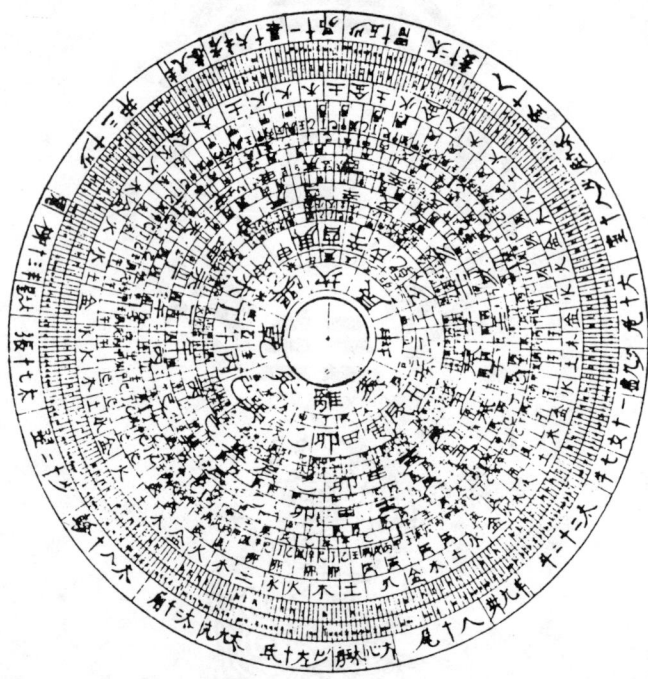

Figure 1.3 The several rings of the Lo-Pan, the plate used in the Chinese geomantric art of Feng-Shui. The several rings of the Lo-Pan are actually elements of the Ganzhi system.

N,W,S,E and NE,NW,SW,SE. Interior to this eight trigrams is the inner circle of the four heraldic supernatural animals (usually Snake, Tiger, Phoenix, "Lung" corresponding to the cardinal points of N, W, S, E) and the innermost symbol of the Yin-Yang, a half white-half black spiral symbol. Outside the Pakua's eight trigrams would be arranged larger circles like the twelve zodiacal Jupiter-cycle animals and the twenty-eight lunar constellations. These cyclic signs are the basis of the Chinese Ganzhi system and also the geomantric art of Feng-Shui and its associated device the Lo-Pan (Figure 1.3).

The Chinese classic I Ching (Book of Changes) is deeply rooted in the Pakua. In the I Ching the eight trigrams would be paired against each other into 64 possible combinations of six lines (Figure 1.4) Both the I Ching and the Pakua, when studied superficially, are often misused in divination and magical rites. But when studied in depth, the I Ching and Pakua are said to contain very profound wisdom.

Only one other symbol other than the Pakua reflects the essence of Chinese culture – the Chinese "Lung" alias the "dragon." Even so, as we shall see, the "Lung" itself derives its auspiciousness from its position within the Pakua.

■ The Binary Secret Of Pakua

The trigrams and hexagrams of the I Ching are arranged in two sequences, a more ancient Fu-Hsi or Early Heaven Array and a later King Wen or Later Heaven Array (Figures 1.4, 1.5). The Fu-Hsi Array of hexagrams is the very arrangement which led the seventeenth century father of calculus, Gottfried Wilhelm Leibnitz, to discover the binary system.

Father Joachin Bouvet, a Jesuit priest in China, showed this sequence to Leibnitz. Leibnitz was astonished to find that when taking 0 for each solid line and 1 for each broken line and reading upwards on each of the hexagrams gave

8 THE CHINESE PAKUA

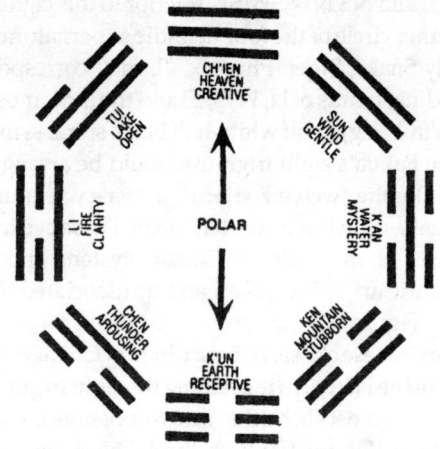

A. *Sequence of Earlier Heaven or Primal Arrangement or Fu Hsi Arrangement*

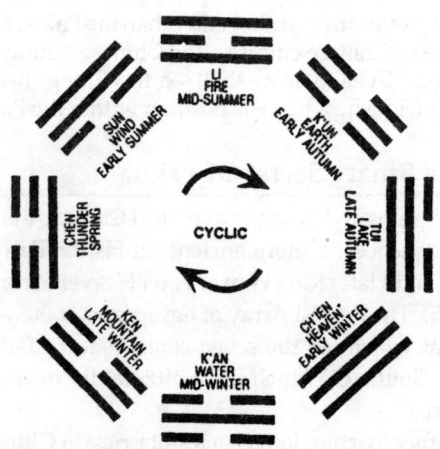

B. *Sequence of Later Heaven or Inner-World Arrangement or King Wen Arrangement.*

Figure 1.4 *The Eight Diagrams*

CHAPTER 1 **ORIGINS OF PAKUA** 9

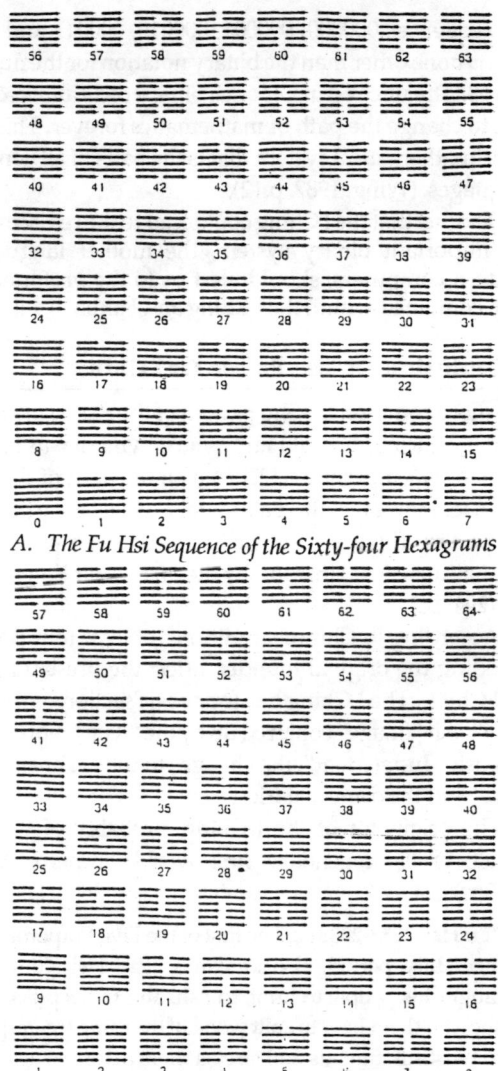

A. The Fu Hsi Sequence of the Sixty-four Hexagrams

B. The King Wen Sequence of the Sixty-four Hexagrams.

Figure 1.5 The 64 Hexagrams of the I Ching

the sequences 000000, 000001, 000010, 000011 and so on. This is none other than the binary notation for the numbers 0 to 63! The uncovering of such binary code allowed Leibnitz to change the path of mathematics forever. This is the same mathematical system that is the basis of all computer languages. (Wing, 1982. p.12).

The fact that the I Ching could lead to the rediscovery of the important binary system, the mother language of modern computers, should alert us to the profound wisdom contained within the I Ching and Pakua.

■ Evolution Of The Pakua Or I Ching

The more common Lo-Shu pattern of the Pakua originated from the ancient "Great Plan" whose symbol was first discovered by Emperor Yu (2205BC) on the back of the Great Tortoise. However, the Pakua, following an earlier Hou-T'u pattern (Figure 1.6), is discovered even earlier on a dragon-horse (the Unicorn) by the first world Emperor Fu-Hsi (2943BC).

According to Chinese traditions, at least four persons, including the original founder, affect the present form of the I Ching. The I Ching has four basic sections – the basic "Kua", the "Image" conjured up by the "Kua" representing the basic "Judgement", the changes to the six lines of each "Kua" and the commentaries.

The originator of the I Ching, probably of the basic "Kua", is the legendary first world Emperor Fu-Hsi (2953BC):

"**Fu Hsi, 2953-2838BC**: The first of the Five Emperors of the legendary period, also known as Pao Hsi Kung ... He taught his people to hunt, to fish, and to keep flocks. He showed them how to split wood of the t'ung tree, and how to twist silk threads and stretch them across so as to form crude musical instruments. From the markings on the back of a tortoise he is said to have constructed the Eight

CHAPTER 1 **ORIGINS OF PAKUA** 11

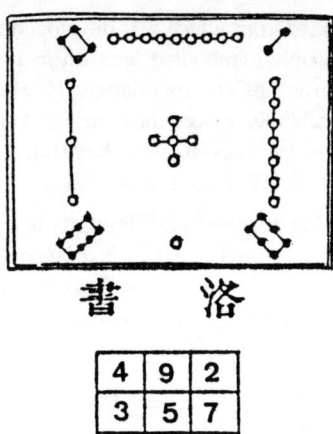

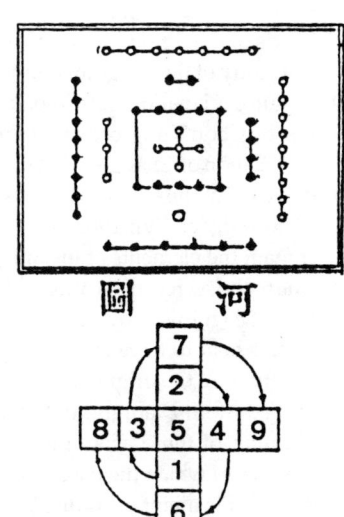

Figure 1.6 The Lo-Shu and Hou T'u of the Pakua.

Diagrams or series of lines from which was developed a whole system of philosophy, embodied later on in the mysterious work known as the Canon of Changes. He also invented some kind of calender, placed the marriage contract upon a proper basis, and is even said to have taught mankind to cook their food." (William 1931, p.167)

After Fu-Hsi, the I Ching received additions made by King Wen the founder of the Chou dynasty (who placed in the "Judgement" of each "Kua") and his son Duke Chou around 1120BC (who appeared to be responsible for the changes to the lines of the "Kua."):

Eight Diagrams: The Pa Kua, or Eight Diagrams, are represented by an arrangement of certain cabalistic signs consisting of various combinations of straight lines arranged in a circle, said to have been evolved from the markings on the shell of a tortoise by the legendary Emperor Fu Hsi, 2852BC. ... Wen Wang, 1231-1135BC, the founder of the Chou dynasty, while undergoing imprisonment at the hands of the tyrant Emperor Chou Hsin, devoted himself to a study of the Diagrams, and appended to each of them certain explanations ... further observations ... attributed to his son Chou Kung, constitute the abstruse work known as the "Canon of Changes", the most venerated and least understood of the Chinese classics, serving as a basis for the philosophy of divination and geomancy, and supposed to contain the elements of metaphysical knowledge and the clue to the secrets of creation. ... "In addition to the series of Eight Diagrams above, Fu Hsi, or some one of his successors, is held to have enlarged the basis of calculations by multiplying the original number eight-fold, thus creating the Sixty-four Diagrams or Hexagrams ... A six-fold multiplication of these again gives ... 384 ... , completing the number to which the diagrams are practically carried, although it is maintained that by a further process of multiplication a series of 16,777,216 different forms may be produced." (William, 1931 pp.121-123)

The fourth and final person recognised as affecting the contents, especially commentaries, of the I Ching was Confucius around 550BC:

> In Chinese literatures four holy men are cited as the authors of the Book of Changes, namely Fu Hsi, King Wen, the Duke of Chou and Confucius. Fu Hsi ... is designated as the inventor of the linear signs of the Book of Changes means that they have been held to be of such antiquity that they antedate historical memory. Moreover the eight trigrams have names that do not occur in any connection in the Chinese language, and because of this they have even been thought to be of foreign origin ... The eight trigrams are found occurring in various combinations at a very early date. ... the present collection of sixty-four hexagrams origin-ated with King Wen, progenitor of the Chou dynasty. He is said to have added brief judgements to the hexagrams during his imprisonment at the hands of the tyrant Chou Sin. The text pertaining to the individual lines originated with his son, the Duke of Chou. This was the status of the book at the time Confucius came upon it. In his old age he gave it intensive study, and it is highly probable that the Commentary on the Decision (T'uan Chuan) is his work. The Commentary on the Images also goes back to him. A third treatise, a very valuable and detailed commentary on the individual lines compiled by his pupils or their successors, in the form of questions and answers, survives only in fragments ... (Wilhelm, 1951 pp.lviii-lix).

The primary eight trigrams, named in a sequence of pairs to form 64 possible combinations or "Kua", go back to the first world Emperor Fu-Hsi, 2943BC. These 64 "Kua" are all which form the original secrets of the Pakua – the interpretations of the "Image" or "Judgement", changes to the lines, and the commentaries are all added much later ... and may not even be perfect interpretations. Just how did King

Wen in 1120BC know how to interpret the original 64 "Kua"? There must have been some oral traditions.

Already, students of the Pakua have found even the later additions by King Wen, Duke Chou and Confucius difficult enough to understand – how much more so are the original deceptively simple 64 "Kua"s.

Wilhelm (1951) notes that the origin of the Pakua may be from outside ancient China:

> Fu Hsi ... is designated as the inventor of the linear signs of the Book of Changes means that they have been held to be of such antiquity that they antedate historical memory. Moreover the eight trigrams have names that do not occur in any connection in the Chinese language, and because of this they have even been thought to be of foreign origin. ... (Wilhelm, 1951 pp.lviii-lix).

■ Purposes Of The I Ching

This enigmatic text of I Ching was compiled by its original founder for specific purposes, some of which we could only today guess at. Two collections belonging to antiquity are known: first, the Book of Changes of the Hsia dynasty, called Lien Shan, which is said to have begun with the hexagram Ken, Keeping Still, mountain; second, the Book of Changes dating from the Shang dynasty, entitled Kuei Ts'ang, which began with the hexagram K'un, The Receptive (Wilhelm, 1951 p.lviii-lix). The difference in purposes of these versions of the I Ching are ill-understood.

The I Ching is, first of all, a divinatory device (Wilhelm, 1951):

- The original purpose of the hexagrams was to consult destiny (p.262)
- ... the Book of Change; hence it enables us to penetrate and understand the movements of the light and the dark, of life and death, of gods and demons. This knowledge makes

possible mastery over fate, because fate can be shaped if its laws are known (p.296)

- that when "someone, on being told the auguries for the future, did not let the matter rest there but asked "What am I to do?" the book of divination had to become a book of wisdom." (p.liii)

However, the I Ching is also meant to be a book of wisdom and philosophy:

1. The master said: Whosoever know the Tao of the changes and transformations, knows the action of the gods (Wilhelm, 1951. p.313)

2. (Wilhelm, 1951. pp.328-329) Chapter II. History of Civilisation: When in early antiquity Pao Hsi [same as Fu Hsi] ruled the world he looked upward and contemplated the images in the heavens; he looked downward and contemplated the patterns on earth. He contemplated the markings of birds and beasts and the adaptations to the regions. He proceeded directly from himself and indirectly from objects. Thus he invented the eight trigrams in order to enter into connection with the virtues of the light of the gods and to regulate the conditions of all beings.

3. The Pai Hu T'ung [written in the Han period by Pan Ku, AD32-92] describes the primitive condition of human society as follows: In the beginning there was as yet no moral nor social order. Men knew their mothers only, not their fathers. When hungry they searched for food; when satisfied they threw away the remnants. They devoured their food hide and hair, drank the blood, and clad themselves in skins and rushes. Then came Fu Hsi and looked upward and comtemplated the images in the heavens, and looked downward and contemplated the occurrences on earth. He united man and wife, regulated the five stages of change, and laid down the laws of humanity. He devised the eight trigrams, in order to gain mastery over the world.

4. "From the markings on the back of a tortoise he is said to have constructed the Eight Diagrams or series of lines from which was developed a whole system of philosophy, embodied later on in the mysterious work known as the Canon of Changes." (William 1931, p.167)

5. "... the abstruse work known as the "Canon of Changes", the most venerated and least understood of the Chinese classics, serving as a basis for the philosophy of divination and geomancy, and supposed to contain the elements of metaphysical knowledge and the clue to the secrets of creation" (William, 1931 p.121-123)

6. Gorn (1904) also noted that the great Yu used the I Ching to help regulate the floods that threaten the Chinese people.

The I Ching wisdom emphasises that the world composes of divine, spirit and the natural realms. The ancient purposes of the I Ching are to keep track of the spiritual as well as natural realms in order to regulate the conditions of all spiritual and natural beings and gain mastery over the world.

The I Ching has an ultimate divine goal:

Whatever goes beyond this indeed transcends all knowledge. When a man comprehends the divine and understands the transformations, he lifts his nature to the level of the miraculous (Wilhelm 1951 p.338)

The Pakua embraces an active positive philoso-phy. It is not a fatalistic passive philosphy. For, there is an undercurrent profound exhortation to all practitioners who seek the wisdom of the Pakua – Destiny can be changed, provided you know the laws of Destiny.

■ Emperor Wu-wang Consulted The Pakua Great Plan

Several books have been written on how to use the Pakua of the I Ching (e.g. Wilhelm, 1951; Wing, 1982). Interested readers should refer to these texts for more details on the consultation of the "Kua"s.

The popular use of the Pakua and I Ching for divination could be attributed to Emperor Wu-Wang usage of the "Great Plan" discovered by Emperor Yu. After some years as co-ruler with Shun, Yu succeeded Emperor Shun as emperor in 2205BC. When Yu was draining the Lo river into the Hwang-Ho, he uncovered a text called the "Great Plan" which was supposed to contain the principles of the Tao. This "Great Plan" was consulted through a divination method known as the Tortoise and reeds.

During the Warring Nations in the dying years of the Chou dynasty, the great Chinese sage Confucius or Kong Fu Tse, around 500BC, compiled and edited a series of more ancient Chinese texts, besides expounding his own ideas, of which his Analects of Confucius is famous. Many of them were lost when in 220BC Emperor Shih Huang-Ti (builder of the Great Wall of China) of the short Chin dynasty ordered the Burning of Books in his persecution and massacres of the Chinese philoso-phers, particularly Confucius. But in 140BC, Kung Wang, a prince of Lu related to Confucius, was demolishing a former building of Confucius when a broken wall revealed a hidden collection of books written in the ancient characters.

One of these books is the Shu King or Book of History (Gorn 1904) (another book is the I Ching or Book of Changes which will have great significance in our discussions – the I Ching was one of the few books which escaped the great Burning of Books ordered by Emperor Shih Huang-Ti around 220BC). The original book is supposed to have one hundred sections, but only fifty-seven survived and form the basic of all modern texts of the Shu King. Although scholars have regarded certain sections as spurious (Creel, 1938), this Shu King is valuable as it contains the history of

China from 2355BC to the end of the reign of Pin Wang in 719BC.

The Shang dynasty (1794 to 1120BC) was coming to an end. Emperor Chow Hsin the last Shang emperor was killed and Wu-Wang started the new Chou dynasty.

Within this Shu King (Gorn, 1904. p.160) is a record of how Emperor Wu-Wang, the founder of the Chou dynasty, consulted Ki-Tse, the former Minister of Instruction of the former Shang dynasty about how to govern his newly acquired nation. Ki-Tse (who, reputedly, was later to be allowed by the emperor to leave China to form the nation of Korea) told the emperor that he heard that in ancient days, Kwan, trying to control the overwhelming flood waters, wrongly disposed of the five factors. The Supreme Ruler was angered and did not communicate to him the "Great Plan" of the nine classifications. The invaluable principles were thus lost, and Kwan therefore was driven into exile. Yu, the son of Kwan, was then appointed to succeed him, and Heaven revealed to Yu the Great Plan of the nine classifications and the immutable principles of right government were regulated."

Emperor Wu-Wang was not unfamiliar with the aspects of the "Great Plan" because he had studied it before. The Emperor gained further insights through humbly seeking the advice of the ex-Minister Ki-Tse. This "Great Plan" composes of Five Factors (which are the five elements of water, fire, wood, metal and earth) and the Eight Regulators (the eight ministries in the government). The nine classifications propose how the Five Factors and Eight Regulators should be applied. The Emperor was urged to act in three-fold consultation with the nobles, the people and the divination method of the Tortoise and reeds, with the status of planned actions determined as follows:

CHAPTER 1 ORIGINS OF PAKUA

King Ruler	Nobles Government	People	Reeds	Tortoise	Status
+	+	+	+	+	Fortunate
+	−	−	+	+	Fortunate
−	+	−	+	+	Good
−	−	+	+	+	Good
+	−	−	−	+	Internally good Externally bad
+	+	+	−	−	Unfortunate

A disagreement of the opinions of the king, nobles and people with the opinion of the Tortoise broods no good – i.e. the advice of the "Great Plan" of the Tortoise was considered supreme in determining the status of any plan of actions. While the divination may appear mystical, there is good sense in leaders consulting various factors including the people before implementing a plan.

The original method(s) of using the "Great Plan" may have been lost and may not be as chancy as seen in today's divination method using the Pakua. Today's version is only the modern remnant of the ancient "Great Plan."

Although fascinating, the I Ching and Pakua are very difficult to comprehend. Despite considerable research, no one could claim to know effectively the secrets and original mechanisms of the Pakua or I Ching. Some practitioners believe that to comprehend the Pakua or I Ching what may be required is a spiritual and psychic approach to utilise the "Great Plan".

2

MAGIC SQUARE OF PAKUA – alias SIGIL Of SATURN

Huang-Ti invented the magic squares to counter and slay the Black Serpent...

■ The Lo-Shu And Hou-T'u Magic Squares

The Shu King mentions that Emperor Yu, 2205BC, marked the back of the Great Tortoise with nine numbers corresponding to the nine classifications to form the Lo-Shu arrangement of the Eight Diagrams or Pakua (Figure 2.1.a).

The Lo-Shu or Later Heaven Array pattern, also known as the "Lo River Writing" and written in red, has a nine-numbers arrangement as seen in Figure 1.6 (also Figures 2.1, 2.2) which corresponds to the typical Pakua of eight trigrams around the ninth central point. The Lo-Shu thus forms what is known as a Magic Square of a 3 x 3 table, where the numbers, added up along any diagonal, line or column, make 15. This is also a swastika or cross form.

The Early Heaven Array of the Pakua is associated with Hou-T'u (Figure 1.6) which is said to be a gift to Fu-Hsi (2943BC) on a dragon-horse which came out of the Yellow River. It is usually written in green. When the odd numbers or even numbers are added up, without considering the central 5, they make 20.

The Lo-Shu pattern is more well known than the Hou-T'u pattern. It forms the basis of several Chinese culture symbolism revolving around the Four Heraldic Animals and the Five Elements. Its profound secrets are also the

CHAPTER 2 **MAGIC SQUARE OF PAKUA** 21

B. *The Lo River Plan*

A. *The Great Tortoise Marking*

4	9	2
3	5	7
8	1	6

C. *Magic Square of 15*

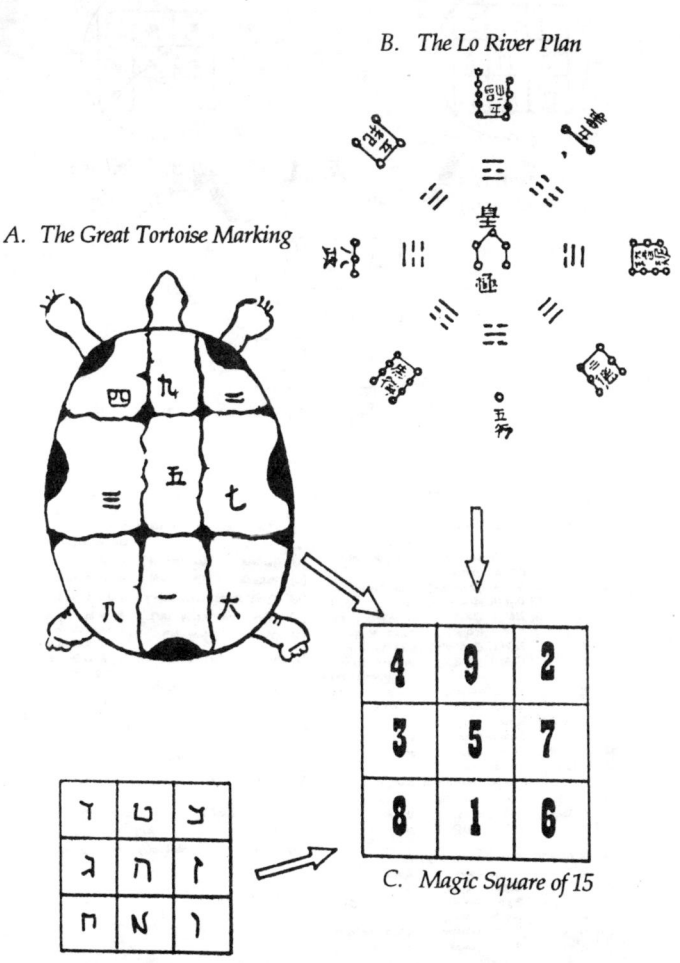

D. *Hebrew Talisman of Saturn (more details in Figure 2.2)*

Figure 2.1 Similarities of Chinese Eight Diagrams to Hebrew Talisman of Saturn

22 THE CHINESE PAKUA

A. Arrangement of first nine alphabets.

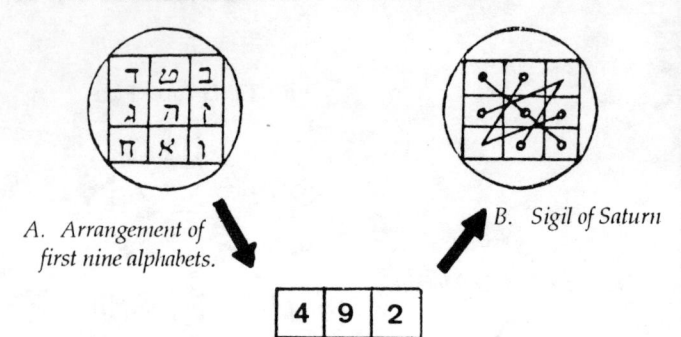

B. Sigil of Saturn

4	9	2
3	5	7
8	1	6

C. Magic Square of 15

D. Hebrew Articulation

2. The letters are as follows:

No.	Form.	Name.	Transliteration and Power.
1.	א	'Aleph (aw'-lef)	' unappreciable
2.	ב	Bâyth (bayth)	b
3.	ג	Gîymel (ghee'-mel)	g hard = γ
4.	ד	Dâleth (daw'-leth)	d [cent
5.	ה	Hê' (hay)	h, often quies-
6.	ו	Vâv (vawv)	v, or w quies-
7.	ז	Zayin (zah'-yin)	z, as in seal [cent
8.	ח	Chêyth (khayth)	German ch = χ [(nearly kh)
9.	ט	Têyth (tayth)	t = ת [cent
10.	י	Yôwd (yode)	y, often quies-
11.	כ, final ך	Kaph (caf)	k = ק
12.	ל	Lâmed (law'-med)	l
13.	מ, final ם	Mêm (mame)	m
14.	נ, final ן	Nûwn (noon)	n
15.	ס	Çâmek (saw'-mek)	ç = s sharp = שׂ
16.	ע	'Ayin (ah'-yin)	' peculiar
17.	פ, final ף	Phê' (/ay)	ph = f = ף
	פ	Pê' (pay)	p
18.	צ, final ץ	Tsâddêy (tsaw-day')	ts
19.	ק	Qôwph (cofe)	q = k = כ
20.	ר	Rêysh (raysh)	r
21.	שׁ	Sîyn (seen)	s sharp = ס = ç
	שׂ	Shîyn (sheen)	sh
22.	ת	Thâv (thawv)	th, as in THIN
	ת	Tâv (tawv)	t = ט = t [= ת

3. The vowel-points are the following:

Form.	Name.	Representation and Power.
(ָ)	Qâmêts (caw-mates')	â, as in all
(ַ)	Pattach (pat'-takh)	a, as in man, (/är)
(ֲ)	Sh°vâ'-Pattach (she-vaw' pat'-takh)	ă, as in hat
(ֵ)	Tsêrêy (tsay-ray')	ê, as in they = y
(ֶ)	Çĕgôwl (seg-ole')	e, as in their / ĕ, as in men = e
(ֱ)	Sh°vâ'-Çĕgôwl (she-vaw' seg-ole')	ĕ, as in met
(ְ)	Sh°vâ' †	(she-vaw') { * obscure, as in [average / silent, as e in made / ƒ, as in machine ‡ / [(misery, hĭf)
(ִ)	Chîyrĭq (khee'-rĭk)	ĭ, as in suppliant, [(misery, hĭf)
(ֹ)	Chôwlem §	(cho'-lem)	ô, as in no = o
(ָ)	Short Qâmêts ‖		o, as in nor = o

(ֳ)	Sh°vâ'-Qâmêts (she-vaw' caw-mates')	ŏ, as in not
(ּ)	Shûwrĕq (shoo-rake')	û, as in cruel
(ֻ)	Qĭbbûts *	(kĭb'-boots)	u, as in full, rüde

Figure 2.2 The Hebrew Talisman of Saturn — The first nine alphabets (A) are equivalent to the nine numbers (D) as arranged in (C). Connecting a line from 1 to 9 gives the Sigil of Saturn (B)

CHAPTER 2 **MAGIC SQUARE OF PAKUA** 23

foundation of powerful Taoist magic. The mystical rituals of Taoist magic are synchronised with the sequences of the numbers within the Lo-Shu Magic Squares.

This Lo-Shu nine numbers plan and its sister chart the Hou-T'u were already part of scholarly study in the later Han dynasty, AD 23-220 (Saso, 1978):

- The Lo-Shu and Hou-T'u were known earlier in the Taoist Wei Apocrypha during the usurper Wang Mang's time of AD 9-23 (Saso, 1978; Needham, 1959. p.56). Taoism, however, went back even further to the time of the Taoist Chang Liang who aided Liu Pang to start the Han dynasty in 206BC.

- The Lo-Shu and Hou-T'u arrangements were also alluded to in the Ta Chuan commentary on the I Ching (Wilhelm, 1951. pp.305-306) and the Ta Chuan was mentioned by the early Han historian Ssuma Chien, 145-86BC (Wilhelm 1951, p.258). The I Ching was compiled by Confucius, 551-478BC. It is evident that when Confucius also compiled the Shu King, the "Great Plan" and "Tortoise" found by Emperor Yu of 2207-2157BC referred therein was the same as the Hou-T'u–Lo-Shu arrangements.

- The Han historian Ssuma Chien also recorded that when the third emperor of the Chou dynasty ascended the throne, circa 1067BC, the treasures of the court displayed in the ascension ceremony included the River Scheme, the Hou-T'u (Wu, 1982. p.52).

- The story of the Hou-T'u being the gift on a dragon-horse from the Yellow River and the Lo-Shu being a gift on a turtle from the River Lo was older than the –5th century as it was mentioned in the Lun Yu (Conversations and Discourses of Confucius) and the Shu King (Needham, 1959. p.56). It was also mentioned in the Mo Tzu beginning of the 4th century. In the end of the 4th century it was mentioned in Chuang Tzu where the nine numbers were first associated with the diagrams, speaking of the nine elements in the Lo-Shu (Needham, 1959. p.56).

■ Lo-Shu And Middle East Kabalic Sigil Of Saturn

Remarkably, this Chinese Lo-Shu arrangement of nine numbers corresponds exactly to the Hebrew Kabalic talisman of the planet Saturn (Figures 2.1.d, 2.2) ruled by the angel "Cassiel" presiding over intelligence of all secret things.

The Hebrew Talisman of Saturn uses the first nine alphabets of the Hebrew language to correspond with the first nine numbers (Figure 2.2). The symbols (or rather "writings") on the Talisman of Saturn are the first nine Hebrew alphabets aleph, beyth, giymel, daleth, he, vav, zayin, cheyth and teyth (Figures 2.1.d, 2.2). The 3 figures along any direction add up to 15. Both the Chinese "Great Plan" and the Hebrew Talisman of Saturn are this same "Magic Square of 15"! (Figures 2.1, 2.2).

If the numbers of the Great Tortoise are connected by a single line starting from 1 and ending with the 9, the symbol created is the sign of the Hebrew Kabalic Sigil of Saturn! (Figures 2.1, 2.2 – "sigil" meaning "geometric diagram or geometry"). The Sigil of Saturn is formed by drawing a line from the first alphabet to the ninth alphabet and omitting the connections between the third-fourth and sixth-seventh alphabets.

This Sigil of Saturn is also the very symbol of the Chinese Nine Emperor Gods.

The Sigil of Saturn is the simplest of the Middle East–Hebrew Kabalic planetary tables (Shumaker, 1972. p.143; King, 1975. p.104) which form part of the Hermetic doctrines attributed to Hermes Trimegistus (Shumaker, 1972. pp.201-249). Hermes was also known as Mercury to the Greek and Thoth to the Egyptians (Shumaker, 1972. p.202) and Enoch the seventh patriarch in the Bible (Seiss,

CHAPTER 2 **MAGIC SQUARE OF PAKUA** 25

1972. pp.22,150-151). Shumaker (1972, p.205) notes that this Hermetic doctrine and the Kabala was a tradition entrusted to Moses at Mount Sinai.

These planetary tables consist of squares of numbers so arranged that addition downward, across and diagonally produces identical sums. Figure 2.3 shows King's illustration of the 3 x 3, 4x 4 and 5 x 5 squares for Saturn, Jupiter and Mars as well as Shumaker's illustration of a 6 x 6 square for the Sun.

This Sigil of Saturn is a Hebrew talisman to help in childbirth, confer safety and power and cause request made of princes and other men of authority to be granted (Shumaker, 1972. p.143). Similarly, just as the Hebrew Sigil of Saturn confers safety, the Chinese Pakua is a universal Chinese talisman to ward off evil influences (Dennys, 1968. p.50).

The method to consult the "Great Plan" is through the use of thirty six sticks of the reed. Divination by reeds (of rods, staff or even arrows) is of very ancient origin and is also mentioned in the Hebrew Scriptures:

> My people ask counsel at their stocks, and their staff declareth unto them ... – Hosea 4.12

> ..to use divination: he made his arrows bright, he consulted with images, he looked in the liver. – Ezekial 21:21

This measurement with reeds or rods also is a significant but ill-understood feature of the Hebrew Temple system prominent in at least two great Biblical books of prophecies, viz the Old Testament Ezekial and the New Testament Revelation:

> And he brought me thither and behold there was a man, whose appearance was like the appearance of brass with a line of flax in his hand and a measuring reed; and he stood in the gate ... and in the man's hand a measuring reed of six

cubits long by the cubit and an hand breadth; so that he measured the breadth of the building... – Ezekial 40:3, 5.

And there was given me a reed like unto a rod; and the angel stood, saying, Rise and measure the temple of God and the altar and them that worship therein ... – Revelation 11:1.

There are mysterious secrets of power in the Pakua which appear to be locked into the sequences represented by the planetary tables. Their uses in both Taoist and Hebrew Kabalic magic rituals indicate that they may represent some coded messages of instructions into the spiritual realm to affect interactions with the physical realm. The Pakua is an aknowledgement that reality in the universe composes of interactions between the spiritual and physical realms.

■ Lo-Shu's Nine Numbers And Pakua's Eight

"Nine" is an auspicious number in the Chinese culture, symbolising completeness and height of greatness.

Although the "Great Plan" in the Tortoise-Reeds divination method has nine numbers corresponding to the nine classifications, the Chinese people is now more familiar with the number "eight" of the Pakua. This Pakua is preserved in the I Ching, one of the books compiled by Confucius (Wilhelm, 1951; Wing, 1982). The exponents of this Pakua realise that the Pakua is actually a derivation of the Tortoise design, being the eight sides of the Tortoise design without the central number. Why the ninth point is commonly missing is not fully known but this may be a reason why the permutations of the Pakua have proved enigmatic to all those who have tried to crack the secrets of the codes in the Pakua.

There may be older forms of the nine-points Tortoise design than the Pakua. One form may be the Tai Hsuan

CHAPTER 2 **MAGIC SQUARE OF PAKUA** 27

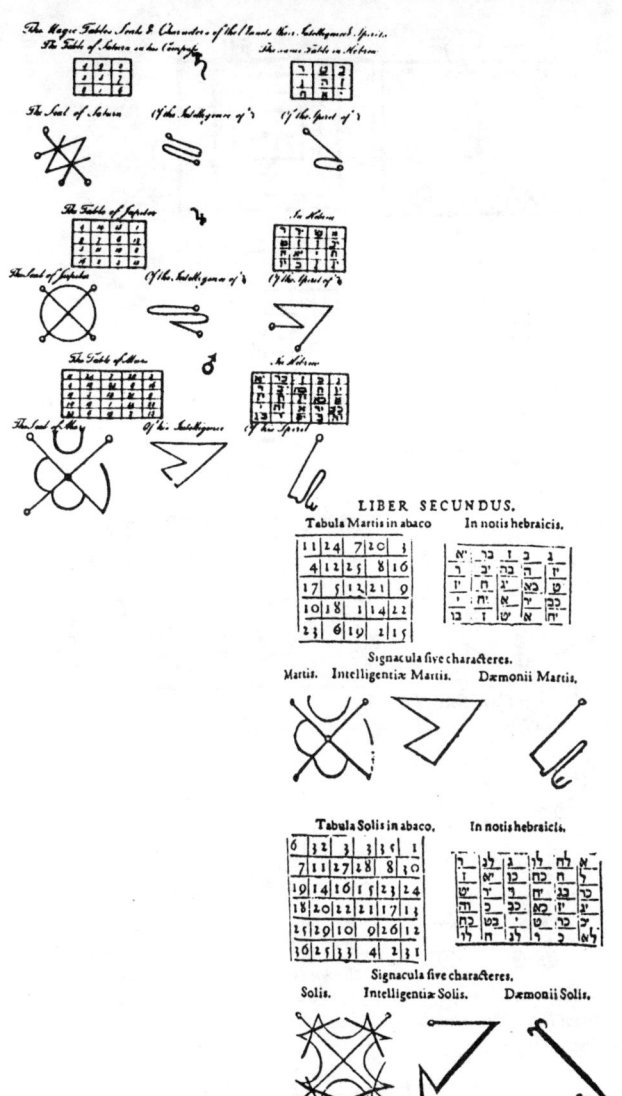

Figure 2.3 Kabalic Planetary Tables (for 3 x 3 to 6 x 6 Magic Squares)

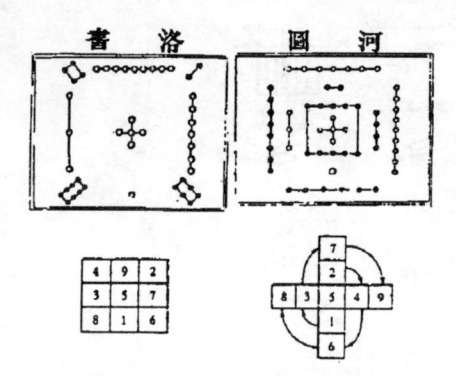

28 THE CHINESE PAKUA

The Lo Shu diagram

The Hou T'u diagram

A magic square from Yang Hui's Hsū Ku Chai Chhi Suan Fa (+1275), after Li Nien

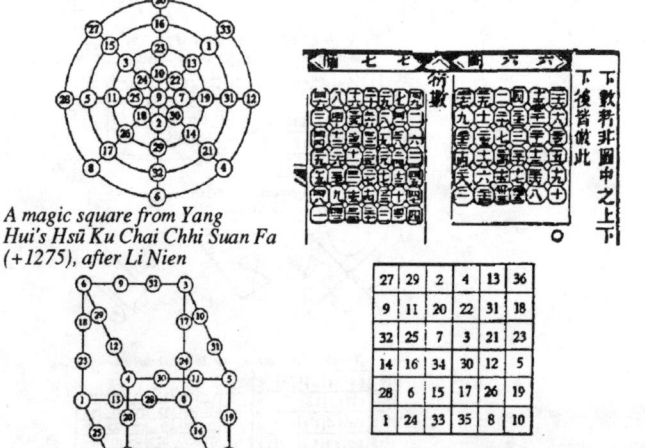

A three-dimensional magic square from Pao Chhi-Shou's Pi Nai Shan Fang Chi

27	29	2	4	13	36
9	11	20	22	31	18
32	25	7	3	21	23
14	16	34	30	12	5
28	6	15	17	26	19
1	24	33	35	8	10

Two magic squares from Chhêng Ta-Wei's Suan Fa Thung Tsung (+1593). The one on the right is shown below in Arabic numericals corrected by Li Nien

Figure 2.4 *Chinese Magic Squares*

Ching which has a set of nine tetragrams with eighty-one permutations (Walter, 1983), a form which Walters (1983) also shows to be reflected in the famous Chinese game of Mahjong. Actually, Taoist priests who are exponents of Pakua magic sometime include the central ninth point in their rituals and even doubled up this central point to derive a tenth point above the basal nine points to form a sort of eight-sided pyramid.

■ Common Origin Of Chinese-Hebrew Kabalic Magic Squares

Of the close remarkable agreement between the Lo-Shu and Hebrew Sigil of Saturn symbols, Gorn (1904, p.170) states in his commentaries of the Shu King, "It is indeed extremely difficult to account for this exactly similar arrangement of both the Hebrew and Chinese figures without supposing both are derived from some common source."

Both the Lo-Shu and Sigil of Saturn are mysterious symbols believed linked to powerful magic. The Chinese and Hebrew cultures must have got the Lo-Shu and Sigil of Saturn Magic Square symbols from some common source(s). Wilhelm (1951, pp.lviii-lix) has noted views that the Pakua could be of foreign origin.

The Shu King in recording the use of the Tortoise for the oracle has been confirmed by the oldest relics of urban civilisation in China found from Anyang of about 1400BC of the Shang dynasty. These relics include marked oracles bones and Tortoise shells, which confirm the Shu King's record of the use of the Tortoise in oracles in times antiquity in Chinese culture.

The earliest mention in the West of Magic Squares similar to the Chinese Hou-T'u and Lo-Shu occurred in the work of Theon of Symrna in A.D. 130 – Needham (1959, p.61) doubted that the Greek work was due to a transmission from Chinese sources. Hebrew Kabalic traditions, however, attributed the Kabalic number systems which include the planetary table of the Sigil of Saturn back to Moses, circa 1491BC, and Enoch, circa 3387BC (also called Hermes Trimegister, i.e. Hermes the Trice Great) (Shumaker, 1972; King, 1975).

There is no reason to doubt the traditions that just as the Chinese Tortoise-Great Plan-Pakua is of ancient origins going back to before Emperor Yu of 2207-2157BC, the Sigil of Saturn also is attributed to as far back as the seventh patriarch Enoch of 3387BC. The common source(s) must have originated as far back as at least 2207-2157BC!

This is long before the birth of the Hebrew nation. The Hebrew nation of Israel was born when Moses led the Hebrews out of Egypt around 1491BC. Remember Shumaker (1972, p.205) has noted tradition linking this Hermetic principle to Moses at Mount Sinai. This is about 400 years before Emperor Wu-Wang ascended the throne as the founder of the Chou dynasty. Emperor Yu, the one credited with finding the "Great Plan" lived about 2200BC about the same time as Abraham (born circa 1996BC).

The Chinese already got this symbol long before the Hebrew nation. Just how did the Hebrews get these same mystic things as the Chinese around these periods about 1,500 to 2,000 years before Christ? Once upon a time, in time past, the Chinese and Hebrew cultures must have met and were the same.

According to Chinese tradition, it was Emperor Huang-Ti (2688BC) who invented Magic Squares (Needham, 1959. p.61). Interesting enough, in the "Five Emperors" arrangement of the Pakua, Huang-Ti is associated with the planet Saturn! This indicates Emperor Huang-Ti could be known by another name to the ancient Hebrews. For, unless the Chinese tradition is incorrect, the Hebrews must have got the Sigil of Saturn from or through Emperor Huang-Ti.

We will see in subsequent chapters that these and other aspects of the Pakua have parallels in the ancient Middle East and Biblical-Hebrew cultures. In the Pakua is also hidden the lost original monotheistic worship of the Supreme God of the ancient Chinese culture. These hidden ancient Chinese secrets also have a lot to tell of the ancient Middle East world and its legends.

3
MYSTERY OF THE PAKUA IN THE GANZHI SYSTEM

■ Introduction

The full secrets of the Pakua cannot be understood without reference to the Chinese Ganzhi system. For the Pakua is part of the Ganzhi system, which is also as mysterious as the Pakua. Time is the essence of life and the ancient Chinese measured time by the Ganzhi system, attributed to Danao, the advisor of the Yellow Emperor Huang-Ti (alias Gongsun or Hsien-Yang; 2677BC) (Wu, 1982). The system was probably older and Danao must have been instructed by the Emperor to polish it up.

The Ganzhi system, which can appear complicated to the laymen mind, is full of cyclic signs, which are particularly associated with Chinese animal symbolism in Chinese astrology as well as the geomantric art of Feng-Shui. The popular Chinese Almanac, the Tong-Shu (Figure 3.1), describes several applications of Ganzhi lore to everyday life.

These cyclical signs of the Ganzhi system play tremendous roles in the Chinese culture and cast vast influence on the everyday life of the Chinese people.

■ Ten Celestial Stems And Twelve Terrestrial Branches

The Ganzhi system composes basically of twenty-two symbols grouped into two sets – ten belonging to "tiangan" (Ten Celestial Stems) and twelve belonging to "dizhi" (Twelve Terrestrial Branches). The "dizhi" Terrestrial

CHAPTER 3 **MYSTERY OF THE PAKUA** 33

Figure 3.1 The Chinese Almanac, Tong Shu — The Chinese Almanac provides advisory and divinatory guidelines on several aspects of the Chinese everyday life. Much of the advice are based on the Chinese Ganzhi System.

34 THE CHINESE PAKUA

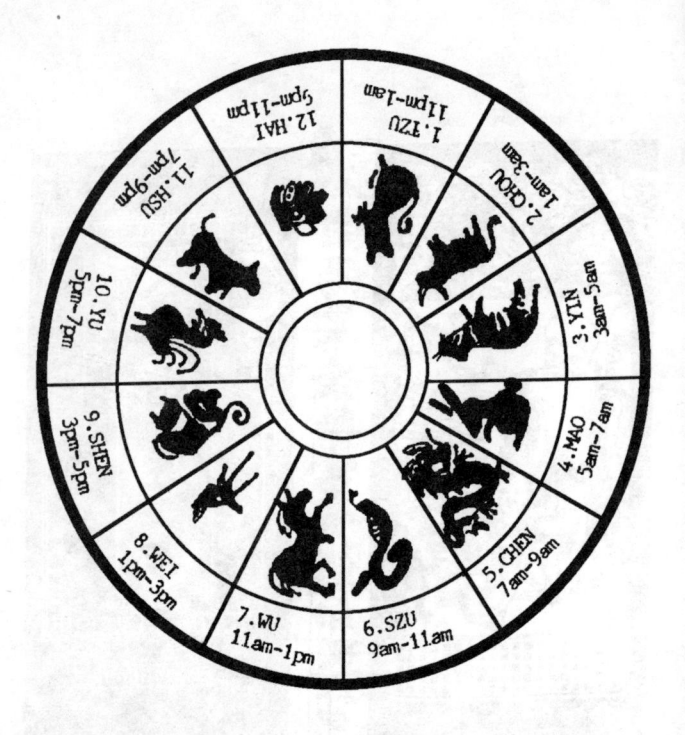

Figure 3.2 The Twelve Zodiac Animals or Terrestrial Branches — They represent angelic forces located at the earthly levels.

CHAPTER 3 **MYSTERY OF THE PAKUA**

Table 3.1a
GANZHI SYSTEM TWELVE TERRESTRIAL BRANCHES ESTIMATION OF TIME

	Animal	Month	Double	Direction	Western Zodiac	Planet
Tzu	Rat	mid-winter	11pm-1am	N	Sagittarius	Jupiter
Ch'ou	Ox	end-winter	1am-3am	N30E	Capricorn	Saturn
Yin	Tiger	early spring	3am-5am	N60E	Aquarius	Uranus
Mao	Hare	mid-spring	5am-7am	E	Pisces	Jupiter
Ch'en	Dragon	end-spring	7am-9am	S60E	Aries	Mars
Ssu	Snake	early-summer	9am-11am	S30E	Taurus	Venus
Wu	Horse	mid-summer	11am-1pm	S	Gemini	Mercury
Wei	Sheep	end-summer	1pm-3pm	S30W	Cancer	Moon
Shen	Monkey	early-autumn	3pm-5pm	S60W	Leo	Sun
Yu	Cock	mid-autumn	5pm-7pm	W	Virgo	Mercury
Hsu	Dog	end-autumn	7pm-9pm	N60W	Libra	Venus
Hai	Pig	early-winter	9pm-11pm	N30W	Scorpio	Mars

Table 3.1b
INTERPRETATIONS OF GANZHI TWELVE TERRESTRIAL BRANCHES SIGNS

	Animal			Gem
Tzu	Rat	yang	small child, beginning	Carbuncle
Ch'ou	Ox	yin	bound hand, binding, sustain	Onyx, white
Yin	Tiger	yang	greeetings, reverence	Sapphire
Mao	Hare	yin	open door, reception of Spring	Chrysolite
Ch'en	Dragon	yang	pregnant and timid	Amethyst
Ssu	Snake	yin	fully formed, seventh month of gestation	Mossagate
Wu	Horse	yang	struggle, opposition	Beryl
Wei	Sheep	yin	fully grown, mature	Emerald
Shen	Monkey	yang	expansion Ruby	
Yu	Cock	yin	vase for fermented drink	Jasper, pink
Hsu	Dog	yang	cutting, destruction, clearing the ground	Diamond
Hai	Pig	yin	propitious time for venturing	Topaz

Branches system is popularly known as the twelve zodiacal animals (Figure 3.2): rat, ox, tiger, hare, dragon, serpent, horse, sheep, monkey, cock, dog, and pig. On the other hand, the more complicated "tiangan" Celestial Stems system composes of the Five Elements, each with a hard or soft aspect. The "tiangan" Celestial Stems system is associated with the Four Heraldic or Supernatural Animals and also represent the Four Seasons.

The interactions of the twenty-two symbols of the Ten Celestial Stems and Twelve Terrestrial Branches control everything in the Universe. The two groups of this Ganzhi system are as follows:

A. Ten Celestial Stems ("Tiangan" or Shih T'ien Kan) also known as Ten Heavenly Stems or Denary series.

1. JIA (hard wood) trees
2. TI (soft wood) hewn timber
3. BING (sun fire) lightning
4. DING (kitchen fire) burning incense
5. WU (mountain earth) hills
6. JI (sand earth) earthenwares
7. GENG (rough metal) metal ores
8. XIN (refined metal) kettles
9. REN (sea water) salt water
10. GUI (rain water) fresh water

These Ten Heavenly Stems reflect the influence of Heavenly forces and relate to the Five Elements as disposed according to the Four Directions of the compass. The "tiangan" therefore illustrates the major influence of space (movement of the tilted earth) in interactions with time to create the four major seasons.

The Ten Celestial Stems are represented by the Milky Way.

B Twelve Terrestrial Branches ("Dizhi") also known as Twelve Earthly Branches or Duodenary series.

CHAPTER 3 **MYSTERY OF THE PAKUA** 37

1.	ZI (rat)	7.	WU (horse)
2.	CHOU (ox)	8.	WEI (sheep)
3.	YIN (tiger)	9.	SHEN (monkey)
4.	MAO (horse)	10.	YOU (cock)
5.	CHEN (dragon)	11.	XU (dog)
6.	SI (serpent)	12.	HAI (pig)

The Terrestrial Branches apply to factors on the Earth plane. The units of the "dizhi" system would be applied to the twelve units of times of the day (each unit being a double hours), the twelve months of the year and the twelve years corresponding to the twelve zodiacal animals. The twelve years compose one full Jupiter cycle. They also mark the twelve terrestrial directions and the location of the earth dragon "ch'i" forces.

Permutating the "tiangan" with the "dizhi" would produce a sixty unit cycle, starting with jiazi (hard wood rat) and ending with guihai (rain water pig). Once the cycle is completed, it is repeated. This cycle is known as the "jiazi" cycle after the beginning of the sixty units which is "hard wood rat."

The permutation of the "jiazi" system is not a perfect permutation of all possible combinations which would lead to one hundred and twenty possibilities and not sixty. The "jiazi" system is really a repeat of the "tiangan" symbols through six times to get sixty units paralleled by a repeat of the "dizhi" system through five times to also get sixty units. This sixty units cycle could be applied to a cycle of sixty days, sixty months or sixty years. It will result in the odd units from the Terrestrial Branches pairing with the odd units from the Heavenly Stems, forming the cycle of sixty years.

The Ganzhi system is also known as the Sexagenary cycle, which is often grouped into 3 cycles (the three

"Yuans" – higher, middle and lower Yuans) to form one hundred and eighty years.

The Ten Celestial Stems compose the oldest known cyclic signs. They featured on the oracles inscriptions (the then oldest Chinese texts of around 1400BC) linked to the calendar The TwelveTerrestial Branches were not fully defined until around the fifth century BC and were first used to designate the twelve hours of the day, then the twelve months and finally the twelve years of the Jupiter cycle. (de Kermadec and Poulsen, 1983. p.26). However, Ho (1975. p.240) notes that the legendary Hsia Emperors used the twenty-two letters of the Ganzhi system to help differentiate the sequence of their Emperors, indicating that the Ganzhi system with both the Ten Celestial Stems and Twelve Terrestrial Branches could be far older; as old as the legendary Hsia dynasty (2203-1766BC).

■ The Twenty Eight Constellations

Outside the two basic groups of the Ganzhi system, there are other refinements of the measurements of the Heaven and Earth. There is the 120 "fen-chin" which are actually extension of the Ganzhi 60 units cycle.

There are the 28 "hsiu" or smaller constellations of uneven sizes related to the 28 mansions of the moon of Western astrology and therefore seems to indicate the position and movement of the moon. They are related to the "tiangan" Celestial Stems system as seven "hsiu" would be allocated to each of the four quadrants of Heaven (Table 3.2). These "hsiu" represent times when the geomancer would regard as most optimal to exert certain measures – something akin to the auspiciousness given to the new and full moon periods, believed to have influences on tidal movements and human sanity.

CHAPTER 3 **MYSTERY OF THE PAKUA** 39

For practical purposes, the Ganzhi system with its two parallel systems of the "dizhi" Twelve Terrestrial Branches and the "tiangan" Ten Celestial Stems are the basis of Chinese astrology. The man would thus be influenced by one animal of the twelve zodiac animals and then also by one of the four-plus-one heraldic animals.

Logistic difficulties of measuring time rendered certain components of the Ganzhi system easier to follow than the rest. Time was obviously easier to measure using a lunar month unit and a solar year unit, into which the Ganzhi system was not fully compatible. There being thirty days to a month, the application of the Ganzhi system to a cycle of sixty days is not practical. Instead of the names, the Chinese found it easier to remember the months by their numericals. It is also easier to compute reigns periods by the number of years after the ascension of the emperor. The Ganzhi system at that ancient time also encountered the difficulty that the year is 365.25 days while the lunar period is 29.5 days – it was only later that the idea of intercalary months were used to reconcile the measurement of time.

There are inherent advantages in the Ganzhi system in that though the western solar year fit in well with the movement of the sun, lunar units are more reflective of short term environmental changes. The lunar units gain a closer approximation to the solar year through the interjection of intercalary months. Through centuries of observation, the Chinese have worked out associations between environmental changes and the lunar, seasonal and solar periods in the 60 years cycle of the Ganzhi system. This is the basis of the Chinese Almanac or Tong-Shu, where the Chinese could guess 60 years ahead the general characteristics of a period through its position in the Ganzhi system. The Ganzhi system develops a mysteriousness owing to its complexity and this unwittingly gives it a misleading sort of fortune-telling quality of a supernatural level. While cer-

40 THE CHINESE PAKUA

Table 3.2

THE TWENTY EIGHT CONSTELLATIONS ANIMALS

No.	Hsiu	Object	Animal	Element	Auspiciousness
East Azure Dragon Sector:					
1.	Chiao	Horn	Crocodile Earth Dragon	Wood	auspicious
2.	K'ang	Neck	Sky Dragon	Metal	inauspicious
3.	Ti	Root	Badger	Earth	inauspicious
4.	Fang	Room	Hare	Sun	auspicious
5.	Hsin	Heart	Fox	Moon	auspicious
6.	Wei	Tail	Tiger	Fire	auspicious
7.	Chi	Basket	Leopard	Water	auspicious
North Black Turtle Sector:					
8.	Nan tou	Ladle	Unicorn, Griffon	Wood	auspicious
9.	Niu	Buffalo	Buffalo	Metal	inauspcious
10.	Nu	Woman	Bat	Earth	inauspicious
11.	Hsu	Void	Rat	Sun	inauspicious
12.	Wei	Roof	Swallow	Moon	inauspicious
13.	Shih	House	Pig, Bear	Fire	auspicious
14.	Pi	Wall	Porcupine	Water	auspicious
West White Tiger Sector					
15.	K'uei	Legs	Wolf	Wood	inauspicious
16.	Lou	Link	Dog	Metal	auspicious
17.	Wei	Stomach	Pheasant	Earth	auspicious
18.	Mao	Lights	Cock	Sun	inauspicious
19.	Pi	Thread	Crow, Raven	Moon	inauspicious
20.	Tsui	Turtle	Monkey	Fire	inauspicious
21.	Shen	Three associates (3 stars)	Gibbon	Water	auspicious
Red Phoenix Sector					
22.	Ching	Well	Tapir	Wood	auspicious
23.	Kuei	Ghost	Goat Sheep	Metal	inauspicious
24.	Liu	Willow	Buck	Earth	inauspicious
25.	Hsing	Star	Horse	Sun	inauspicious
26.	Chang	Fishing net, square	Stag	Moon	auspicious
27.	I	Wings	Snake	Fire	inauspicious
28.	Chen	Chariot	Earthworms	Water	auspicious

1 to 7 and their multiples correspond to the seven days of the week, starting with Thursday, and the seven planets Jupiter, Venus, Saturn, Sun, Moon, Mars and Mercury.

CHAPTER 3 **MYSTERY OF THE PAKUA**

tain supernatural aspects may exist, much of the predictive elements of the Ganzhi system are born out of the ancient wisdom in natural observations about the environment, including those of Man.

■ Four Heraldic Animals Of The Ten Celestial Stems

The Five Elements with their dark Yin and light Yang aspects in the "tiangan" Ten Celestial system are symbolised by the Pakua Four Heraldic Animals, viz. Black or North Snake-White or West Tiger-Red or South Phoenix-Azure or East Dragon, with the centre fifth point occupied by another dragon, the Yellow Dragon. The Four Heraldic Animals also correspond respectively to the Four Major Seasons of Winter, Summer, Autumn and Spring. This symbolism is shown in Figure 3.3 and their major characteristics in Table 3.3.

The Pakua is primarily the cyclic signs of the Ten Celestial Stems.

The Five Elements and their associated Four Heraldic Animals represent an ancient knowledge of how heavenly forces could be manipulated to affect earthly destinies. The central rituals of Taoist magic, following the sequences of the Lo-Shu, consists in the ability to call up these forces of these Spirit-Generals and indicate that these Pakua Five Elements-Four Heraldic Animals are indeed the essence of supernatural powers. Which is why the Chinese call them the Four Supernatural Animals.

The combination of the Twelve Terrestrial Branches with the Ten Celestial Stems comprehensively symbolises the interactions of heavenly and earthly forces in the regulation of everything in the life of mankind. The Taoist priest would summon the heavenly or spirit powers through the heraldic animals but he also has to recognise

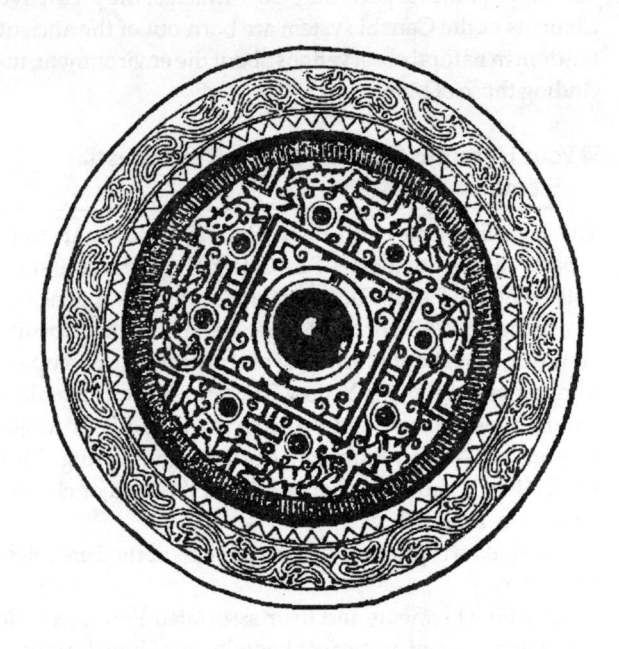

Figure 3.3 Cloud-Bordered Han Mirror with Four Supernatural Animals — The Mirror contains the Four Supernatural Animals of Dragon, Tortoise-Snake, Tiger and Bird. The other four animals appear to be a winged deer, another deer with longer horn, another long-tailed crested bird and another bird.

CHAPTER 3 **MYSTERY OF THE PAKUA**

Table 3.3
GANZHI SYSTEM TEN CELESTIAL BRANCHES ESTIMATION OF DIRECTION

	Wood	Fire	Earth	Metal	Water
Direction	East	South	Centre	West	North
Colour	Blue-green	Red	Yellow	White	Black
Sacred Animal	Dragon	Phoenix	Dragon Ox	Tiger	Snake Tortoise Dark Warrior
Class of Animals	Scaly	Feathered	Naked	Hairy	Shell
Domestic Animals	Sheep	Fowl	Ox	Dog	Pig
Orifice	Eyes	Ears	Mouth	Nose	Anus, Vulva
Planet	Jupiter	Mars	Saturn	Venus	Mercury
Emperor	Fu-Hsi	Shen-Nung	Huang-Ti	Shao-hao	Chuan-Hsu
Qualities	Formidable	Burning	Cultivation	Changeable	Soaking
Weather	Wind	Heat	Sunshine	Cold	Rain
Organ	Liver	Heart	Spleen	Lungs	Kidney

44 THE CHINESE PAKUA

Celestial Stems

Terrestrial Branches

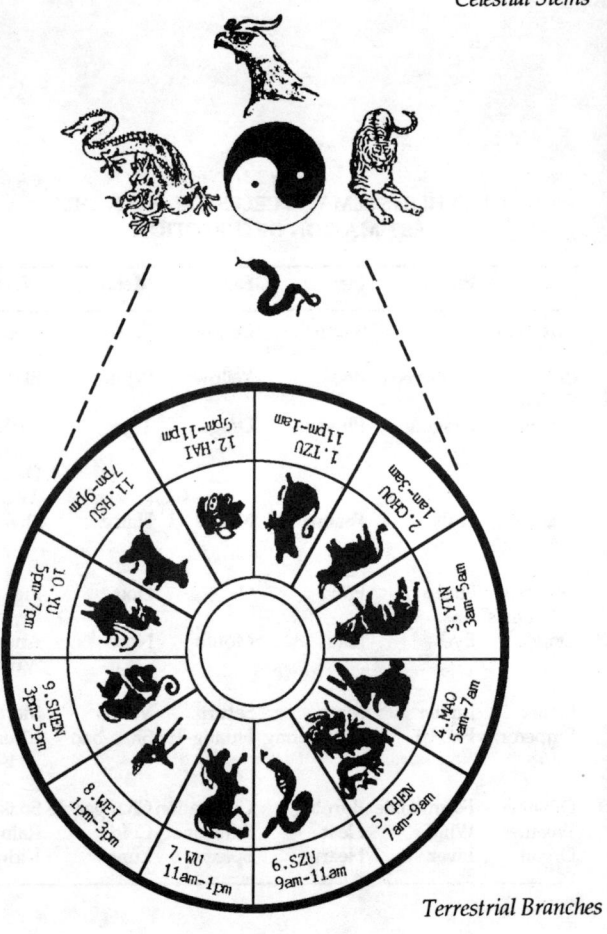

Figure 3.4   The Ganzhi System is an interaction between the forces of the Celestial Stems with their Twenty-Eight Constellations and the Terrestrial Branches. This interaction is invoked in the Fang-siang-che Ceremony (Bear Dance).

CHAPTER 3 MYSTERY OF THE PAKUA

Table 3.4

ORIGIN OF HEBREW ALPHABETS FROM GANZHI SYSTEM

	Ganzhi System 22 symbols	Sefer Yetsirah* 22 Hebrew Alphabets
	Ten Celestial Stems	**First and Second Books**
	Five Elements (with Yin and Yang)	(First Book) Three Elements
1.	JIA (hard wood)**	Alef
2.	YI (soft wood)	Mem
3.	BING (sun fire)	Shih
		(Second Book) (Conditions controlling elements)
4.	DING (kitchen fire)	Beit
5.	WU (mountain earth)	Gimmel
6.	JI (sand earth)	Daled
7.	GENG (rough metal)	Kaf
8.	XIN (refined metal)	Peh
9.	REN (sea water)	Resh
10.	GUI (rain water)	Taf
	Terrestrial Branches	**(Third Book)**

The twelve simple Hebrew letters covering the twelve minor compas directions and also the twelve months and the twelve organs of man. They also are equivalent to the twelve constellations

1.	ZI (rat)	Rest of Hebrew alphabets (12)
2.	CHOU (ox)	
3.	YIN (tiger)	
4.	MAO (hare)	
5.	CHEN (dragon)	
6.	SI (serpent)	
7.	WU (horse)	
8.	WEI (sheep)	
9.	SHEN (monkey)	
10.	YOU (cock)	
11.	XU (dog)	
12.	HAI (pig)	

*Jewish (Book of Creation) (Sharf, 1876 p 25-26) grouped the twenty two letters as above
**The first symbol of the GANZHI system is also a GAMMADION symbol and possibly correspond to "alef or alpha."

the earthly forces represented by the twelve zodiacal animals which especially reflect the characteristics of the person.

The ancients know that the Ten Celestial Stems and Twelve Terrestrial Branches rule the entire destiny of Man.

■ The Twelve Zodiac Animals

The association of the twelve years with the twelve animals arose from a belief that the different years come under different animal spirits' influences which could be reflected by the behaviour of the corresponding animals. That is, the characteristics of these animals symbolise the nature of the different years.

Although the Twelve Terrestrial Branches of the animals are said not to be defined until the fifth century BC, they may be linked with the Bear Dance of the Chou Li (Waterbury, 1952. pp.11-12). An official called the "Inspector of the Region or Universal Preserver" would impersonate a Bear, wearing bear dress and went into houses to drive away demons and diseases. This Fang-siang-che, accompanied by twelve persons disguised as various animals and birds, was also invoked during the Han dynasty to drive away great calamity. The twelve animals were said to represent the summoning of the animal spirits of the various localities. A ram and a cock would normally be sacrificed at the gate.

The Bear could be the Chinese polar system of Ursa Major along with the North Pole Star and other polar stars. Thus, the Fang-siang-che ceremony was really an invokement of the full Ganzhi system viz. the "tiangan" Ten Celestial Stems represented by the Bear and the "dizhi" Twelve Terrestrial Branches represented by the twelve animals (Figure 3.4)

The Fang-siang-che ceremony would be performed only during times of very great calamities. These great calamities could be caused by irregularities along both the Heavenly and Earthly fields. So, during the Fang-siang-che ceremony, the priest had to summon the forces of both Heaven and Earth, as represented by the two different groups of animals.

Ganzhi Link Between Chinese And Hebrew Languages – And True Origin Of Alphabetic Language

A curious and very remarkable aspect of the Ganzhi system is that it finds strong parallels in the Hebrew Kabala system (Table 3.4) and may hold the secrets of the origins of the alphabets!

The Hebrew language has an alphabetic system of twenty letters. The Hebrew Sefer Yetsirah (Book of Creation) (Sharf, 1976. pp.25-26) groups the twenty two letters as follows:

- First book : alef, mem, shih. The three mother letters meaning the elements of air, water, fire
- Second book : the seven doubles letters of beit, gimmel, daled, kaf, peh, resh and taf. They represent the seven necessary qualities and possible situations
- Third book : the twelves simple letters covering the twelve minor compass directions and also the twelve months and twelve organs of man. They also are equivalent to the twelve constellations.

It would be noticed that the Kabalic third book of twelve letters are very alike the Twelve Terrestrial Branches of the Ganzhi system (Table 3.4) The combination of the first and second books of the Kabalic letters are also rather similar to the Ganzhi Ten Celestial Branches, both involving also the elements!

The Ganzhi system is believed to influence the whole universe and this is the same significance the Hebrew Kabala gives to the Hebrew letters. The sifrot, composing of the numbers one to ten and the twenty two letters of the Hebrew alphabet, is the story of the universe. The sifrot are the means which God used in the creation of the universe. The letters, which He created too, are the material of the universe: they are 'otiot ha-yesod'; the "foundation-letters."

■ The Ganzhi System Of Twenty-two Symbols Is The Same As The Hebrew Kabalic Twenty-two Letters!

The Hebrew alphabets must have developed from an adaptation of the kind of symbols found in the Ganzhi system.

The comparison also throws unique light on the origins of the alphabets. It is known that the oldest writings were pictorial in nature, like the Sumerian-Egyptian-Chinese writings, and alphabetic writings emerged later (Buttrick, 1954). The comparison shows that alphabetic language must have arose as an adaptation of pictorial symbols, especially those used in sacred rituals.

Such striking similarities also mean that the Chinese and Hebrew languages must have close kinship which reflects either some transmission from one to the other or an origin from some common source(s).

However, for an alphabetic system to evolved from the Ganzhi symbols, there must have been a prior period of development. As the early portions of the Hebrew Bible were written from 1400BC onwards, the Hebrew script must have existed a few hundred years before and the elements of the Ganzhi system must be in the Middle East even earlier. The Ganzhi system must have been in the Middle East as early as 2000BC.

The tradition of the Ganzhi system goes back to the time of the Hsia dynasty (2203-1766BC). Chinese writings were found in China only as early as 1400BC on Shang oracle bones writings, but not before. These oracle bones Chinese writings were already well developed, indicating prior existence through a period of time of at least a few hundred years.

The implication is that the Chinese writings came from where the Ganzhi system already earlier existed – the Middle East!

4

THE FOUR HERALDIC ANIMALS OF THE PAKUA

■ The Four Heraldic Animals Of The Pakua

A very powerful cyclic layer of significance, and the most auspicious one, of the Pakua Lo-Shu pattern is that the cardinal points of North, West, South, East are associated with the Chinese Four Heraldic Animals the Snake, Tiger, Phoenix and "Lung" (Figure 4.1). These Four Heraldic Animals of the Pakua with strong relationships to the Five Elements occupy important positions in several aspects and rituals of the ancient Chinese culture.

In important Taoist rituals, the power of these Four Heraldic Animals are always summoned.

The ancient Chinese has considered the "Lung" as the "chief of the Four Spiritual Animals." The Four Spiritual Animals are 1. The Ling or Unicorn, 2. The Phoenix 3. The Tortoise 4. The Dragon. (Plopper, 1935. p.47). The Unicorn, the Phoenix, the Tortoise, and the Dragon are the four spiritual creatures. (Plopper, 1935. p.113).

The arrangements of the Four Supernatural Animals and the Four Spiritual Animals are not essentially different. This is because the Snake is often replaced by the Tortoise (Black Warrior). The hairy animal representing the West could be the Tiger, the Bear or the Unicorn (Hsu and Ward, 1984. p.467).

What is not well-known and would be shown in this book is that the variants of the Four Heraldic Animals arrangement also contains fundamental secrets about the history of ancient China! The Four Heraldic Animals

CHAPTER 4 **FOUR HERALDIC ANIMALS** 51

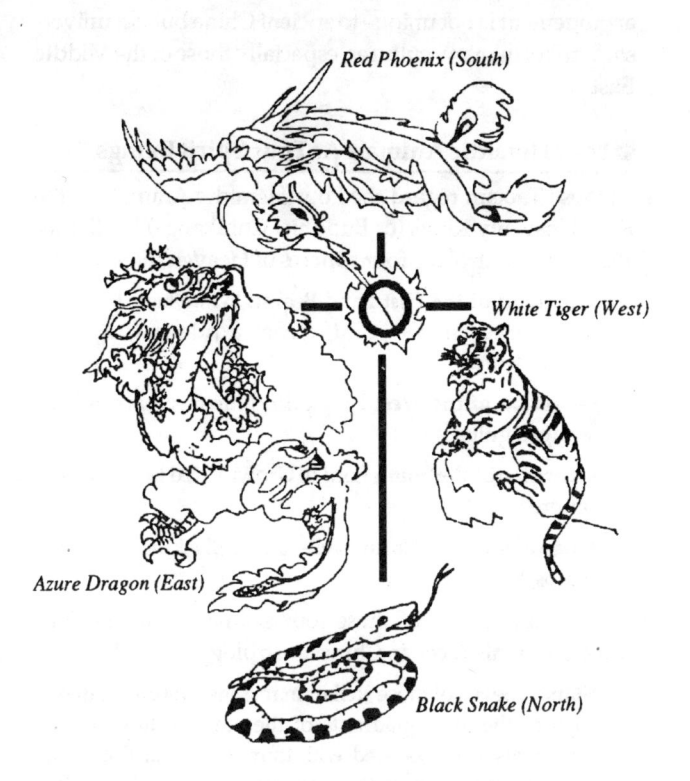

Figure 4.1 The Chinese Four Supernatural Animals of the Celestial Stems. They represent the four major spheres of highest angels, located at the Heavenly level. The Snake is often replaced by the Tortoise which is also known as the "Black Warrior."

arrangement is not unique to ancient China but is a universal symbol in many cultures, especially those of the Middle East.

■ Four Heraldic Animals As Four Spirit Beings

Chinese Taoism regard the Four Heraldic Animals as the Four Heavenly Kings (or Buddhist Chinkangs) (Williams, 1931) who control the four spheres of Heaven (Figure 4.2):

Guardian of the East Land Bearer. White face, ferocious appearance, copper beard, carries a jade ring, a spear, magic sword

Guardian of the West Far-Gazer. Blue-face, carries four-stringed guitar

Guardian of the South Lord of Growth. Red face, holds an umbrella.

Guardian of the North Well-famed. Black face, has two whips, bag, and snake.

The association of these four animals with the four directions is also seen in Chinese astrology:

Stars: ... Seven of those stellar 'mansions' were allocated to each of the four quadrants of the vault of heaven. The quadrants are associated with four animals ... The Azure Dragon presides over the eastern quarter, the Vermillion Bird, i.e. the Chinese phoenix over the southern, the White Tiger over the western and the Black Warrior, i.e. the tortoise – over the northern ... The morning sun is in the east, which hence corresponds to Spring; at noon it is south which suggests Summer. By similar parallelism the west corresponds to Autumn and the north to Winter (William, 1931. pp.336-340)

These Four Beings are also associated in the worship of the Nine Emperor Gods – the East, West, South, North and Centre are guarded by the Green, White, Red, Black and

CHAPTER 4 **FOUR HERALDIC ANIMALS** 53

魔禮紅
Mo-Li Hung
Guardian of the South

SOUTH
Red Phoenix
Red Dragon
(Gabriel)

魔禮青

Centre
Yellow Dragon

WEST
White Tiger
Blue Dragon
(Michael)

EAST
Azure Dragon
Green Dragon
(Brahma
four-faced
cherubim of
Ezekiel)

魔禮海

NORTH
(Throne of God)
Black Tortise
Warrior-Snake
Black Dragon

Mo-Li Ch'ing
Guardian of the East

Mo-Li Hai
Guardian of the West

魔禮壽

(Lucifer,
as representative of God)

Mo-Li Shou
Guardian of the North

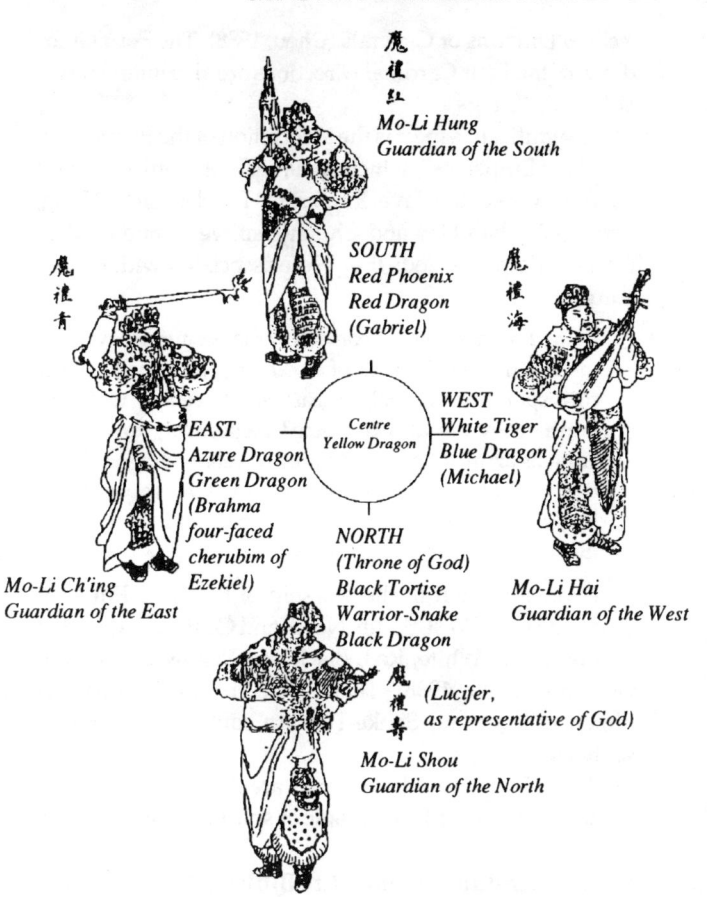

Figure 4.2   The Four Supernatural Animals as the Four Buddhist Chinkangs or Four Taoist Heavenly Kings.

Yellow Dragons or Generals (Cheu, 1988). The Four Guardians of the Four Cardinal Directions are also interchangeable with "Lungs"

A significant aspect is the association of the Pakua with the "Five Emperors", which is the basis of many powerful charms. When the Five Emperors, Fu-Hsi, Shen-Nung, Huang-Ti, Shao-Hao and Chuan-Hsu were canonised as the Five Emperor Gods they were associated with certain animals:

> In the Five Elements according to the Former Heaven Sequence, the five elements of wood, fire, earth, metal, water correspond respectively to east, south, centre, west and north. They are also connected respectively to the five animals azure dragon, red phoenix, yellow dragon, white tiger and black snake-tortoise and the five emperors Fu-Hsi, Shen-Nung, Huang-Ti, Shao-hao and Chuan-hsu. (Skinner 1982, Table 5. pp.58-59)

Remember that in the worship of the Nine Emperor Gods, the East, West, South, North and Centre are guarded by the Green, White, Red, Black and Yellow Dragons or Generals (Cheu, 1988). That is, the spiritual animals of Phoenix, Tiger and Snake-Tortoise could also be represented by "Lungs".

These Four Heraldic Animals are the source of power summoned during Taoist magic or spiritual rituals.

■ Four Heraldic Animals Are Biblical Angelic Four Beasts

The Four Heraldic Animals is also a significance concept in other ancient cultures in the Middle East.

The Bible mentions four angelic beasts around the throne of God:

> And before the throne ... were four beasts full of eyes before and behind. And the first beast was like a lion and the

CHAPTER 4 **FOUR HERALDIC ANIMALS** 55

second beast like a calf, and the third beast had a face as a man and the fourth beast was like a flying eagle. And the four beasts had each of them six wings about him and they were full of eyes within and they rest not day and night saying Holy, holy, holy, Lord God Almighty which was, and is, and is to come (Revelation 4:6-8)

Now the cherubims stood on the right side of the house when the man went in and the cloud filled the inner court ... And when I looked behold the four wheels by the cherubims, one wheel by one cherub and another wheel by another cherub: and the appearance of the wheels was as the colour of a beryl stone ... And every one had four faces: the first face was the face of a cherub, and the second face was the face of a man, and the third the face of a lion and the fourth the face of an eagle ... And the cherubims..stood at the door of the east gate of the Lord's house ... (Ezekial 10:3,9, 14, 19 – verse 9 indicates there were four cherubims)

Figure 4.3. (right) illustrates these Ezekial's Four Heraldic Animals in Biblical and Jewish Kabalic symbolism – this is also the Four Animals the Four Gospels are associated with (Figure 4.4). Figure 4.3 (left) illustrates another Kabalic arrangement of the Four Heraldic Animals which are also found in the ancient Babylonian-Assyrian culture. These winged angelic creatures include the lion, the calf and the eagle.

A host of angelic creatures compose those marvellous creatures known as "cherubs or cherubims." These cherubs or cherubims have many forms. Peloubet (1947) wrote:

Cherub, Cherubim. The symbolical figure so called was a composite creature-form which finds a parallel in the religious insignia of Assyria, Egypt and Persia, e.g. the sphinx, the winged bulls and lions of Nineveh, etc. A cherub guarded paradise. Gen 3:24. Figures of cherubim were placed on the mercy seat of the ark. Ex. 25:18. A pair of

56 THE CHINESE PAKUA

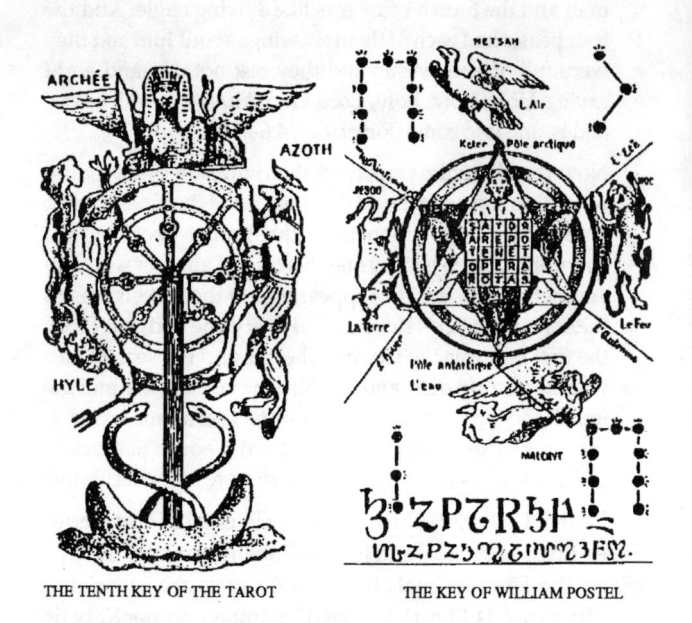

THE TENTH KEY OF THE TAROT   THE KEY OF WILLIAM POSTEL

Figure 4.3   *The Kabalic equivalent of the Chinese Four Supernatural Animals — Note the opposition of the bottom Snakes against the top winged Sphinx is similiar to the Chinese opposition of the top Phoenix against the bottom Snake. At the east, the Kabalic horned bearded fix-tail creature is actually the Chinese Dragon. The kabalic creature at the West is a Dog, which is the Chinese domestic equivalent of the Tiger.*

CHAPTER 4 FOUR HERALDIC ANIMALS 57

The symbol of Matthew is the Man, the King and Man that is Christ. It is the Gospel to the Jews, of the past, seeing Christianity as the fulfilment of Judaism. It is a didactic Gospel of discourses on Christ as the Messiah of the Jew.

The symbol of Mark is the Lion, reflecting courage, dignity and energy. It is the Gospel to the Romans, of the present and incident. It is an anecdotal Gospel showing Christ as the Son of God and Lord of the world.

The symbol of Luke is the Ox, for power, sacrifice. It is the Gospel for the Greeks, of the future, of universal gratuitiousness. It is a historic Gospel of the priestly, mediatorial Good Physician and Saviour of Mankind.

The symbol of John is the Eagle, whose eyes pierce the mysteries of God's Truth. It is the Gospel of eternity. It is the spiritual Gospel of Christ as the Eternal Son and Incarnate Word.

Figure 4.4   The Four Animals of the Four Gospels

colossal size overshadowed it in Solomon's temple with the canopy of their contiguously extended wings. 1 Kings 6:27 ...

It is remarkable that with such precise directions as to their position, attitude and material, nothing, save they were winged, is said concerning their shape. On the whole it seems likely that the word "cherub" meant not only the composite creature-form, of which the man, lion, ox and eagle were the elements, but, further, some perculiar and mystical form. Ezekial 1:6...

The Biblical, Middle East and Kabalic philosophy thus describe angels as looking like animals. The "Lung" and other heraldic animals of the Pakua are such angelic creatures.

The Shan Hai Ching (from early 1st millenium BC) associated the Double "Lungs" with carrying agents bringing messages back and forth between heaven and earth. Oracle bones inscriptions also show that Shang-Ti the Supreme God was believed to have been served by many officials including the "messenger phoenix." (Chang, 1983. pp.65-68). The "Lung" and the Phoenix are therefore regarded as the messengers of God. So, they are really the same as angels of the Bible – for the word "angel" means "messenger of God."

■ Kabalic Four Directions And Angelic Beasts

In its Tenth Key of the Tarot (Figure 4.3, left), the Kabala associates four animals with the cardinal points (Levi, 1825-1875):

1. Top, South Woman headed Sphinx. Woman front, lion forebody and claws, eagle wings and ox backbody and tail. (Chinese parallel = phoenix)
2. Left, East Kerub – Bull-Horned Bearded Man headed Sphinx. Bull-Horned Bearded Man front, backbody-tail of fish (Chinese parallel = "Lung")

3. Bottom, North Typhon. The double serpents. (Chinese parallel = snake)
4. Right, West Dog-headed Sphinx. Dog head, man's body. (Chinese parallel = tiger)

These Kabalic arrangements of four animals are thus very strikingly similar to the Chinese Pakua arrangement of the Four Heraldic Animals. It is very evident that the Pakua symbol of the Four Heraldic Animals has universal existence and parallel similar significance in many cultures, including those of ancient China and Middle East.

They could not have arose independently but must have originated from common sources. There can only be a diffusion of this Pakua Four Animals symbol into the different cultures.

■ The Pakua Is A Universal Gammadion

The above variants of the Four Directions symbolism of the Pakua are actually the Gammadion principle, which is basically the Cross or Swastika symbol (MacKenzie, 1926). The Christian Cross, which is the Heirophant Cross, is also a Gammadion symbol. The Buddhist Swastika is also a Gammadion. Of the Gammadion, MacKenzie (1926) wrote:

> The swatiska is of considerable antiquity in Elam (southwestern Persia), in Asia Minor, and in the Aegean and Danubian "culture areas" ... It appeared comparatively early in Central, Western and Northern Europe, as well as in India ... in China and Japan ... in pre-Columbian America. There is, however, no trace of the swastika proper in Egypt ... Neither the Sumerian nor Babylonian made use of it in lower Mesopotamia. Nor did it appeal to the Assyrians in the North... The symbol recurs times without number on the prehistoric pottery of Cyprus and the Trojan plain; but no trace of it has ever been found in

Egypt, in Assyria, or in Babylonia ... Was it an invention of the Hittite people ...? (pp.2-5)

In brief, the ancient world might be divided into two zones, characterised, one by the presence of the Gammadion, the other by that of the Winged Globe as well as the "crux ansata". (p.1)

The Pakua Gammadion is a sacred symbol of universal existence among several ancient cultures.

5

PAKUA AS RECORDER OF ENVIRONMENTAL CHANGE

... the Luopan ... no one is really competent to give a scientific explanation of it because no scientific research has been carried out on this subject (Lee, 1986. p.110)

■ Family Of Eight Persons Represented In Pakua

The Pakua, through the Ganzhi system, categorises the cyclic changes in major environmental traits in the 60 years cycle. These are general concepts. The remarkable thing is that the Pakua is also able to take into account localised physical factors which influence the environment. This is the root of the geomantric art of Feng-Shui and the Lo-pan, whose earliest forms appeared to be based on sundials (Needham, 1959).

There are evidence that the Pakua, as a device to track time and direction, is also a device to measure environmental influences.

It is been discussed that the eight trigrams of the Pakua have two different arrangements (Figure 1.4). The eight fundamental trigrams correspond to image (environmental), direction and family relations as follows:

62 THE CHINESE PAKUA

Trigram	Image	Direction		Family
		Former Heaven	Later Heaven	
Ch'ien	Heaven	S	NW	Father
Chen	Thunder	NE	E	Eldest Son
K'an	Water Clouds Rain Spring	W	N	Middle Son
Ken	Mountain	NW	NE	Youngest Son
K'un	Earth	N	SW	Mother
Sun	Wind-Wood	SW	SE	Eldest Daughter
Li	Fire Sun Lightning	E	S	Middle Daughter
Tui	Lake	SE	W	Youngest daughter

Each trigram has a characteristic of a natural force and also a characteristic of a certain position within the human family. Each of the 64 "Kua" of the I Ching, being the association of a pair of the eight trigrams, is therefore the summation of the interactions of the meanings derived from the natural forces and the family positions.

In the Ganzhi system, the Pakua's influence relates to the Ten Celestial Stems, which overlap the Twelve Terrestial Branches. The above association of the Pakua with the natural forces and family characteristics must be an extension of the Ten Celestial Stems influence. That is, each aspect of the Ten Celestial Stems receives a representation of its actual power through comparing with the power of a natural force as well as that of the family position.

The Pakua contains the symbolism of a family of eight with the father, mother and their three sons and three daughters. Deep in the roots of ancient China history there must have been a famous legend about a family of eight. The Pakua's family of eight is remarkably close to the Middle East legend of the eight members-family of Noah who

CHAPTER 5 RECORDER OF ENVIRONMENTAL CHANGE 63

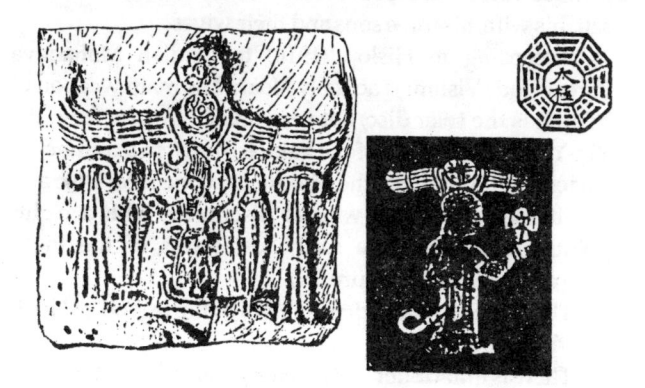

Figure 5.1 Winged Disc Symbols — Hittite Winged Disc has a characteristic eight-points star in centre (above, left), Ancient Chinese chieftains had the Falcon on their war banners. The eight-points star is reminiscent of the Chinese eight-sided Pakua (above, right). Egyptian Winged Disc with two serpents at disc (Below, first row). Eight sections discs in Syrio-Hittite disc (Bottom, left) and Babylonian disc (Bottom, right).

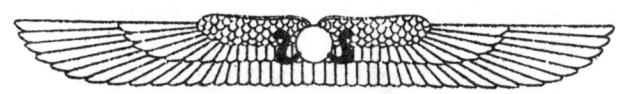

Winged disk from the Temple of Ediou, Egypt.

escaped the Great Flood! Noah's family consisted of himself, his wife, his three sons and their wives.

According to Hislop (1916) the Indian Mahadeva (Great God) Vishnu is actually Noah. The main weapon of Vishnu is the solar disc, not very much different from the Yin-Yang disc symbol of the Pakua. In fact, in a number of ancient civilisations in the Middle East, the solar disc and an alternate form, the winged disc, often with a eight-points central star, are really lost forms of the Eight Diagrams or Pakua (Figure 5.1)

The Pakua is the ancient symbol of the legend of Noah and the Flood.

There is little doubt that in its original form the family of eight of the Pakua is equivalent to the Middle East legend of Noah's family. This remarkable symbolism of a family of eight is another of the clues that the Pakua is connected with ancient Middle East or Biblical Hebrew traditions.

■ Changes In Sequences In I Ching Caused By Climatic Factors

Significant changes have occurred in the sequences of eight basic trigrams and 64 hexagrams of the I Ching. Philosophers, already puzzled about the basic Pakua, are understandably puzzled by the reasons underlying these changes.

There was a change to the eight trigrams arrangement from the Early Heaven Array to the Later Heaven Array (Figure 5.2):

- In what is probably a very ancient saying, the eight primary trigrams are named in a sequence of pairs that, according to tradition, goes back to Fu Hsi – that is to say, it was already in existence at the time of the compilation of the Book of Changes under the Chou dynasty. It is called the Sequence of Earlier Heaven, or the Primal Arrangement ... Ch'ien, heaven, and K'un, earth, determine the north-south axis. Then follows the axis Ken-Tui, mountain and lake ... Chen, thunder and Sun, wind ... Li, fire and K'an water ... Within the Primal Arrangement the forces always take effect as pairs of opposites ...

- Here the sequence of the eight trigrams is given according to King Wen's arrangement, which is called the Sequence of Later Heaven, or the Inner-World Arrangement. The trigrams are taken out of their grouping in pairs of opposites and shown in the temporal progression in which they manifest themselves in the phenomenal world ... It is highly probable that section 5 represents a cryptic saying of great antiquity that in the passage below has received an interpretation referable no doubt to the Confucius school of thought ... (Wilhelm, 1951. pp.266-269).

■ Order Of Mutual Production Changed To Mutual Conquest

The Hou-T'u and the Lo-Shu also reflect the change in the order of the trigrams within the Pakua in terms of the interaction of the Five Elements (Skinner, 1982. pp.55-57; de Kermadec, 1983. pp.82-83) (Figure 5.2)

- The first portrays the relationships of the five elements in the Former Heaven Sequence ... The sequence of the Hou-T'u is thus one of giving birth. The elements give birth to each other [Wood-Fire-Earth-Metal-Water-Wood = The mutual production order] ...

- On the other hand the Lo-Shu ... Later Heaven Sequence ... indicates the destructive order of the elements. Each element destroy another in the sequence shown [Wood -jaundice- Earth -plague- Water -death in youth- Fire -natural calamities- Metal -wasting away and injury- Wood = The mutual destruction order]

The Former Heaven Sequence stands for the Heavenly order, whilst the Later Heaven Sequence treats the less perfect cycle of seasons and manifestations on the earth itself

66 THE CHINESE PAKUA

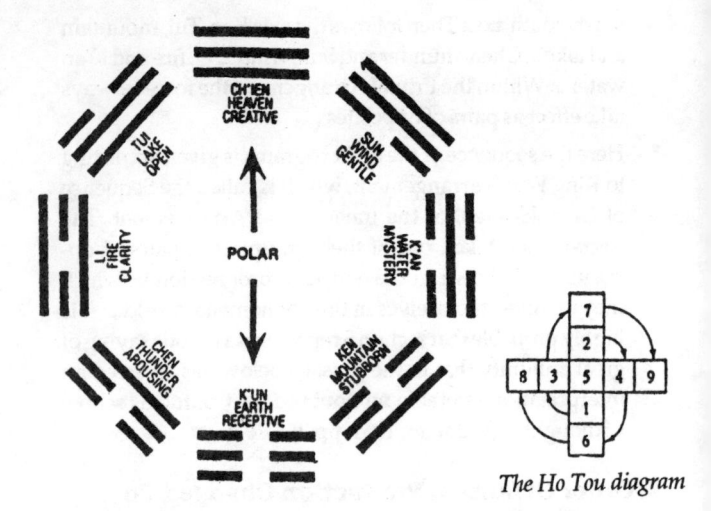

A. *Sequence of Earlier Heaven or Primal Arrangement or Fu Hsi Arrangement*

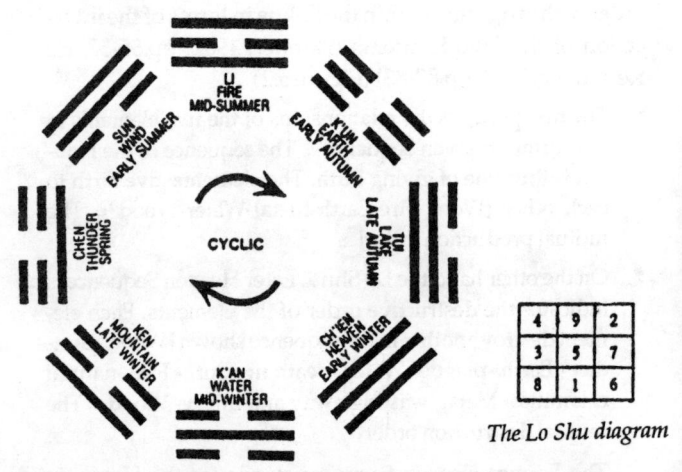

The Ho Tou diagram

B. *Sequence of Later Heaven or Inner-World Arrangement or King Wen Arrangement.*

The Lo Shu diagram

Figure 5.2 *The Eight Diagrams and their changes*

CHAPTER 5 RECORDER OF ENVIRONMENTAL CHANGE

and is thus prominent in the Earth section of the Feng-Shui compass (Skinner, 1982. p.64). The Former Heaven Sequence is the ideal version, whilst the Later Heaven Sequence is the practical application of the trigrams to the earth ... The Later has the more practical application to the strategically important Earth ch'i ... The Former Heaven Sequence corresponds with the Hou-T'u diagram whilst the Later Heaven Sequence corresponds with the Lo-Shu diagram. (Skinner, 1982. pp.61-63)

It appears that the period of the Early Heaven Array was one when the natural elements were harmonious and conducive for human living. But environmental conditions changed and the elements become hostile. An understanding of the hostile aspects of the elements become more important, including the methods to combat the adverse effects of the hostility. Hence, the emergence of the Later Heaven Array.

These changes may have to do with changed conditions brought about by the Great Flood. There are speculations that before the Flood the earth's climate was very equitable and human beings lived long life. But after the Great Flood, the climate became harsher and more prone to extremes. Fu-Hsi's arrangement must be applicable to conditions before the Great Flood. King Wen of the Chou dynasty took steps to realign the applications of the I Ching with changed conditions after the Flood.

This is not an unreasonable theory as the Great Yu claimed to regulate the floods following the principles of the I Ching according to the Lo-Shu or Later Heaven scheme (Gorn, 1904). Flooding appears to be an early problem for human living and flood control became a crucial role of the ruling families. It is likely that much of the I Ching may also relate to environmental and climatic issues.

■ Relationship Of Later Heaven Array To Phases Of Solar Year

An evidence that the changed Pakua has to do with changed climatic conditions is seen in the Lo-Shu's numbering.

In the Lo-Shu, there are nine groups of dots representing numbers. These are usually shown in a three by three magic square. The virtues of the square include that the numbers in any rank, file or diagonal always add to fifteen which happens to be the number of days in each of the twenty-four phases of the solar year. These nine chambers the nine palaces of the Ming T'ang, the temple through which the Emperor was supposed to circulate according to the season of the year. The trigrams provide indications of the best rooms of a house for specific purposes or for specific members of the family. (Skinner, 1982. pp.61-63)

The unique numbering could thus be a move to synchronise the use of the permutations of the Pakua with the solar year, likely as a device to keep track with the changes in the seasons.

■ "Li" For Fire Moved From East To South

The Pakua is associated with natural climatic elements like Thunder, Water-Clouds-Rains, Fire-Sun, etc. Another evidence of the climatic role as the basis of the change is reflected by the change in the position of the hexagram "Li" for "Fire".

When King Wen took the initiative to alter the sequences of the hexagrams, there was one change which could be related to the changes in the geography of the Chinese people. In the Fu Hsi's Early Heaven Array of the trigrams, the trigram Li (Fire and Light) was at the east. But in King Wen's Later Heaven Array, the trigram Li is at the south.

A little thinking would uncover one reason for this change. Fu Hsi's Early Heaven arrangement was when the Chinese people were in a land where the sun rose from the east. But during King Wen's time (Later Heaven) the people had moved to a place where the sun shined from the south! This simple change reveals that the Chinese people originally came from a region where the sun indeed rose and shine in from the east – in Mesopotamia. Whether they be buildings or temples, the Middle East people, including the Jews, arranged their doors to face east and the Chinese arranged their doors to face south!

Hence, the change of the position of "Li" for "Fire" is a Pakua memory of the migration of Chinese race from Mesopotamia.

■ Memory Of Climatic Changes Caused By Flood

The Pakua is a memorial of the universal legend of the Flood. It contains the symbol of the legend of the eight members family of Noah. The changes from the Early Heaven to Later Heaven Arrays testify to major changes in the world climatic conditions which must have been brought about by factors associated with the legend of the Flood.

Then, special aspects of the changes show that the Chinese originally came from a region where the sun shines in from the East.

The ancient Chinese realign the Pakua to maintain it as a device to measure time and direction and their cyclic environmental influences. In the process, the ancient Chinese unwittingly left behind a historical testimony of the major climatic changes caused by the Flood.

6

THE ESOTERIC THUNDER MAGIC OF PAKUA

■ Five Elements As Basis Of Pakua Magic

Why do the Chinese hang up the Pakua, often with the image of Taoist Pope Chang Tao-Ling riding the tiger, over their household doors to ward off evil? (Figure 1.2)

While the Pakua, through the highly mathematical I Ching and Ganzhi system, would be seen as a philosophical symbol, it is also the basis of the powerful Taoist magic. For that is what the PAKUA also is, a mystic device to manipulate powerful, unseen spirit forces.

The Chinese would be generally fascinated by two major forms of magic based on the Pakua and Ganzhi system:

1. One art of divination is the famous art of Feng-Shui, based on that locational characteristics are mainly influenced by wind and water. The art is used to determine the auspiciousness of the location for a particular person of family.
2. The other is Chinese "fortune-telling." This could be the astrological system based on the Ganzhi system of the Ten Celestial Branches and Twelve Terrestrial Branches. It could also extend to Chinese palmistry and facial features.

Both are methods of peering at destiny and both methods have their arsenal of tools to modify destiny.

The fundamental concept of Pakua magic is that the world is composed of qualities symbolised by the Five Elements of Wood, Fire, Earth, Metal and Water. These Five Elements are the Four Cardinal Points of the Pakua with the

CHAPTER 6 THUNDER MAGIC OF PAKUA

fifth as the centre and are matched with the Four Heraldic Animals plus the "Golden Lung" as the centre. The magical use of the Five Elements is based on either of these premises:

1. The Mutual Production Relationship, where wood produces fire, fire earth, earth metal, metal water and water wood. This is the Early Heaven or Fu-Hsi Array of the Pakua. It is also called the Prior or Anterior Heavens Array. The Hou-T'u is its fundamental design.
2. The Mutual Destructive Relationship, where wood overpowers earth, earth conquers water, water fire and fire metal. This is the Later Heaven or King Wen Array. It is also called the Posterior Heavens Array. The Lo-Shu is its fundamental design.

There is a difference in the nature of the spirit forces behind the two forms. The Taoist distinguishes between the spirits of the visible Posterior Heavens from the heavenly worthies of the eternal Prior Heavens. (Saso, 1978. p.241). When the world was governed by "heavenly worthies" during the Prior Heaven Pakua, evil thoughts and actions were alien. The coming of contending forces leading to evil is signaled by the emergence of the Posterior Heaven forces.

The Lo-Shu's arrangement is reflected in the designs of important buildings. The main gates of the grounds of palaces and temples are arranged according to the Four Directions. The Lo-Shu is the basis of the nine halls of the mysterious "Ming Tang" which determine the living position in the palace which the Emperor was to frequent according to the seasons (Figure 6.1, after de Kermadec and Poulsen, 1982. p.7). The familiar tall columnar pagoda, often with seven or nine storeys, is a Five Elements design to manipulate the Feng-Shui of the locality.

The permutations inherent in the Ganzhi system and the Mutual Production or Mutual Destruction Relationships represent two special major aspects of the influence of the Pakua. The terms of the Five Elements of the Four Heraldic Animals are devices to remind the practitioner of the nature of the particular sphere of influence he is calling on.

■ Demon Fighting and Black Magic

The common Chinese may fear the malevolent influence of spirits and the use of black magic by one's enemies. During sickness and misfortune the Chinese may turn to the magical arts for solutions. When normal precautions have failed, the cause would be attributed to demons and the magician's aid is then sought. It is in combating and manipulating the spirit forces that Pakua's magic is spectacularly used.

The Taoist priest-magician has his familiar Pakua emblem. The use of the Pakua for magic could conjure up the image of black magic and is a subject filled with emotional overtones. Unfortunately, because the true magical art of the Pakua is profound and secretive, charlatans are many and there are always ample gullible victims. The vast majority of priests really know nothing of its true magic. They have learnt a small assemblage, sufficient for them to perform the normal rites for birthdays, marriages, blessings of business and funerals. Adequate for a living but never meant to be directed against the true demonic forces.

For dealing with demonic forces, the Master of the Pakua knows he always has to prepare prior to the actual rites to battle the evil. There may be a number of days of cleansing, of fastings and prayers before the battle. He must know how to summon other unseen powers to assist. Anything less expose both the Master and his victim to great danger.

In this the Pakua is especially related to the two Masters; Chung Kuei the Demon Queller and the Taoist Pope Chang Tao-Ling riding the Tiger.

CHAPTER 6 **THUNDER MAGIC OF PAKUA** 73

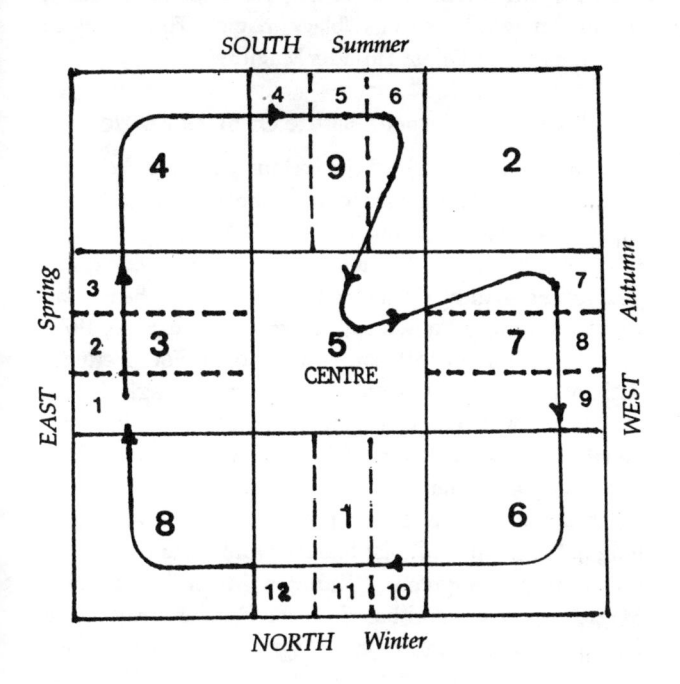

Figure 6.1 The Ming Tang Palace of the Emperor — The Lo-Shu Magic Square positions determine the section of the palace and empire he would be in according to the seasons. The small numbers determine his approximate accommodations in the palace according to the seasons, while the larger odd numbers determine the approximate locations of the empire the Emperor could visit.

The Pakua Thunder Magic

Even though the common people could not understand the nature of the forces involved they have correctly sensed harmful magical forces as "black magic." The enemy of "black magic" is Pakua Thunder Magic.

Mao Shan-Serpent Nature Of Black Magic

To counter "black magic" the serious Taoist has to learn what it is. The Taoist lores identify the epitome of "black magic" as "Mao Shan" magic. "Mao Shan" magic, using a horizontal array of the eight trigrams with a moving changeable and highly flexible powerful serpent head (the trigram Chen), is known as "Serpent" magic (Saso, 1978. pp.2325, 260), a clue to its source in one of the Four Heraldic Animals. For "Mao Shan" or "Serpent" magic is the manifestation of malevolent forces of the Dark Snake of the North, the direction from which dark waters, winds and other evil come from.

In order to counter the powerful evil "Mao Shan" magic, the genuine Taoist Master would use the highly secretive but supreme "Thunder Magic." "Thunder Magic" is circular and based on the circular array of the Pakua. In "Mao Shan" the eight trigrams are also used, but they are lined into a horizontal array with "Chen" Arousing Thunder as the deadly evil "Serpent Head" – this is a reason why the Chinese traditionally associate evil demons with a straight line.

In Thunder Magic, the formation is arranged into a powerful circle to form an impregnable circle against the "Serpent Head." This circle is, of course, the popular notion of drawing a magic circle around a person to protect him. It is also why the Taoist Master walks in a circular clockwise pattern in his magic rituals. It is also why the Chinese households hang up the Pakua over the doors to ward off evil.

Pakua Thunder Magic is primarily an art to combat the Serpent black magic. Thus, the legend about Thunder Magic and the slaying of a great serpent (Saso, 1978. p235).

The Rituals Of Thunder Magic

The system of the Taoist rituals would depend on the exponent and the temple. But the systems follow some basic procedures which may involve up to a few days:

DAY 1

1. Posting up a memorial to initiate the ritual outside the temple or reading it within the temple. The stage could be a courtyard of the temple or a temporary square would be set up.

   This may be immediately followed by a number of cleansing of the site and a concert.

DAY 2

2. Then the priest in charge would perform the Announcement to summon the spirit forces.
3. The Invocation would then welcome the unseen guests.

   It may be accompanied by Flag-Raising, Noon Offering and Division of the Lamps. This Invocation would include rituals to combat malevolent forces and is best done at night.

DAY 3

4. Land of the Way ritual. This is the most important step in the system of rituals. The Taoist proceeds to stand before the Way to send his message-despatch. It is the emotional highpoint and centre of the rites.

   The ritual makes much use of the magic square of the Lo-Shu.

It is best done at dawn when the cock crows.

5. There may be a procession after the rite of the Land of the Way.

   The previous day's rites would be repeated.

Though there seem countless rituals of Taoist magic, the main rituals are based on the sequences of the numbers of the Lo-Shu. An example of the Lo-Shu role is seen in a powerful pattern of "Thunder Magic" dance of the Taoist Master illustrated in Figure 6.2. In this star-walk of the "Constellation of the Eight Trigrams" he would murmurs at each step in sequence (Lagerway, 1972. pp.84-85):

1. I carry heaven's generals on my head
2. I command heaven's soldiers
3. I sound heaven's drum
4. I broadcast heaven's voice
5. I strike heaven's bell
6. I hurl the flaming chimes
7. I lay my hand on the astral murderers
8. I set in motion my primordial essence
9. Officers and generals of the various bureaus come quickly to the altar

The ritual is a summoning and manipulation of the forces of the Four Directions. Crucial to the success of the whole ritual is that "the power of the thunder is first stored by a meditation." (Saso, 1978. p.242).

The Thunder of Phoenix Seal

Often, there are yellow papers charms with writings in red or black ink. A powerful paper charm could have the character for "Thunder" written on it (Figure 6.3). The charm therefore invokes the power of the Thunder.

The yellow paper charm may have the sentence "Nine phoenix symbol for the destruction of filth" (Lagerway, 1972. p.73) This is because the Thunder Magic is related to the power symbolised by the "Nine-Phoenix." Figure 6.4 illustrates the Thunder God; this so-called god, known for proverbial ugliness, is a bird-like deity. Thunder God is actually the Phoenix!

"Thunder Magic" against "Mao Shan" is the fiery South-Phoenix against the dark North-Serpent of the Pakua.

■ Memorial Of Lao Chun's Ancient Battle Against Evil

The magical Taoist Thunder rituals are actually repetitions of some ancient battles!:

> As the modern high priest repeats the combat of Chang Tao-Ling, so did Chang Tao-Ling imitate that of the Human Sovereign. The Human Sovereign (Lao-Chun) also called Lao-Kuei, Old Demon, having won his battle with the demons of the Six Heavens (Lagerway, 1972. p.28).

What is this ancient battle? Who is thus "Human Sovereign" "Lao-Chun" or "Lao Kuei"?

"Human Sovereign" is a term for third world Emperor Huang-Ti (also "Golden Lung")! "Human Sovereign" is the third of the triad Emperors, viz. Heaven Emperor Fu-Hsi, Earth Emperor Shen-Nung and Human Emperor Huang-Ti.

This ancient battle has to do with a battle against forces represented by the Serpent as a legend attributed the founding of all Thunder Magic sects to Hsu Hsun, a legendary Taoist said to have died in AD374. But the legend about Thunder Magic and the slaying of a great serpent do not

78 THE CHINESE PAKUA

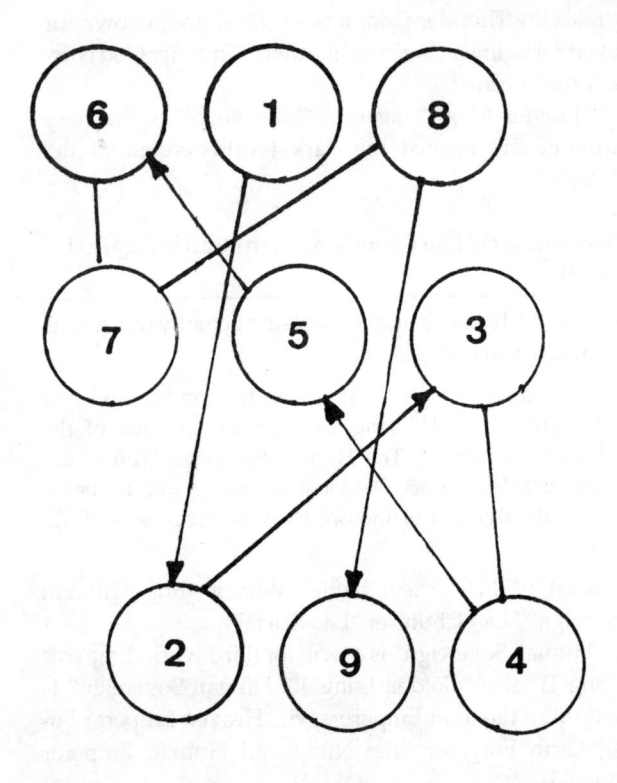

*Figure 6.2 Star-Walk of constellation of Eight Trigrams —
(The number '9' is the symbol for the Phoenix
which is invoked to destroy the evil)*

occur in Taoist writings until the mid-Sung about 1100. (Saso, 1978. p.235)

It appears that in this ancient battle, a pact was made with the four major angels of the Pakua. The four tables (directions, writs) are the four generals with whom Chang Tao-Ling made his covenant; they hold the earth together. But the centre is of celestial origin, that holds everything together. (Lagerway, 1972. p.32)

The ability to call on the influence of the Four Heraldic Animals or Generals of the Pakua is the focus of Pakua Thunder Magic against the Mao-Shan Serpent.

■ Link Of Lao Chun's Battle To Dragon Boat Festival

The origin of Thunder Magic is linked to the Dragon Boat Festival. At the time of the Summer Solstice and the longest day on the 5th day of the 5th moon is the popular colourful festive Dragon Boat Festival (Lai, 1984). The Dragon Boat Festival emphasises the water element of "Lung" with its various aspects of rains, clouds and even floods.

Different groups of people would race each other in "Dragon" boats races. Accidents frequently occur during these races. It is said that an accident has to happen so that there would be a human sacrifice to appease the spirits and that this human sacrifice is the true significance of the festival.

The Memory Of Chu Yuan Of Warring States

The festival is now popularly instituted in memory of a statesman named Ch'u Yuan a native of Ying who drowned himself in the River Mi-lo in 295BC. During these Warring States Period some 2,300 years ago Ch'u Yuan or Qu Yuan, was a minister and councillor to the king of Ch'u. He was also a patriotic poet whose motherland was the

80 THE CHINESE PAKUA

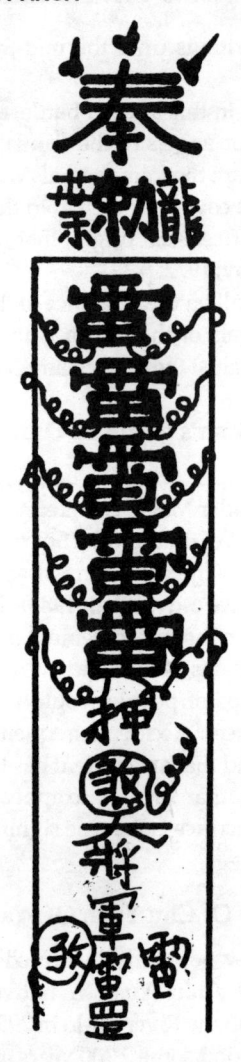

Figure 6.3 The Five Thunder Seal Charm

CHAPTER 6 THUNDER MAGIC OF PAKUA 81

Figure 6.4 The God of Thunder – (Note the wings and clawed feet. The Thunder God is actually the Phoenix, which is the Kabalic symbol of the Holy Spirit of God).

State of Chu in the southern part of China. He was born around 340 BC at a time when Chinese society was in the throes of cataclysm. He frowned upon the corruptness of the aristocrats in the state. After having been falsely accused by one of the petty princes of the state, and as a protest against the corrupt condition of the government, he drowned himself in the river.

The people, who loved the unfortunate courtier for his virtue and fidelity sent out boats in search of the body, but to no purpose. They threw rice into the river for his soul. But his ghost appeared and said that the fish ate up all the rice. So the people then prepared a peculiar kind of rice called "tsung" made of glutinous rice and wrapped in silk (which became leaves later) and setting out across the spot of tragedy, and to sacrifice to the spirit of the loyal statesman. This mode of commemorating the event has been carried down to posterity as an annual holiday. (Williams, 1931. p.114).

It is said that the boatmen continued to honour the memory of Ch'u Yuan; hence the boat races and the Dragon Boat Festival.

Eberhard (1972. pp.83-85) postulates that Ch'u Yuan's family descended from the Tai tribe of Ch'u as his poems contained several allusions to Tai's sacrificial and ceremonial songs. What is significant is that the Tai tribe of ancient times used to trap strangers, especially bearded ones and therefore often scholars, to be sacrificed on this day. The stranger would be treated well but he would know his role preserved for that day. It happened that a girl may fall in love with the stranger and the couple might escape to China.

Ch'u Yuan's act might be a voluntary human sacrifice.

CHAPTER 6 THUNDER MAGIC OF PAKUA

Dragon Boat Festival An Ancient Time of Human Sacrifices

The Dragon Boat Festival is strongly connected to ancient rites of human sacrifices:

- It is said that the equivalent of this festival in some parts of China is stone throwing between two groups wading in the waters (Eberhard, 1972. p.85). There would be songs and dancings until a person got killed by the stones.

- There are links of this festival with tales of young girls being sacrificed to the "river god" on this day.

  There was a tale of sorcerers dressing up a young girl and sending her down a raft to be married to the river god. She naturally got killed in the rapids and waterfalls. A wise governor then sent the sorcerers first to ask if the river god approve of the chosen bride. As the sorcerers did not return, the intended girl victim was saved and the custom stopped ever since.

- There is also a legend of the rich girl Meng-Chiang pining for her dead lover at the Great Wall of China connected with this day (Eberhard, 1972). Emperor Shih Huang-Ti had conscripted thousands of men to build the Great Wall and innumerable numbers died and their bones. were buried into the walls. Han Chi-Liang was the only son and tried to escape the conscription. In his hiding he met the girl and both were married. But the police chief took him away to the Great Wall. The girl managed to locate her husband's bones with her tears which turned the bones red.

  This legend is sometimes connected with the famous "Keng Hua" the desert Christmas cactus whose lovely blooms opened only for the deep nights, poignantly reminding of the delicate forlorn love. Once again a king was walking in the garden during the mourning for his later father. He heard crying in the garden and saw a beautiful girl weeping. The girl too was crying for her dead father. The king wanted to marry her but both found that they were brother and sister and the match was forbidden. The king insisted on the marriage and locked up the girl in a desert fortress to be readied for the marriage. On the wedding eve, the girl escaped into the desert. When the soldiers found her, she was dead, surrounded by the desert cacti which were blooming in that night.

The 5th Day of the 5th Moon of the Dragon Boat Festival appears to have a strong connection with an ancient concept of the tragedy of love.

The Chinese ceremonial fertility bath of iris broth for both men and women is said to be connected to the river sacrifice of this day (Eberhard 1972 p 90). Instead of bathing in an orchid bath or drinking wine seasoned with iris, one could hang up the artemesia (Eberhard, 1972. p.92).

■ Ancient Festival To Bring Rains

The festival may have an earlier origin, and may be inaugurated with the object of propitiating the beneficent "Lung", in the hope that he would send down sufficient rain for the crops (Williams, 1931. p.114)

The reasoning is logical as this period is the period of the longest day and of the strongest heat of the year. As Eberhard (1972, pp.78-79) notes, despite the superficial gaiety of the festival, there is "an element of fear and horror hidden in every ceremony ... Man is on the defensive against dangerous enemies, overwhelming dark powers."

This Fifth Month Festival or Summer Festival or Dragon Boat Festival is one of the three main folk festivals of China, apart from the Spring Festival and the Mid-Autumn Festival. It falls on the 5th day of the 5th month and is an age-old festival. This festival had been observed long before Qu Yuan was born and the many customs observed on that day had something to do with "Lung".

CHAPTER 6 **THUNDER MAGIC OF PAKUA 85**

Figure 6.5 Pakua with Chang Tao-Ling riding the White Tiger — Hang over main door to ward off evil influence.

Figure 6.6 Paper Charm against evil influences of the Five Poisonous Animals. — The charm is suspended from the roof on the 5th day of the 5th moon. The charm appears to spring from the invocation of the power of the Pakua. This 5th day of the 5th moon is also the Dragon Boat Festival and the time when the Taoist Pope Chang Tao-Ling rides out on his tiger to quell evil.

CHAPTER 6 **THUNDER MAGIC OF PAKUA** 87

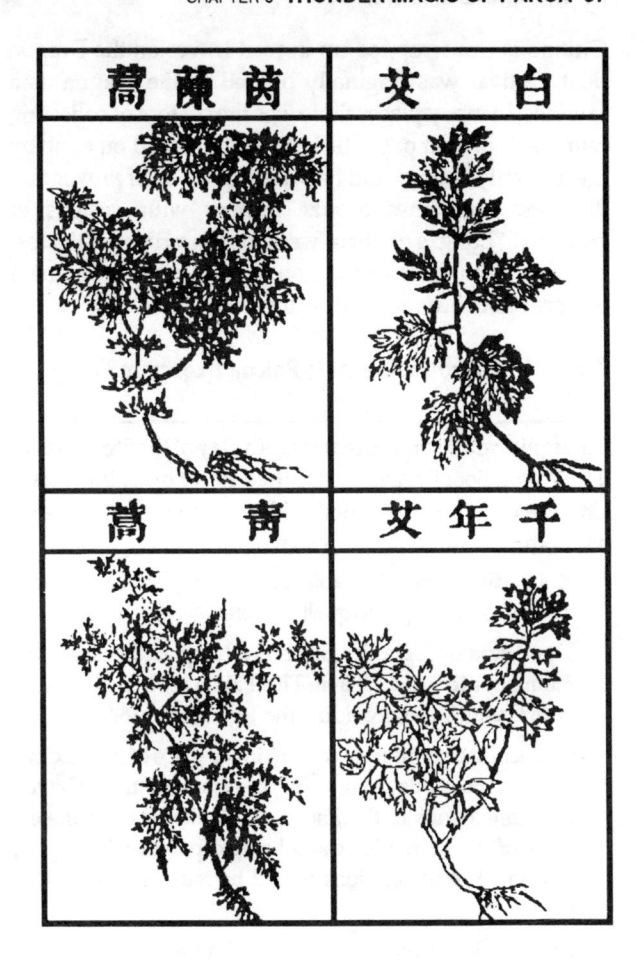

Figure 6.7 *Artemisia argyi (pai ai)* — From Pen Tshao Kang Mu (AD1596). Hanged up on 5th Day of 5th Moon to ward off evil. The plant contains santonin, used against nematode parasites and also in moxa cautery.

88 THE CHINESE PAKUA

Glutinous rice wrapped up in reed leaves on the Dragon Boat Festival was originally offered to the dragon as a sacrifice. In many places there was the custom of collecting rain water on that day. The holy water spread on earth by the heavenly "Lung" and had the reputation of preventing diseases. Sometimes bronze mirrors with designs of crouched "Lung"s on them were cast on a river on the festive day. With these mirrors on hand rain would come if one prayed to heaven for it. (Xing, 1988. pp.36-37)

■ Five Poisonous Animals Pakua Exorcism Of Demons

But significant to note is that this 5th Day of the 5th Moon of the Dragon Boat Festival is also the date for other important Chinese customs associated with warding off evil ... and use of the Thunder Magic design of the Pakua:

- It is the time when the Taoist Pope Chang Tao-Ling would ride out on his Tiger to quell demons.

    The Pakua or Eight Diagrams is often placed outside the main door to ward off evil. This Pakua is often illustrated with Chang Tao-Ling riding the Tiger (Figure 6.5).

    Or the illustrations may contain in the place of the Pakua a huge red cock busy killing the poisonous animals. The red cock (analogous to the Phoenix) is believed to be the essence of male Yang force and hence capable of destroying the evil. The illustrations would be red print on yellow papers.

- Or the Pakua may be illustrated with the Five Poisonous Animals, viz. snake, scorpion, toad, centipede and spider, also to ward off evil (Figure 6.6)

    This symbol would be placed on the roofs on the 5th Day of the 5th Moon to ward off the evil influences of these Five Poisonous Animals. It is a general charm against evil as a whole.

CHAPTER 6 THUNDER MAGIC OF PAKUA

- Sometimes the five animals are placed in a jar till one is left alive. That survivor would be killed and dissolved in wine or food. It is said that taking this preparation would ward off evil.

  One drinking the preparation would also fall in love with the server. In fact several love charms could be prepared on the 5th Day of the 5th Moon such as small stones from the magpies nests.

- During the initial few days of the 5th Moon, the Demon-Queller, Chung Kuei, is sometimes invoked.

- Artemesia, a plant believed to ward off evil, is also placed outside the main doors to ward off evil on this 5th Day of the 5th moon (Figure 6.7). Several sayings connected to this are:

  If on the 5th Day of the 5th Month Festival you do not wear artemesia you will die away from home

  On the 5th Day of the 5th Moon, if you do not stick up artemesia you will hardly eat any new wheat

  On the 5th Day of the 5th Month stick it in the gourd or fire will come

  On the 5th Day of the 5th Month you do not stick up artemesia you will become a clam-shell when you die

Despite the apparent gaiety of the Dragon Boat Festival, the 5th Day of the 5th Moon, indeed the whole 5th Moon, is a time of danger. One should not climb a roof, beds and mattresses must not be exposed to the sun on this day (Eberhard, 1972. pp.96-97)

The use of the Pakua against the 5 Poisonous Animals (which include the Serpent) on the 5th Day of the 5th Moon is the same as the Pakua Thunder Magic legend of Human Sovereign "Lao Chun" or Huang-Ti alias "Golden Lung" destroying the Serpent.

There is also a relationship between this ancient battle against evil with some water or rain crisis. "Lung" would be called upon not only to provide rains for the crops but also to protect the people against diseases. Perhaps this could be linked to diseases which come in the wake of lack of water for washings and bathing as well as diseases which come with the hot weather conditions of rainless times.

■ 5th Day Of 5th Moon Is A Universal Festival

It is significant to realise that this period of the 5th Day of the 5th Moon, the Summer Solstice, is also known in several cultures even in the West as the time of the Harvest Festival and may be equivalent to the time of Saturnalia and the May Pole Dance. The May Pole Dance itself could be another form of the Thunder Magic Dance. The indigenous people of South East Asia, like the Kadazans of East Malaysia, also have harvest festivals around the same periods – which in ancient times were connected with head-huntings. Just as the ancient Chinese associate this day with human sacrifices, the western Harvest Festival is also associated with human sacrifices.

This day is evidently some very ancient memory among many cultures of a universal event of a great evil. The element of human sacrifice is strong. An ancient event where a tradition of a tragedy of a great love also featured.

As Xing (1988) speculates, the many customs observed on that day have something to do with "Lung" – some ancient events in which "Lung" participated. This memory of "Lung" must have migrated into China from somewhere... and along with it the Pakua and its esoteric powerful Thunder Magic...

7

THE FIVE EMPERORS PAKUA TALISMAN

The five elements are incomplete ... Proverb 712 (Plopper, 1935. p.118)

■ The Way Of The Talisman

As an abstract religion, Taoism would have appealed little to the average man who, pressured by the needs of everyday living, has no leisure time to devote to his own perfection and ultimate immortality. However, Chang Tao-Ling, the first Taoist Pope, found a way to popularise the religion among the common people through the invention of charms and talismans.

There is a great variety of charms and talismans. Originally, they were written on bamboo slips but are now written on paper or silk. These invoke blessings or ward off evil.

The Pakua, itself and/or the mirror a powerful talismanic emblem, is associated with a series of charms where the number "eight" features (Figure 7.1). One set are the emblems of the Eight Immortals. Another set are the Eight Treasures, which are the Pearl, Lozenge, Stone Chime, Horns, Coin, Mirror, Books and Leaf, symbolising respectively Power, Victory, Felicity, Happiness, Protection, Marriage, Wisdom and Health. The Buddhist also have their set of Eight Buddhist Emblems.

The Pakua has a "Five Emperor Gods" variant (Figure 7.2).

The "Five Emperors" Pakua

This "Five Emperor Gods" version of the Pakua features strongly in Taoist talismatic art as another way of manipulating the forces of the Five Elements:

In the Five Elements according to the Former Heaven Sequence, the five elements of wood, fire, earth, metal, water correspond respectively to east, south, centre, west and north. They are also connected respectively to the five animals azure dragon, red phoenix, yellow dragon, white tiger and black snake-tortoise and the "Five Emperors" Fu-Hsi, Shen-Nung, Huang-Ti, Shao-hao and Chuan-hsu. (Skinner, 1982. Table 5, pp.58-59)

Both Fu-Hsi and Shen-Nung are also Chinese Gods of Medicine, while Shen-Nung is also God of Agriculture (Plopper, 1935; Werner, 1922). The "Five Emperor Gods" could be invoked for health and blessings.

Basically, the Taoist Thunder Magic ritual is the summoning of the "divine soldiers of the Five Emperors" (Lagerway, 1967. p.35). The universe is believed to be divided into five camps, each presided by one or the other of the "Five Emperors." In some of the rituals, these "Five Emperors" could be directly invoked.

The "Five Emperor Gods" symbol is very old:

Prominent among the Stars worshipped are the Five Planetary Stars, the homes of the Five Emperors. About 2500BC the Emperor Chuan Hsu Kao Yang appointed six princes to govern the Five Regions of the universe, together with the five elements of which it is composed. These officials were later deified as the Five Emperors presiding over these regions. [These six princes were the four sons (Chung, Kai, Hsiu and Hsi) of his predecessor Shao-hao, his own grandson, Li and Kou Lung the son of Shen Nung]. (Plopper, 1935. pp.41-42)

CHAPTER 7 **FIVE EMPERORS PAKUA TALISMAN** 93

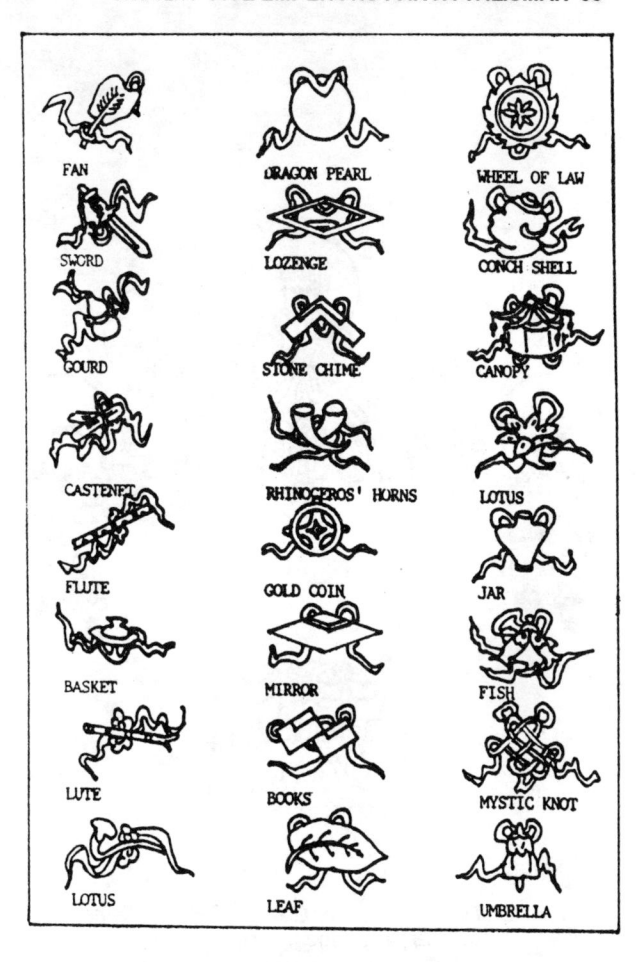

Figure 7.1 Talismantic Emblems of "Eight" Group — Left are the eight emblems of the Eight Immortals. Central column are the Eight Treasures. Right column are the Eight Buddhist Emblems.

94 THE CHINESE PAKUA

Figure 7.2 The Five Emperors Gods — The "Five Emperors" are Fu-Hsi, Shen-Nung, Huang-Ti, Shao-Hao and Chuan-Hio. The "Five Emperors" charm is a "Five Fortunes" charm. Paper strips of five colours with various images and writings are based on the "Five Emperors" significance.

The "Five Emperors" Fu-Hsi, Shen-Nung, Huang-Ti, Shao-hao and Chuan-hsu are also inter-equivalent with five other rulers (Plopper, 1935. p.42):

- Chung, Li, Kou-Lung, Kai and Hsiu-Hsi.
- Tsi-Hou, Chu-Yung, Hou-T'u, Ju-Shou, and Hsuen-Ming. These are more properly the assistants of the "Five Emperors."

These "Five Emperors" are also called the Gods of the Five Planetary Stars, Jupiter, Mars, Saturn, Venus and Mercury.

The "Five Emperor Gods" symbol, covering an era from 2943 to 2207 BC, has instilled itself so strongly into the Chinese memory that it features in various Chinese magical arts. Its connection with the Five Elements is obvious; wherein the "Five Emperor Gods" Pakua symbol derives its auspiciousness.

■ Fortune Telling With Song Of The Four Emperors

A well known method of fortune telling called the Song of the Four Emperors is described in the Chinese Almanac, the Tong-Shu. This is based on the Five Elements or Five Emperors.

In the Ganzhi system, the day of the person's birth could be used to define which of the four seasons the person is born into. These four seasons are called the "Four Emperors" for Spring, Summer, Autumn and Winter, corresponding to the elements of Wood, Fire, Metal and Water.

A person born around the close of one season and the emergence of the following season is also under the influence of the Centre which is Earth.

By using the hour of the person's birth, the person could be assigned to one of the positions along the body of the Emperor of the season (Figure 7.3) and his fortune foretold:
1. Forehead
2. Shoulder, left and right
3. Belly, left and right
4. Hand, left and right
5. Sex
6. Knee, left and right
7. Foot, left and right

This fortune is under the influence of the Pakua's "tiangan" or Ten Celestial Stems level. There are seven categories of positions on the Emperor's body and these correspond to the seven animal assistants of each of the Four Heraldic Animals forms of the Four Emperors. The total of twenty-eight categories for the Four Emperors are the equivalent of the Twenty-Eight Constellations.

■ Talismans Of The "Five Emperors"

Among the myriads of charms, including those based on the "eight" of the Pakua, there is also a powerful series of talismans based on the "Five Emperors" Pakua. The number "five", rather than the congenial "eight", is more appropriate to the serious task of fighting and annihilating evil.

"Five Elements" talismans could be directly based on the "Five Emperors" or they could use papers of five colours, as below.

Five Emperors Charms

There is a "Five Emperors Gods" paper charm. Though its basic power is against famine, it is also credited with the ability to ward off diseases, of which cholera appears to be their speciality (Burkhardt, 1982. p.205). The Five

CHAPTER 7 **FIVE EMPERORS PAKUA TALISMAN** 97

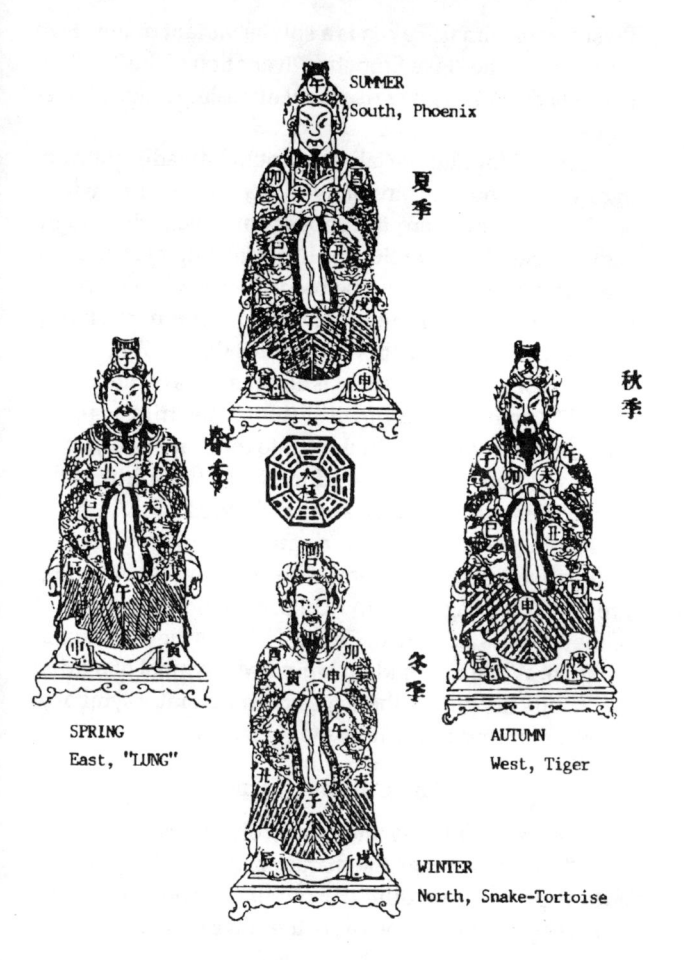

SUMMER
South, Phoenix

夏季

秋季

春季

SPRING
East, "LUNG"

冬季

AUTUMN
West, Tiger

WINTER
North, Snake-Tortoise

Figure 7.3 The Four Emperors of the "Song of Four Seasons"
— The position on the Emperor's body is
determined by the hour of birth. The same hour of
birth would be placed on different parts according
to the season of birth.

Poisonous Animals Pakua is a special variant of the "Five Emperors." The "Five Emperors" variation of the Five Elements of the Pakua gives rise to an interesting range of talismans.

A powerful Chinese talisman could be made by stringing five old Chinese coins of five different emperors with a small knife. These are the copper coins with the square central hole. For example, five different emperors coins of the Manchu period could be used. Such a talisman could worn on the body or they could be wrapped in red paper and kept on one's body to ward off evil (Figure 7.4).

This coin-sword talisman is also the basis of the "coinssword". Old brass or copper coins could be string together with an iron core to stiffen them into the shape of a sword. They could be hung or waved to invoke the spirits of the reigning Emperors to keep away evil spirits.

Another "Five Elements" charm is the image of Chang-Hsien shooting at the sun-rat with an arrowless bow (Figure 7.5). This image with five children clinging to the robes of the archer is a charm of Chang-Hsien as the protector of children. While the children would be a symbol of marital and family happiness, the acquisition of the rat, a symbol of wealth, is an endowment for the big family.

Five Colours Charms

Another way to apply the power of the "Five Emperor Gods" would be to sign the character "Fu" for "Happiness" onto papers of five different colours (Figure 7.6). These colours would be the colours of the "Five Emperors":

Golden or orange for Centre
White or pale yellow for West
Green or deep yellow for East
Blue or deep purple for North
Red or Pink for South

CHAPTER 7 FIVE EMPERORS PAKUA TALISMAN 99

Figure 7.4 The Five Emperors coins charm — Five old Chinese copper coins of five different emperors are stringed with a small blade. It is a powerful charm against evil influence.

100 THE CHINESE PAKUA

Figure 7.5 Chang Hsien, Protector of Children — Chang Hsien uses a bow without arrow to shoot at the black rat with scarlet wings. Five children hold on to his red robes. The talisman may include a brace of red cats with double tails.

Instead of the character "Fu", the image of the God of Wealth could be used (Figure 7.7). They represents the Five Fortunes or Blessings of longevity, wealth, health, virtue and to live out one's allocated span.

Papers of five colours are also used to write various talismantic charms. The five colours talisman would be pasted onto the door or wall to bring both luck and happiness.

Other messages and wishes could be written onto these papers of five colours and burnt as offerings to departed souls. Paper money with the "Five Devils" are common currency to be burnt for the departed souls.

During the Dragon Boat Festival, rice dumplings wrapped in leaves are offered to Chu Yuan, who sacrificed himself on this day (Lai, 1984). The dumplings are wrapped with sharp edged leaves to form sharp edges and points so as to scare off the demons. Originally, to ward off the demons, these dumplings were also wrapped with strings of five colours, viz. red, yellow, blue, black and white.

In western meditation, these five colours are also the components of blessings derived from positive thinking (Ponder, 1967. p.108):

> Colour healing was an ancient science and was practised in the healing temples of Egypt, India and China ...

Ponder (1967, p.112) outlines how specific blessings could be invoked through association with the appropriate five colours; as follows:

Golden	Happiness and wealth
White	Purity, honesty and spiritual aspects
Yellow	Health, vitality and strength
Blue	Achievement and intelligence
Pink	Love, marriage and social harmony

(Orange)   (Yellow)   (Blue)

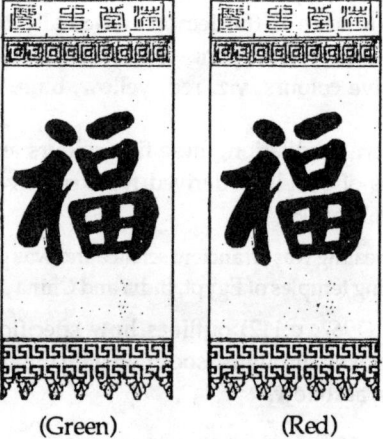

(Green)   (Red)

Figure 7.6 "Fu" Five Fortunes Talisman — Paper strips of five different colours with the character "Fu" for "Happiness" written on them. The five fortunes or blessings are wealth, longevity, health, virtue, living one's lifespan.

CHAPTER 7 FIVE EMPERORS PAKUA TALISMAN 103

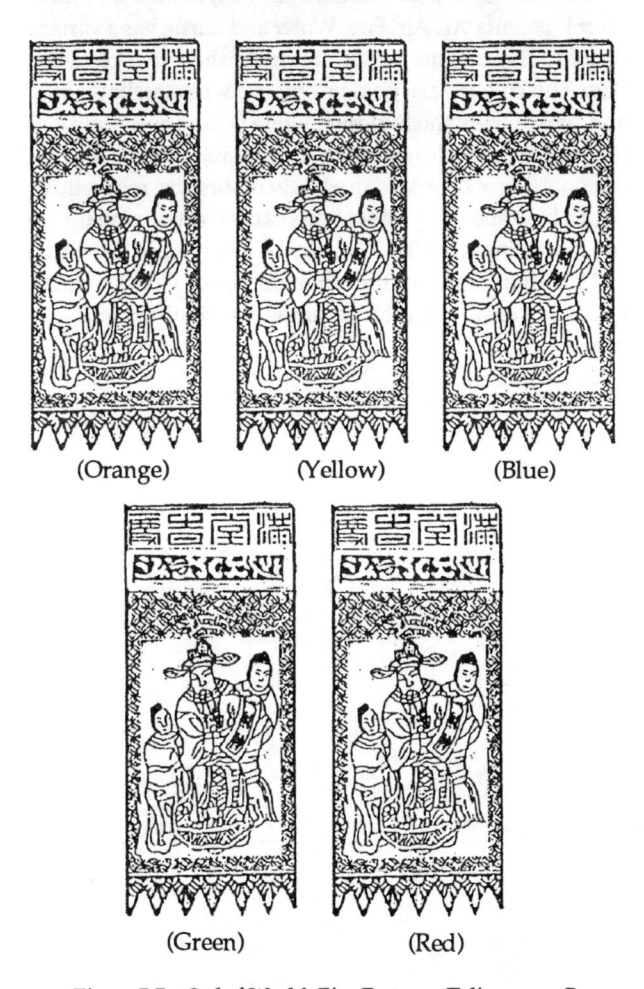

(Orange)   (Yellow)   (Blue)

(Green)   (Red)

Figure 7.7 God of Wealth Five Fortunes Talisman — Paper strips of five different colours with the God of Wealth. The five fortunes or blessings are wealth, longevity, health, virtue and living one's lifespan.

104 THE CHINESE PAKUA

It is curious to note that the Buddhist, though they have Four Elements viz. Air, Fire, Water and Earth, has a variant of these five-colours paper charm as their five coloured flag. The colours are golden orange, white, yellow, blue and pink; where the Buddhist white is the Taoist pale yellow, while the Buddhist yellow is the Taoist green. The first national flag of China also had five colours, viz. red, yellow, white, blue and black, the colours of the strings tying up the rice dumplings for Chu Yuan on the Dragon Boat Festival.

The five colours of the "Five Emperors Gods" symbol have universal significance among several ancient cultures.

⊙ PART B ⊙
ROLE OF PAKUA IN THE DEVELOPMENT OF THE HISTORY AND LANGUAGE OF ANCIENT CHINA

The several variants of the Pakua found in Chinese writings and records are examined. The examination reveals why the Pakua is indeed the device of time and direction because the ancient Chinese use the variants of the Pakua to mark major epochs in the ancient history of China.

These variants of the Pakua are also components of the Chinese ideograms. According to Chinese tradition, the first man, First World Emperor Fu-Hsi, used the Pakua or Eight Diagrams to invent writing. The Chinese tradition is not wrong, for the Pakua, through the Ganzhi system, is intimately involved with the origins, not only of the Chinese writings, but also of the alphabetic languages!

8   Debate Over Beginnings Of Ancient Chinese History
9   The Five Emperors And Three Dynasties
10 First World Emperor Fu-Hsi, Originator Of Pakua Alias "Lung" At The East
11 Basis Of The Chinese Ideograms
12 Middle East Legends In Chinese Ideograms
13 The Gammadion-Pakua Ideograms

8

DEBATE OVER BEGINNINGS OF ANCIENT CHINESE HISTORY

Of all the numerous problems with which the scientific research of China is concerned, the problem of the early origin and development of Chinese civilisation is the most important, and at the same time the most fascinating (Berthold Laufer, 1914. The Journal of Race Development 1914, 5.2.160)

■ Reliability Of Ancient Chinese History

It has been shown that the Pakua symbolism of the eight members family is a memorial of the legend of Noah's family of eight who escaped the Flood. This indicates an ill-understood ancient purpose of the Pakua; it is also a historical device to record major epochs in the ancient Chinese history! The Pakua have many secrets to tell about important stages of the ancient Chinese history.

A major problem with ancient Chinese history, which goes back to 2943BC, is that archaeological evidence indicate Chinese civilisation began in China only around 1400BC. An important question, therefore, is how reliable are the ancient Chinese historical records?

Many nations have historical records that span back to antediluvian times (around and before the Great Flood year of 2348BC) (Farmer et al, 1977). Although remnants of agriculture and livestock keeping, indicative of Neolithic cultures, could be traced much earlier, archaeological digs indicate that actual world urban civilisations started in Mesopotamia and Egypt around 2900-2334BC. (Table 8.1) Urbanised civilisations started to spread to the Indus Valley in India around 2350 to 1750BC and then to China only with the beginning of the Shang Dynasty in 1400-1122BC

There have been theories that the Chinese people are believed to be migrating through Khotan (Eastern Turkestan in Central Asia) from Akkadia (of Mesopotamia) (Werner, 1922. p.13) – this route was the overland Old Silk Trade Route between China and the West (Figure 8.1).

There are the legendary "Three Divine Rulers" (San-Huang), namely the "tian-huang", Heavenly Emperor Ruler Fu-Hsi (2943BC), "ti-huang", Terrestrial Emperor Shen-Nung (2828BC) and "tai-huang", Primal Emperor Huang-Ti (2688BC). They are not to be confused with the Three Sage Emperors "Yao, Shun and Yu" (respectively 2355, 2255 and 2205BC). There is also a minor tradition of the Nine Emperors Gods as the first nine human sovereigns during antediluvian (pre-Flood) times.

But the more reliable history of ancient China could be defined by the two major eras represented by the "Five Premier Emperors" and the "Three Dynasties." (Table 8.2). The term "Five Premier Emperors" (Wu-Ti) starts with Emperor Huang-Ti (2688BC), and proceeds to Shao-Hao (2588BC), Chuen-Hio (2504BC), Yao (2355BC), and Shun (2255BC). The "Five Premier Emperors" should not to be confused with another famous term the "Five Emperor Gods" which is associated with the Pakua, covering the era ruled by Fu-Hsi, Shen-Nung, Huang-Ti, Shao-Hao and Chuen-Hio from 2943 to 2504BC

The "Three Dynasties" are the Hsia (2205-1766BC), Shang (1766-1122BC) and Chou (122BC-AD246).

Sinologists encounter these fascinating controversial issues in ancient Chinese history:

- Do the legendary Hsia dynasty and the pre-Hsia emperors exist?

CHAPTER 8 **DEBATE OVER BEGINNINGS** 109

Table 8.1
HISTORY OF ANCIENT CIVILISATIONS OF EGYPT, MESOPOTAMIA, INDIA, CHINA
(modified after Farmer et al, 1977)

Year	Egypt	Mesopotamia	India	China
5500-4300		Eridu irrigated agriculture		
5000				Yangshao hunting to village agriculture, millet
4300-3500		Ubaid		
4000			livestock	
3500-3100		Early Uruk temple building		
3100-2900		Uruk IV and III		
3000-			early Harappan agriculture	Early Lung-shan, rice
FLOOD era				**FLOOD era**
3000-2300	Old Kingdom(1)			
2900-2334		*Urban civilisation* Early Dynasty city walls		
2700-2600		Kings of Kish		
2600		1st Dynasty Ur		
2350-1750			*Urban civilisation* Indus Valley	
2334-2154		Akkad Dynasty(4)		
2112-2004		3rd Dynasty Ur		
2017-1763		Isin and Larsa		
2050-1800	Middle Kingdom			
1894-1595		1st Dynasty Babylon(5)		
1750-1550	Hyksos invasions (7)		(2)	
1600-1400		Dark Ages		
1600-1122				*Urban civilisation* Shang Dynasty urbanisation, temple
1565	New Kingdom (8) Hyksos driven out			
?-1157		Kassite Dynasty		
1122-256				Chou Dynasty
1122-771		(6)	(3)	Western Chou
883-627		Assyria		
771-256				Eastern Chou

1 Great Pyramids, 2800-2400 BC
2 Rigvedas, with 1028 hymns to Aryan gods, refers to period around 1700 BC
3 Ramayana & Mahabhrata refers to period around 1000-700 BC
4 Sargon of Akkad, 2279 BC
5 Hammarubi, 1792-1750 BC
6 Aramaic script, around 1000-900 BC
7 Hyksos may be term for Hebrews! Said to include Apiru or Hebrews page 94
8 Moses led Israel out of Egypt, 1500 BC. Moses said to led Hyksos groups out page 94

110 THE CHINESE PAKUA

Table 8.2
COMPARATIVE HISTORY OF ANCIENT CHINA AND BIBLICAL HISTORY
(modified after Gorn, 1904 and Bullinger, 1964)

Year	CHINA		Year	BIBLICAL
			4004-3074	Adam
			3874-2943	Seth
			3769-2864	Enos
			3679-2769	Cainan
			3609-2714	Mahal-aleel
			3544-2582	Jared
		Era of Nine Human Sovereigns worshipped as Nine Emperor Gods? (2)	3387-	Enoch
	Yiu-Chao-Shi others		3317-2348	Methusaleh
			3130-2353	Lamech
			2948-1998	Noah
2943	Fu Hsi			
2828	Shen Nung			
2688	Huang Ti			
2588	Shao-hao			
2504	Chuen-Hio			
2425	Ti-kao, father of Yao		2448	birth of Japeth
2355-2255	Yao		2447	birth of Ham
			2446-1844	Shem
2348			2348	Great Flood
2315-2205	Shun		2346-1908	Arphaxad
2287	Shun as Minister of State		2311-1878	Salah
2285	Shun as Co-Regent with Yao		2281-1817	Eber
2255	Shun as sole Emperor		2247-2008	Peleg
2207-1766	Hsia Dynasty (others: BC 2203-1766)		2219-1978	Reu
2207-2157	Yu		2185-1965	Serug
2157-2144	Chung-kung		2155-2008	Nahor
	Siang		2126-1921	Terah
	Shaou-kung		1996-1821	Abraham
	Chu		1944	Abraham 1st Call
	Hwae		1921	Abraham 2nd Call
	Mung		1912	Abraham left Egypt
	Si		1910	birth of Ishmael
	Puh-kiang		1896	birth of Isaac
	Kiung		1859	Sarah died
	Kin		1836	birth of Jacob
	Kung-kia		1812	FAmine of Genesis 26
	Kao			
	Fa			
-1764	Kieh		1792-1750	(Hammarubi of Babylon)
1794-1120	Shang Dynasty (others: 1400-1120 BC)		1500	Exodus, Moses Led Isreal out of Egypt
1150-0249	Chou Dynasty			
0249-0220	Chin Dynasty			
	Shih Huang-ti Built Great Wall of China			
0220-	Han Dynasty			

1 Archaeological evidence show urban civilisation arose in China only after 400 BC
   Intrapolations of dates before 1400 BC are thus unreliable and speculative
2 The nine human sovereigns could be the nine patriachs from Adam to Lamech
   There were also celestial and terrestial rulers before them and these may be angels

- Is the ancient Chinese civilisation primarily an internal development within ancient China or do significant aspects came from the Middle East?
- The Chinese history is most factual starting with the actual historical records of the Chou dynasty (1150-249BC). Extant historical records of China before this period, back to as far as the world first Emperor Fu-Hsi in 2943BC, have been treated with caution as they are said to be from legendary, subjective and speculative sources.

The Chinese Pakua symbolism is not unique to China but has universal significance in ancient cultures in the Middle East. The Chinese Pakua is very similar to the Middle East-Hebrew Sigil Of Saturn, the twenty-two symbols of the Ganzhi system to the Hebrew Kabalic Sifrot of twenty-two alphabets and the Pakua Gammadion Four Heraldic Animals to Middle East Kabalic Four Animals. These universalism are very strong evidence of diffusion of major culture symbols from common ancient sources. Serious consideration should be given to theories of ancient Middle East roots for the ancient but comparatively newer Chinese civilisation.

It will be necessary to have a fresh look at the ancient Chinese history.

■ Where Were The Hsia And Earlier Emperors?

Archaeological evidence have shown that ancient Chinese urban civilisation started only around 1400BC But no relics have been found for the so-called legendary Hsia dynasty and earlier kings. Earlier archaeological relics concern only primitive artifacts of Neolithic Yuan-Shao and Lungshan cultures, none of which could be the basis of the pre-Shang Hsia dynasty and earlier emperors. Where were the so-called civilised Chinese of the legends before the Shang dynasty?

Farmer *et al* (1977, pp.28-29) notes: "... the Shang dynasty (traditional dates 1766-1122BC, but 1600BC is more realistic for the year of the founding) ... The oldest surviving Chinese literary works containing information on ancient Chinese history were composed in approximately their present form only in the second half of the first millennium B.C. or later. These works contain what appear to be edicts, regulations, descriptions, songs and poems, and other matter pertaining not only to the Shang and the succeeding Chou dynasty, but to a Hsia dynasty that was supposed to have preceded the Shang and to several mythical rulers who were believed to have ruled even earlier than Hsia. If there really was a Hsia dynasty, it would have corresponded to the late Lungshan period in north China, but no archaeological evidence of it has been found. Until and unless this happens, it must be assumed that the Hsia state was at best a small rival state or tribe defeated by the Shang. The Shang dynasty, however, is known archaeologically from a large and rapidly growing number of excavated sites."

Farmer *et al* (1977, p.66) also notes: "According to the literary sources the Shang king P'an-keng assumed the throne in 1401BC and crossed the Yellow River to reestablish his court in a new capital near modern Anyang. The kings remained there until the Chou conquest in 1122BC. All the archaeologically found Shang documents were written during this period. For the two centuries of Shang rule prior to the move to Anyang there is no contemporary written documentation.." This point is significant as it is easy for writers of a period to rewrite more ancient tales either through falsifications or well-meant embellishments.

Creel (1938, 1958) notes the lack of archaeological evidence. Creel (1958, p.53) states: "It seems quite probable in fact that the whole genealogy of the Hsia rulers and every detailed circumstance of Hsia tradition which has come down to us is a falsification of later times. But it also seems certain that there was in early China a state of the name of Hsia. It was probably endowed with a relatively high degree of culture and may like the Shang state which came after it, a cultural if not political leader in the north Chinese area. But there is not yet a scrap of archaeological evidence concerning the Hsia people. Many attempts have been made to link them with excavated Neolithic sites, but so far without success. From the archaeological and scientific point of view, the curtain rises on Chinese history with the Shang dynasty people living at Anyang in the fourteenth century BC"

Problems Of Personification And Euhemerisation

Where do fantasy end and facts begin in the history and mythologies of ancient civilisations? These same problems face Sinologists examining ancient Chinese history:

- Personification, the process where purely abstract features like culture and historical periods were personified into non-existent legendary figures.
- Euhemerisation, the process where mythologies became the basis of recovery of historical facts. Personification could be followed by euhemerisation, i.e. the non-existent became myths and myths became "facts."
- Anthromorphism, the process whereby real ancient human beings and events were mythologised. That is, facts became myths.

The term "Euhemerisation" is ironical, because Euhemerus, from whom the term was coined after, actually maintains that the origin of myth is to be found in actual history, and that the gods and demigods of mythology were, to start with, actual human beings. However, "euhemerisation" denotes precisely the opposite process: the transformation of what were once myths and gods into seemingly authentic history and human beings. (Derk Bodde, 1961 in Samuel Noel Kramer, 1961. p.372).

The issue of "personification" takes that the legendary emperors and heroes in Chinese history are not real persons but are personifications of periods or kinds of cultures.

- Hirth in "The Ancient History of China" expressed his disbelief that Fu-Hsi and Shen-Nung existed. Hirth (1908, p.13) wrote: "For us the legendary emperors from Fu-Hsi onward are nothing more than symbols of the earliest development of Chinese civilisation, as the inventors imagined it, possibly in connection with old traditions."

- The fragmentary texts remaining from this collection are not consistent in describing who the Three Emperors were. They are sometimes said to be Fu Hsi, the heavenly emperor; Nu Kua (the wife of Fu Hsi) the earthly emperor and Shen Nung, the emperor of mankind. In another text the heavenly emperor is called Fu Hsi, the earthly emperor is Shen Nung and the emperor of man is Huang-Ti. The three emperors are described as having twelve heads, eleven heads and nine heads, respectively, but the term "head" is interpreted as a single ruler in a dynamic succession of emperors. Thus the heavenly Emperor was a dynastic reign of twelve kings, the earthly emperor a series of eleven kings and the emperor of humanity a series of nine kings" (Saso, 1978. pp.20-21)

- The names of the so-called Three Sovereigns reveal their legendary characters as well as their contribution to culture. They have sometimes been called the Supreme Sovereign (T'ai-huang), the Heavenly Sovereign (T'ien-huang) and the Earthly Sovereign (Ti-huang). They have also been identified with such figures as Fu-Hsi (Animal Tamer), Sui-jen (Fire-maker) and Shen-nung (Divine Farmer) who bear names that bespeak their merits. As a

CHAPTER 8 DEBATE OVER BEGINNINGS

group these figures might represent the personifications of certain stages in the development of early culture, and are hailed as culture heroes in later texts ... according to them, the Three Sovereigns and the Five Emperors belong to the realm of mythology but became regarded as human beings during the later Chou period ... The sage Shun is associated with the phoenix and has been regarded as the ancestor of the Bird Tribe, while the Flood-controller Yu allegedly identified with the mythical Kou-lung (Dragon) has been called the ancestor of the Reptile Tribe". (Kung, Hans and Ching, Julia, 1988. pp.9-10)

Exponents of "personification" could go as far as to regard almost all religious ancient cultures as naive, as these religions' earliest figures would be non-existent:

With regards to the beginning of Chinese history, one may assume that, just as the Biblical accounts of an original earthly paradise cannot be taken as historical, neither can the Chinese myths of a Golden Age be understood as fact. And, as in the case of the stories of the Old Testament Patriarchs – Abraham, Isaac and Jacob – one can similarly not expect to verify the legends of the three Sovereigns and Five Emperors (culture-heroes, primitive inventors) in their historical details ... (Kung and Ching, 1988. pp.102-103)

The "personification" theory ignores evidence for anthromorphism; i.e. historical figures do become legends:

The Chinese God of War, Kuan Kung, was a general during the time of the Three Kingdoms of the third century A.D.

Going back to more ancient times, several human beings who fought during the Chou conquest of the Shang around 1122BC (Low, 1989) became gods; their exploits no less "legendary" and "supernatural" as those of the legendary Yellow Emperor Huang-Ti before them.

Bilsky (1975) shows that during the late Chou era, the state rulers tended to canonised their human ancestors into deities and even quoted their lineages from a number of the so-called legendary emperors. That is, many old Chinese gods are usually former human ancestors of the ruling families.

The "personification" theory of the ancient emperors also ignores the fact that Chinese emperors often changed their names and restyled their names as indicative of their reigns. Hence, Chinese appellations of reigns periods are often based on transformation of their emperors' names. There may be no real objections against Hirth's (1908) and Saso's (1978) arguments that names like Fu Hsi, Nu Kua, Shen Nung and Huang-Ti could denote reigns styles but first these reigns names are based on real original founders-persons.

In fact, legends should have alerted culture historians as to the existence of real historical figures and events within the legends. Euhemerus was right – legends are usually based on real historical figures and events. The task is therefore not to brush aside legends but to detect their facts of history.

■ Historical Reality Of Hsia And Legendary Emperors

Chang (1983, p.4) has an interesting viewpoint of the reliability of the ancient Chinese records:

> The Three Dynasties form the first period of Chinese history for which we have both texts and archaeological remains. This is not strictly true for the Hsia dynasty, since we have not yet discovered written records left by the Hsia themselves, whereas we do have such records from both the Shang and Chou. But many later records pertaining to the Three Dynasties have been confirmed in essence by the

CHAPTER 8 DEBATE OVER BEGINNINGS

Shang and Chou records, and the textual information on the Hsia may thus be considered much more reliable than anything that exists for the prehistoric (pre-Hsia) period.

What the later records said about earlier events in Shang and Chou have thus been directly vindicated by Shang and Chou relics. These later records are therefore in essence truthful – so what they have to say about earlier periods prior to Shang and Chou are likely to be truthful too – the Hsia and past legendary Emperors must be real.

Wu (1982), making a critical study of the ancient Chinese historical records, notes that the careful Han historian Ssuma Chien and Confucius, equally as careful, accepted the legendary emperors as historical:

- Thus, so far as Paoxi [Fu-Hsi] is concerned there is sufficient evidence that he could have been a real historical personality. And supported by the documentation above, we may even visualise his attempt at inventing the written word ... (p.52)

- For the house of Shennong had ruled immediately before the Yellow Emperor and this fact was recorded by Sima Qian himself in the very first chapter of the "Historical Records" ... Scanty as these materials are, conceivably Sima Qian must have had more not less. But even with these, there seems to be ground to maintain that Shennong and his house are true historical figures that had played a very important role before the rise of the Yellow Emperor. Notwithstanding, Sima Qian chose not to make any mention of them, except for a brief reference to the last of the line, whom the Yellow Emperor had fought and vanquished (p.54)

- From this, Confucius's estimates of the Five Premier Emperors' position in antiquity can clearly be seen. He himself had studied all the records relating to them in the imperial archives; he was able to give the lineal descent of each of them; and he had no doubt that they were true historical figures who had played significant roles in shaping early China ... Confucius never cared to be a historian, but he was always mindful of truth and accuracy. So he confined his own accounts of them to what he knew for certain. And that was very meager indeed (p.56)

- ... when Sima Qian, in the course of writing the "Historical Records" examined the books stored in metal cabinets inside stone chambers in the imperial palace, apparently he found only "pudie" (lineal tablets) and "dieji" (tablet records) which began with the Yellow Emperor. Presumably again, those tablets bore no records about the Three Primeval Emperors. And consequently, except for this one occasion cited above the great historian never referred to them again throughout his long comprehensive history (p.50)

■ Evidence Of Ancestral Lineages And Details

Contradictions and so-called inconsistency in exploits and personal details in the records compose no argument against existence of the legendary figures. Even in modern times, contradictions and exaggerations exist in reports about the same person or event.

The many exploits and personal details constitute another main difficulty in the view that the legendary emperors were non-existent and personifications of reign periods:

- The "personification theory" has a very serious weakness in ignoring the implications of separate lineages of Shen-Nung and Huang-Ti recorded in very ancient times. If the names of Shen-Nung and Huang-Ti were personifications of culture periods, then there would be no descendants especially from Shen-Nung whose culture period was supposed to be immediately followed by that of Huang-Ti.

CHAPTER 8 DEBATE OVER BEGINNINGS

Even rulers of states in the late Chou era claimed descendency from these so-called legendary emperors.

- Many Chinese clans today still preserve their lineages from the ancient legendary emperors. For example, the "Summary of the Genealogy of Wang's Clan" (Wang Shiow-Nan, 1981) lists Emperor Huang-Ti the so-called legendary Yellow Emperor as the ancestor of the Wang Clan. There are great details recorded about the background and lineages of the legendary emperors

- The Chinese language characters preserve the name Ch'iang of the clan of Shen-Nung (Weiger, 1965. p.253). The clans of Fu-Hsi and Shen-Nung are referred to in ancient Chinese records: "When Pao Hsi's clan was gone, there sprang up the clan of the Divine Husbandman ... " (Wilhelm, 1951. p.330 – "Divine Husbandman" in Chinese is Shen-Nung)

Such references to the clanship and descendants of Shen-Nung and Fu-Hsi indicate Fu-Hsi and Shen-Nung were real and the founding leaders of their clans.

Both Shen Nung and Huang-Ti were also claimed as ancestors by various State ruling families during the Warring States times of the later Chou dynasty (Bilsky, 1975).

- Walls and Walls (1984, p.40) notes that Huang-Ti and Shen-Nung were related as half-brothers, while Fu-Hsi and Nu Kua were brother and sister as well as husband and wife.

- The several exploits of Huang-Ti, legendary as they seem, were many and very difficult to explain unless Huang-Ti was a real person. Similarly, the known exploits of Fu-Hsi and Shen Nung were often personal in nature. It is difficult to ignore the real existence of these persons.

As Wu (1982, p.56) notes, details in lineages constitute strong evidence of the existence of the legendary emperors.

■ Overlooking Evidence Of Migration Of Chinese Civilisation From Middle East

The problem leading to the personification and euhemerisation theories is that history of Chinese civilisation appeared in China proper only around 1400BC Hence, it is argued that Chinese records before then must be fictitious. This argument fails to take into account alternative theories like that the Chinese migrated from Mesopotamia in the West into China.

Events prior to 1400BC could have occurred outside China; all events about legendary emperors and heroes and events may not be within ancient China.

Students of ancient cultures should note the striking similar and universal existence of several major symbols of many ancient cultures, including those of China and the Middle East. These point to the diffusion of culture symbols from some common sources. The newer Chinese civilisation received many culture symbols from the more ancient Middle East through Chinese migration from the Middle East.

9

THE FIVE EMPERORS AND THREE DYNASTIES

■ Dawn Of Ancient Chinese History

The ancient Chinese history proper composes of the eras of the "Five Premier Emperors" (Emperor Huang-Ti, Shao-Hao, Chuan-Hio, Yao, and Shun) and the "Three Dynasties" of the Hsia (2205-1766BC), Shang (1766-1122BC) and Chou (122-246BC).

There are also the earlier "Three Divine Rulers" (San-Huang), namely "tian-huang", Heavenly Emperor Ruler Fu-Hsi (2943BC), "ti-huang", Terrestial Emperor Shen-Nung (2828BC) and "tai-huang", Primal Emperor Huang-Ti (2688BC). Also, a minor tradition of the "Nine Emperor Gods" referring to the first nine human rulers before the Flood.

However, Chinese civilisation began in China only around 1400BC – there must be a migration of Chinese people from somewhere. There have been theories that the Chinese people are believed to be migrating through Khotan (Eastern Turkestan in Central Asia) from Akkadia (of Mesopotamia) (Werner, 1922. p.13) – this route was the overland Old Silk Trade Route between China and the West (Figure 9.1).

■ Theories Of Migration Of Chinese From Mesopotamia

Keightley (1983, pp.xix-xx) enumerates the various theories of the western origins of Chinese civilisation:

122 THE CHINESE PAKUA

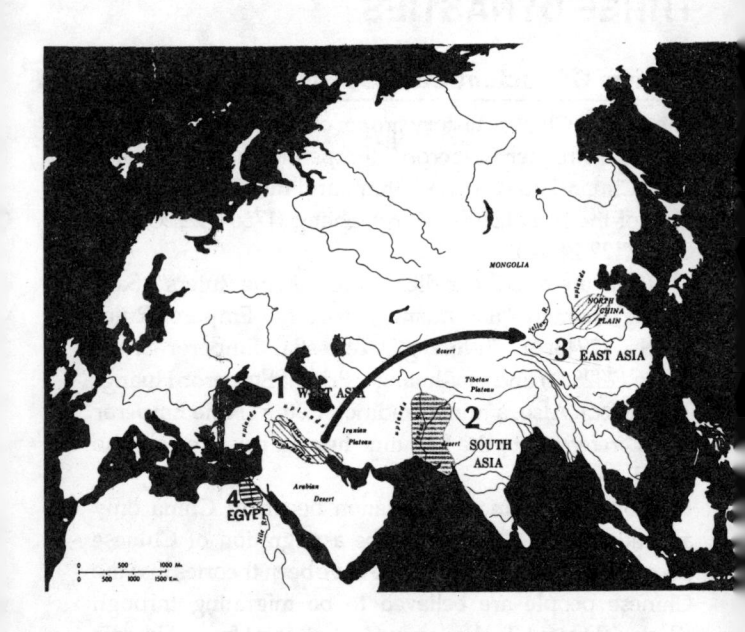

Figure 9.1 The Bronze Age Civilisations — (arrow denotes probable migratory journey of original Chinese people from Mesopotamia through Turkestan in Central Asia).

CHAPTER 9 FIVE EMPERORS & THREE DYNASTIES 123

- Joseph de Guignes claimed in 1759 that the Chinese originally came from Egypt.

- Terrien de Lacouperie, in a series of works written over a hundred years later, became interesingly convinced that the Chinese "are themselves intruders in China proper" (1887) "that the early civilisation and writing of the Chinese were simply derivations from those of Elam and Chaldea", and that Chinese civilisation was "a loan, a derivation, an extension eastward from a much older form of culture in the west" (1894).

- Lauriston Ward (1954) found it impossible to escape the conviction that many of the fundamental elements of Chinese culture had their origins in the countries near the Mediterranean sea.

- Loehr (1979, Encylopedia Brittanica) hypothesised that ceramics, the idea of script, and the technique of bronze casting were originally transmitted to China from such regions as Iran or south Russia.

Hirth (1908, pp.17-20) also notes:

- Professor de Lacouperie's theory that the Chinese descended from the Bak people in Babylon and that Huang-Ti the Yellow Emperor was really Kudur Nakhunte the Elamite chief god.

- Baron von Richtofen's theory that the Chinese originated from southwest of eastern Turkestan.

During the Manchu times, Roman Catholic Jesuits in China, seeing the several striking similarities, not only argued that the ancient Chinese culture contains much Christian truths, but also postulated that the Chinese were originally "men from Judea" and that the Chinese term "Middle Kingdom" is actually Palestine! (Rule, 1986).

The Bactriano-Margianic Complex

The disclosure of the Chinese excavations after the Cultural Revolution especially the radiocarbon datings were known to Russian cultural historians. Despite Chinese Communist Sinologists' attempts to maintain an internal basis for the origin of ancient Chinese history, Jettmar (1983) summing up the Russians' general conclusions notes that "Chesnov (1977) proposes that the development of China took place under the patronage of the south up to the Shang period but thereafter under Western patronage ... its authors were only too conscious of the counterclaims that would follow ... "

Jettmar (1983) capitulates older theories that several Chinese cultural features, like of weapons, other war tools like chariots were distinct of Central Asian regions:

> "... the Bactriano-Margianic Complex had been known through the research of Soviet authors in Afghanistan and south central Asia ... Amiet's research ... has shown that this complex dates back to the third millenium BC ... The Bactriano-Margianic Complex is important as a center of diffusion for the horse and chariot in the steppe ... I think it is possible that China adopted the use of the horse and chariot as a symbol of nobility from the same complex ... This complex could also have transmitted to East Asia "Western" cultivated plants (barley and wheat) along with certain domestic animals, particularly the horse."

Dogs' and pigs' bones, but not horses' bones abound in the Neolithic Yuan-Shao and Lungshan cultures. Horses bones are found only in the Shang dynasty relics. Sauries and Stephen (1979, p.4) state "The first culture to both ride and harness the horse were the Chinese; they were also first to exploit him ..." They (p.16) also note a curious historical fact:

CHAPTER 9 **FIVE EMPERORS & THREE DYNASTIES** 125

"Later, in 1750BC the Hittites exploded into Egypt on the force of their light, horse drawn chariots, routing the pharoah and founding a dynasty that lasted five centuries. They followed with notable victories over Babylon and Assyria, and their equestrian technique spread swiftly across the Near East ..."

Thus, the horse and the war chariot were already a reality in the Middle East around 1750BC (and probably earlier) while they were to be found in China only at least a few hundred years later with the Shang dynasty in 1400BC Yet, ancient Chinese chronology traces horses back to Emperor Huang-Ti (2688BC) who is credited with the invention of the chariot (Chang, 1983. p.42). If the third world Emperor Huang-Ti was really the inventor of the war chariot then this legendary man must be in the Middle East not ancient China!

The evidence of the Bactriano-Margianic Complex, especially of the horse and chariot, support the theory of diffusion of major Chinese cultural symbols from the older Middle East. It means that ancient China witnessed the migrations of people from the Middle East, hence the introduction of Middle East cultural symbols into ancient China.

■ The Legendary Emperors

The Chinese civilisation has the oldest recorded continuous unbroken history since 2943BC (as claimed) up to the present (Table 8.2). Gorn (1904) in his commentary on the Shu King started with the legendary first and second world Emperors, Fu-Hsi (2943BC) and Shen-Nung (2828BC), and then to the third Emperor Huang-Ti (2688BC)

The three world emperors, known as the Three Emperors, seemed to rule one after another. But there are indications that while the period between Fu-Hsi and

126 THE CHINESE PAKUA

Shen-Nung was quite long, Huang-Ti was contemporary to Shen-Nung (Walls and Walls, 1984; Hirth, 1908, p.12):

"Fu-hi's period of hunting life must have lasted several generations before it led to the agricultural period represented by the name Shon-nung; and this period in turn could not possibly have led within a little more than one hundred years to the ernomous progress attributed to Huang-Ti" (Hirth, 1908.p.14)

Some 1260 years after Fu-Hsi the throne fell to Shen-Nung, "God of Agriculture" who taught the people the art of agriculture and the use of herbs as medicine (Li, 1914. p.3)

Illustrations of these first three Emperors show that only Emperor Huang-Ti has Chinese features, for the first two world Emperors do not look like Chinese and look like barbarians. (Figure 9.2). This is an indication that China's first real Emperor was Emperor Huang-Ti and the previous Emperors Fu-Hsi and Shen-Nung were not Chinese but foreign rulers.

After Emperor Huang-Ti are the Three Sage Emperors Yao, Shun and Yu. The Shu King, (Gorn, 1904. p.52), starts its narration on history with these three great rulers Yao, Shun, Yu. It was during the times of these three rulers that much efforts were put into controlling the effects of great floods.

Yao began to reign in 2355BC (Gorn, 1904. p.4) But, previous to Yao, the emperors and patriachs of China are known to be: Ti-Kao, 2425BC, Chuen-Hio, 2504BC; Shao-Hao, 2588BC; Huang-Ti, 2688BC; Shen-Nung, 2828BC; Fu-Hsi, 2943BC Before Fu-Hsi there were the non-human rulers Yiu-Chao-Shi and others whose dates were unknown. (Gorn, 1904. p.17).

Shun was born in 2315BC, became Minister of State in 2287BC, Regent under Yao in 2285BC, Emperor in 2255BC and died in 2205BC He was suceeded by Ta Yu, the great Yu,

CHAPTER 9 **FIVE EMPERORS & THREE DYNASTIES** 127

A. *The San Huang or Three Divine Emperors — The San Huang are the First, Second and Third World Emperors, Fu-Hsi, Shen-Nung and Huang-Ti*

Fu Hsi *Shen Nung* *Huang Ti*

B. *The Three Sage Emperors.*

Yao *Shun* *Yu the Great*

Figure 9.2 The Legendary Emperors of Ancient China.

who founded the Hsia dynasty. (Gorn, 1904. pp.20-21) Shun ascended the throne in the year 2255BC when he began to reign alone after the death of Yao. In the year 2222BC therefore he had reigned for 33 years and he here requests Yu to take a share in the government, (Gorn, 1904. p.27)

The Noachian Flood occurred around 2348BC and only Noah and his family escaped through the Flood. The Chinese Emperors Yao (reign 2355-2255BC), Shun (reign 2285-2205BC) and Yu (reign 2205-2157BC) were said to be greatly involved in rectifying the effects of great floods. These floods must be after the famous Noachian Flood. The Shu King does not mention a great flood of the order of the Noachian Flood. That is, the reigns of the Emperors Yao, Shun and Yu must be after the Noachian Flood of 2348BC

■ The Legendary Hsia Dynasty (2205-1740BC)

After Yu, came the period of Chung-kung, 2157-2144BC (Gorn, 1904. p.72) Between Chung-kung, 2157BC and Kieh, whose reign terminated in April 1764BC there were twelve Emperors, namely: Siang, Shaou-kung, Chu, Hwae, Mung, Si, Puh- kiang, Kiung, Kin, Kung-kia, Kao and Fa. These do not enter into the records of the Shu king (Gorn, 1904. p.79)

Transmission of dynastic rule through family lineage started with Yu. A formal "Hsia dynasty" should start with Yu. The lack of archaeological and authentic Hsia documents not only indicate the Hsia dynasty is legendary but open the Hsia dynasty to being regarded as a fabrication of the Chou dynasty to justify Chou successful rebellion against the Shang emperor. Imperial falsifications of historical records could occur, for example, Emperor Chien Lung destroyed several historical writings critical of the Manchu dynasty.

Despite probable falsifications of Hsia legends, it is difficult to push aside all those legends of Hsia events. It

CHAPTER 9 **FIVE EMPERORS & THREE DYNASTIES**

would be very difficult to palm off a list of so-called important Hsia and pre-Hsia figures unless they were known in some forms in that ancient times. If the Hsia dynasty actually existed in some form, the lack of archaelogical evidence for it within China may only indicate the Hsia dynasty occurred outside China while the Chinese people was still migrating into China. Hsia rulers may have been disposed before the Shang arrived into China where the Hsia former ruling family might have remained in one small Hsia state therein which seemed mentioned in one Shang document. What happened to the Hsia also happened to the Shang. The Li Chi indicate that during the Chou dynasty the duke of Sung represented the kings of Shang while the rulers of Ku represented those of Hsia (Legge, 1967. p.423).

The Shan Hai Ching, a document from the 1st millenniumBC, provides an interesting clue to the possible whereabouts of the Hsia dynasty:

> "Beyond the sea in the southwest, south of the Red River and west of the shifting sands, a man wears two green snakes on his ears and rides on two lung-dragons, and his name is K'ai, the Lord of Hsia ..." (Chang, 1983. pp.65-66)

The above landmarks given by the Shan Hai Ching actually located the Hsia dynasty southwest of ancient China. "Shifting sands" mean "deserts" and "west of the shifting sands" in the southwest of ancient China would bring one to Mesopotamia! The "Red River" would be the Red Sea region near Egypt. So, "south of the Red River" of Mesopotamia would locate the Hsia dynasty in Egypt!

This could explain a number of things about the Hsia dynasty:

- It explains why the dynasty was called "Hsia" which means "summer" and denotes a hot region – like Egypt.

  Although the Shou Wen's dictionary defines "Hsia" as "the people of the Central nation" the ideogram "Hsia" is of a man working with two bare feet and two bare hands and has the meaning "summer season." The Hsia is said to be husbandmen or agriculturists and not nomads. (Wu, 1982. pp.107-108)

- In ancient times, the Chinese chieftains usually carry Yu flags embroided with the Falcon. The Falcon is a sacred emblem of ancient Egypt.
- Why archaeological relics of the Hsia dynasty itself could not be traced within China proper.

Keightley (1983, pp.xix-xx) has noted that Joseph de Guignes claimed in 1759 that the Chinese originally come from Egypt – he could be correct as the Hsia dynasty seems to be in Egypt!

■ The Shang Dynasty (1794-1120BC) and Chou Dynasty (1150-249BC)

Then came the Shang dynasty (1794 to 1120BC: Gorn, 1904. p.76) which was eclipsed by the Chou dynasty in 1150BC This Chou dynasty, spanning some 900 years, is the longest dynasty of China's history. Its final years constituted the epic era of the Warring States when both Confucius and Lao Tzu left their impacts. There was a brief rule by the Chin dynasty which saw the Great Wall of China built by the Chin Emperor Shi Huang-Ti. Then came the glorious Han dynasty spanning 400 years up to about A.D. 220.

Eberhard (1972, p.68) regards the Chou dynasty as originating from Turkish stock and that the Chou preserved parts of their ancient Turkish heritage. Several of the early Chou customs have parallels in the western Turkish areas. The Chous forged an alliance of Turks and Tibetans to conquer the Shang.

The records of the Chou dynasty (1150-249BC) are the start of the reliable historical records of China, for the earlier records, albeit continuous with the Chou records, are nevertheless legendary in nature. There are also some indications that some of the emperors separated in the ancient Chinese chronology were actually contemporaries.

■ The Three Sages

During the later period of the Chou dynasty that were born the three men who would significantly affect the Chinese thought, religion and culture: Confucius, Lao Tzu and Buddha. Plopper (1935) briefly summarises the life of these three men:

> Confucius was born in 551BC during the Chou dynasty. His father was 64 years of age and his mother only 14 at his birth ... Confucius was both an official and a teacher. However, he did not remain in official life any length of time, as it appeared to be impossible to inaugurate his reforms. It is said that he did not hold office for more than two years during his entire life ... He died in 478BC ... His tomb and a magnificent temple in his memory are still in the possession of the Kung family and yearly numbers travel to the little city of Chufou in Shangtung to visit them. pp.16-17,

> Lao Tzu was born about 604BC The details of his life, that are known, are very few. It is known that he resided in Lo, the capital of the Chou dynasty, as State Historian ... Confucius during his travels, had an interview with him there. When Lao Tzu saw the house of Chou was in decay he left the country. As he passed the border, a custom house official, Yin Hsi, requested him to write a book. The Tao Te Ching was the result. Where or when he died no one know ... p.17,

> A Chinese tradition says that Buddhism appeared in China about the year 217BC ... Gautama the founder of the Buddhist religion, was born about 542BC at Kapilavastu in India. He was the son of a Sakyan king. After 29 years of court life in response to a vision he left his home, wife, and

son on a search after peace and salvation ... After 45 years of active ministry he died at the age of eighty ... pp.17-18,

There are traditions that Confucius visited Lao Tzu (Rule, 1986. p.172; Legge, 1967; Lee, 1986. p.9). Confucius is known to acknowledge the superiority of Lao Tzu and compare Lao Tzu to the Azure Dragon (Lee, 1986. p.9; Plopper, 1935. p.52). Confucius was said to have gone and ask Lao Tzu about the "Tao" but found Lao Tzu's understanding too profound for him to understand (Lee, 1986. p.9). According to traditions, Lao Tzu even reproved Confucius for confining Li to the practices of men and holding it to be a natural principle (Plopper, 1935. p.218). Being State Historian of the Chou dynasty at Lo, Lao Tzu was thus familar with the ancient Chinese books in the Imperial library, where he was the keeper of the records (Rule, 1986. p.172; Lee, 1986. p.9). Wu (1982, p.38) writes:

> It had to wait for Confucius, 551-479BC to open up this vast hoard of knowledge to the public. Early in his life, under the sponsorship of his leige lord, the Duke of Lu, he took a special trip to the imperial city to study the institutions of Zhou as well as those of previous dynasties. He was recorded to have met Lao Tzu there and studied under him, perusing no doubt all the books and documents in the latter's charge and probably taking copious notes of them ... as a result of these studies upon his return to Lu in old age he was able to produce those works which are known as the Confucian Classics ...

Therefore, it must be from Lao Tzu that Confucius learnt of the more important ancient Chinese documents, hence Confucius's compilation of certain Chinese classics. Thus, it may be said that Lao Tzu imparted one line of Chinese thought through Confucius; the other more mystical line was to eventually emerged through Chang Liang (who helped Liu Pang found the Han dynasty around

220BC) and his eighth descendent, Chang Tao-ling, the attributed founder of Taoist mysticism who lived around the first to second century A.D.

■ Historical Significance Of The "Five Emperors" Pakua

One most significant and sacred variant of the Pakua is the "Five Emperor Gods" (Figure 7.2). This "Five Emperor Gods" version of the Pakua not only features strongly in Taoist talismanic art, but also marks a most important turning point of the ancient Chinese history.

Fu-Hsi, Shen-Nung, Huang-Ti, Shao-Hao and Chuen-Hio are the "Five Emperor Gods" of the four cardinal plus central points in the Eight Diagrams or Pakua. The "Five Emperor Gods" symbol is very old as it was related to the action of Emperor Chuan Hsu Kao Yang (2500BC) who appointed six princes to govern the Five Regions of the universe, together with the five elements of which it is compose. (Plopper, 1935. pp.41-42)

Legend Of Huang-Ti And The Four Directions

The Pakua symbol of the "Five Emperor Gods" is significant as it is linked with an ancient legend of Emperor Huang-Ti. According to Chinese tradition, Emperor Huang-Ti was the one responsible for assigning the directions of the Five Emperors (Wu, 1982; Walls and Walls, 1984). This he did after a series of battles.

According to the legend, Huang-Ti and Shen-Nung, who seems to be half-brothers, governed each one half of the world. Then was disagreement and Huang-Ti defeated Shen-Nung (Walls and Walls, 1983). Huang-Ti became Supreme Lord and took the centre and placed his son Shao-hao to the west, his grandson Chuan-hsu to the north. Shen-Nung moved south to become God of the South. Fu-Hsi was in the East.

Though Huang-Ti appeared contemporary to Shen-Nung, at least Fu-Hsi was no longer living around Huang-Ti's time. Therefore, the use of the Five Emperors' names must be symbolical – they likely represent some major racial or national differences. That is, the assignment of the different emperors to the different directions of the world is really another way of saying that the major races were assigned to different parts of the world.

This legend indicates a worldwide event. An ancient worldwide territorial allocations occurred.

The legend indicates that Huang-Ti managed to assume a powerful worldwide position whereby he could assign the races to the different parts of the world. Huang-Ti took and remained in the centre and he was the "Golden Lung". The Chinese remember Huang-Ti, in his role of sending the races to the Four Directions, as a four-faced man riding the chariot (Walls and Walls, 1984). Huang-Ti is also illustrated as riding the chariot of the Big Dipper (Figure 9.3) as a memorial of his dispersing the races to the Four Directions.

Are there other legends in other races of such a similar ancient division of races? Yes! A version is preserved in the ancient Biblical history!:

> Now these are the generations of Noah, Shem, Ham and Japeth and unto them were sons born after the flood ... By these were the isles of the gentiles divided in their lands; every one after his tongue, after their families, to their nations ... Out of that land went forth Asshur and builded Nineveh ... the families of Canaanites spread abroad. And the border of the Canaanites was from Sidon ... unto Gaza ... even unto Lasha ... And unto Eber were born two sons; the name of one was Peleg; for in his days was the earth divided; and his brother's name was Joktan ... the sons of

CHAPTER 9 FIVE EMPERORS & THREE DYNASTIES   135

A Han relief depicting the Yellow Emperor riding in his chariot, The Big Dipper.

Figure 9.3 Emperor Huang-Ti riding his chariot, Big dipper
— This is a memorial of Huang-Ti's action in
dispersing the races to the Four Directions of the
Pakua. another symbol remembering the same
event is the "Five Emperor Gods" Pakua.

Joktan. And their dwelling was from Mesha as thou goest unto Sephar a mount of the east ... These are the families of the sons of Noah after their generations in their nations and by these were the nations divided in the earth after the flood ... (Genesis 10:1-32)

This remarkable Bible passage tells of the division of the earth according to the families of Noah. This incidence of division occurred during the time of Peleg, about 2246 to 2008BC This period is not far from the contemporary period of Huang-Ti (2688BC). This Biblical division of the races is same incident as Emperor Huang-Ti dispersing the races to the Four Directions! A very important ancient world event of worldwide migrations occurred!

Evidence discussed earlier indicate Emperor Huang-Ti could only be credited with the invention of the chariot if he was not in ancient China but in Mesopotamia. Furthermore, the legendary role of Emperor Huang-Ti in dividing the races to the Four Directions is also the same event recorded in the Bible about the division of the human races just after the Flood. Emperor Huang-Ti ruled not in ancient China but in ancient Mesopotamia!

In this division, the Chinese people were assigned the East position, the position assumed by Emperor Fu-Hsi, the "Azure Lung." It is probably around this time that the races started to migrate – and the Chinese people arrived in ancient China. The close of the "Five Emperors" also marks the end of an era where humanity previously lived close together in ancient Middle East.

What are the reasons for the worldwide dispersion? It may have something to do with dwindling food supplies in an overcrowded ancient Middle East.

The "Five Emperor Gods" era thus marks a signal change in the history of the Chinese people. The Pakua "Five Emperor Gods" symbol is an ancient Chinese memory of the ancient worldwide event of the separation of the human races. The hidden symbolism of the "Five Emperor Gods" Pakua contains the very secret of the origin of the Chinese people in Mesopotamia and their migration from Mesopotamia.

10

EMPEROR FU-HSI, ORIGINATOR OF PAKUA

■ The First World Emperor, Fu-Hsi

The dawn of Chinese civilisation has not yet come to China in 1400BC, and there is Emperor Fu-Hsi, 2943BC, the mystic originator of the Eight Diagrams or Pakua. Who is Fu-Hsi?

The "Five Emperor Gods" Pakua preserves significant revelation about Fu-Hsi, who is "Lung" at the East.

Looking at the ancient history of China we will find that Emperor Huang-Ti ordered Chu Jung (Fire Emperor) to fight Hui Lu (Fire God) who was actually lived just before the time of Ti-Kao, the father of Emperor Yao. Around this time, Huang-Ti also had a famous series of battles against Chih You (Walls and Walls, 1984). Also note:

> "Fu-hi's period of hunting life must have lasted several generations before it led to the agricultural period represented by the name Shon-nung; and this period in turn could not possibly have led within a little more than one hundred years to the ernomous progress attributed to Huang-Ti" (Hirth, 1908. p.14)

> Some 1260 years after Fu-Hsi the throne fell to Shen-Nung, "God of Agriculture" who taught the people the art of agriculture and the use of herbs as medicine (Li, 1914. p.3)

The comparisons indicate a strong possibility that Shen-Nung, Huang-Ti, Ti-kao, Yao and even Shun were contemporaries even though they were designated as successive separate Chinese emperors. However, Fu-Hsi lived

EMPEROR FU-HSI, ORGINATOR

in a much earlier era distinct from that of Shen-Nung and Huang-Ti.

■ The Works Of Fu-Hsi

Emperor Fu-Hsi was credited with starting a whole series of very fundamental and essential social practices like marriage, cooking, making clothes and keeping livestocks and hunting-fishing. That is, Fu-Hsi was involved with the very beginnings of humanity.

> **Fu Hsi:** "2953-2838BC The first of the Five Emperors of the legendary period, also known as Pao Hsi Kung ... He is said to have been miraculously conceived by his mother, who, after a gestation of twelve years, gave birth to him at Ch'eng-chi in Shensi. He taught his people to hunt, to fish, and to keep flocks. He showed them how to split wood of the t'ung tree, and how to twist silk threads and stretch them across so as to form rude musical instruments. From the markings on the back of a tortoise he is said to have constructed the Eight Diagrams or series of lines from which was developed a whole system of philosophy, emobodied later on in the mysterious work known as the Canon of Changes. He also invented some kind of calender, placed the marriage contract upon a proper basis, and is even said to have taught mankind to cook their food." (Williams, 1931. p.167)

(Wilhelm, 1951: pp.328-329): When in early antiquity Pao Hsi [same as Fu-Hsi] ruled the world he looked upward and contemplated the images in the heavens; he looked downward and contemplated the patterns on earth. He contemplated the markings of birds and beasts and the adaptations to the regions. He proceeded directly from himself and indirectly from objects. Thus he invented the eight trigrams in order to enter into connection with the virtues of the light of the gods and to regulate the conditions of all beings.

The Pai Hu T'ung [written in the Han period by Pan Ku, AD32-92] describes the primitive condition of human society as follows:

> In the beginning there was as yet no moral nor social order. Men knew their mothers only, not their fathers. When hungry they searched for food; when satisfied they threw away the remnants. They devoured their food hide and hair, drank the blood, and clad themselves in skins and rushes. Then came Fu Hsi and looked upward and comtenplated the images in the heavens, and looked downward and contemplated the occurrences on earth. He united man and wife, regulated the five stages of change, and laid down the laws of humanity. He devised the eight trigrams, in order to gain mastery over the world.

Fu-Hsi was also credited with the invention of Chinese writing and that mystical Pakua or Eight Diagrams which form the centre of Chinese religious culture:

Written Characters: The origin of the written language of China is of great antiquity. After events had been recorded by knotted cords (not unlike the Peruvian quipos) and notched sticks, a writing proper began, like the Egyptian, with 'wen' images, forms of visible objects, or ornaments; the first legendary Emperor Fu Hsi, 2953BC, the third Emperor Huang-Ti, 2698BC and the Stateman Ts'ang Chieh, 2700BC, are the traditional inventors of the k'o t'ou tzu, or "tadpole characters," and the niao chi wen, or "bird'tract script," consisting of undulating marks. The historic ku wen or ancient writings, imitative of natural forms, are found on stones and metallic vases, and are the prototypes of the subsequent sinograms ... "History relates that, at the moment Fu Hsi was seeking to combine the characters proper to express the various forms of matter and the relation between things physical and intellectual, a wonderful horse came out of the river, bearing on his back certain signs of which the philosophic legislator formed

CHAPTER 10 EMPEROR FU-HSI, ORGINATOR 141

the Eight Diagrams which have preserved his name." (Williams, 1931. p.410)

Eight Diagrams: The Pa Kua, or Eight Diagrams, are represented by an arrangement of certain cabalistic signs consisting of various combinations of straight lines arranged in a circle, said to have been evolved from the markings on the shell of a tortoise by the legendary Emperor Fu Hsi, 2852BC ... Wen Wang, 1231-1135BC, the founder of the Chou dynasty, while undergoing imprisonment at the hands of the tyrant Emperor Chou Hsin, devoted himself to a study of the Diagrams, and appended to each of them certain explanations ... observations ... attributed to his son Chou Kung, constitute the abstruse work known as the "Canon of Changes", the most venerated and least understood of the Chinese classics, serving as a basis for the philosophy of divination and geomancy, and supposed to contain the elements of metaphysical knowledge and the clue to the secrets of creation. ... "In addition to the series of Eight Diagrams above, Fu Hsi, or some one of his successors, is held to have enlarged the basis of calculations by multiplying the original number eight-fold, thus creating the Sixty-four Diagrams or Hexagrams ... A six-fold multiplication of these again gives ... 384 ..., completing the number to which the diagrams are practically carried, although it is maintained that by a further process of multiplication a series of 16,777,216 different forms may be produced." William, 1931 p. 121-123)

In Chinese literatures four holy men are cited as the authors of the Book of Changes, namely Fu Hsi. King Wen, the Duke of Chou and Confucius. Fu Hsi is a legendary figure representing the era of hunting and fishing and of the invention of cooking. The fact that he is designated as the inventor of the linear signs of the Book of Changes means that they have been held ot be of such antiquity that they antedate historical memory. Moreover the eight trigrams have names that do not occurr in any connection in the

142 THE CHINESE PAKUA

Chinese language, and because of this they have even been thought to be of foreign origin. (Wilhelm, 1951. p.lviii)

Here, in what is probably a very ancient saying, the eight primary trigrams are named in a sequence of pairs that, according to tradition, goes back to Fu Hsi – that is to say, it was already in existence at the time of the compilation of the Book of Changes under the Chou dynasty. It is called the Sequence of Earlier Heaven or the Primal Arrangement ... (Wilhelm, 1951. pp.265-266).

8. Therefore: Heaven creates divine things; the holy sage takes them as models. Heavens and earth change and transform; the hole sage imitates them. In the heavens hang images that reveal good fortune and misfortune; the holy sage reproduces these. The Yellow River brought forth a map and the Lo River brought forth a writing; the holy men took these as models. – the last sentence of the section, referring to two legendary events occurring in the time of Fu Hsi and Yu respectively ... [Like Fu Hsi, one of the legendary rulers of China, He (Yu) is credited with having found the first dynasty of China, the Hsia dynasty, said to have lasted from 2205 to 1766BC] – (Wilhelm, 1951. pp.320-321)

If a man like Fu-Hsi did not arise there would be no Chinese culture! Then came the second world emperor Emperor Shen-Nung, who taught the people only a few more things:

3. When Pao Hsi's clan was gone, there sprang up the clan of the Divine Husbandman [Shen-Nung, who is said to have taught the people agriculture] He split a piece of wood for a plowshare and bent a piece of wood for the plow handle, and taught the whole world the advantage of laying open the earth with a plow ... (Wilhelm, 1951. p.330)

5. When the clan of the Divine Husbandman was gone, there sprang up the clans of the yellow Emperor, of Yao, and of Shun ... (Wilhelm, 1951. p.331)

CHAPTER 10 EMPEROR FU-HSI, ORGINATOR

The invention of agriculture by Shen-Nung is an important watershed in world's history. It indicates that Emperor Fu-Hsi lived in an era where agriculture was not necessary! Before the invention by Shen-Nung it was apparent that, besides the animal food from hunting and fishing, the people thrived on plant food through simple plucking and collection. Formal agriculture which included the use of farming tools like the ploughshare started with Shen-Nung.

Something significant happened to world climate and physical conditions between Fu-Hsi and Shen-Nung, possibly during Shen-Nung's time, to warrant the invention of agriculture.

■ Identity Of Emperor Fu Hsi, The First Man

When the Jesuits were in China, they made intense research into the ancient Chinese records and came to believe that Fu-Hsi was the Biblical Enoch (Rule, 1986. p.162). However, this interpretation may not be correct.

Emperor Fu-Hsi lived at the very dawn of the history of mankind. There are some conflicting legends about Fu-Hsi and his sister-wife Nu-Kua (Figure 10.1). According to legend, Fu-Hsi and his sister Nu-Kua were the first two human beings:

> It is true that there exist one or two other explanations of the origin of things which introduce a personal creator. There is, for instance, the legend ... which represents Nu Kua Shih (also called Nu Wa and Nu Hsi), said to have been the sister and successor of Fu Hsi, the mythical sovereign whose reign is ascribed to the year 2953-2838BC, as having been the creator of human beings when the earth first emerged from Chaos ... Ssuma – Cheng, of the eight century A.D., author of Historical Records and of another work on the three great legendary emperors Fu Hsi, Shen-Nung and Huang-Ti gives the following account of her : "Fu Hsi was

succeeded by Nu Kua who like him had the surname Feng. Nu Kua had the body of a serpent and a human head with the virtous endowments of a divine sage. ... Another account separates the name and makes Nu and Kua brother and sister, describing them as the only two human beings in existence. At the creation they were placed at the foot of the K'un Lun Mountains. Then they prayed, saying, "If thou, O God, hast sent us to be man and wife, the smoke of our sacrifice will stay in one place; but if not, it will be scattered." The smoke remained stationary ... (Werner, 1922. pp.81-82).

Fu-Hsi was reputed to be born of the Thunder God and a mortal girl named Hua Xu (Walls and Walls, 1983). Walls and Walls (1983) also note that Nu-Kua and her brother were the first two human beings on Mount Kun-Lun and were eventually married.

Is Fu-Hsi identifiable with Pan Ku, the other figure of Chinese mythological creation? This may not be as Pan Ku is believed to be a spurious invention : The most conspicious figure in Chinese cosmogony is P'an Ku. He it was who chiselled the universe out of Chaos. According to Chinese ideas, he was the offspring of the original dual powers of Nature, the yin and the yang ... which having in some incomprehensible way produced him, set him the task of giving form to Chaos and "making the heavens and the earth. ... But though the Chinese creation myth deals with primeval things it does not itself belong to a primitive time. According to some writers whose views are entitled to respect, it was invented during the fourth century A.D. by the Taoist recluse Magistrate Ko Hung, author of the "Shen hsien chuan" (Biographies of the Gods) ... (Werner, 1922. pp.76,79).

Fu-Hsi and his "younger sister" Nu-Kua were thus the world first two human beings and were also husband and wife.

CHAPTER 10   **EMPEROR FU-HSI, ORGINATOR**   145

We have earlier noted that while comparisons indicate a strong possibility that Shen-Nung, Huang-Ti, Ti-Kao, Yao and even Shun were contemporaries, But Fu-Hsi lived long before Shen-Nung, at least 1260 years earlier. If the dates of Shen-Nung-Huang-Ti to Shun cluster around 2800 to 2200BC, then Fu-Hsi lived around 4000 to 3400BC

Who is Emperor Fu-Hsi? Emperor Fu-Hsi was the Biblical Adam!

Fu-Hsi, the Chinese first man, was Adam the Biblical first man, who lived from 4000BC to just before 3000BC The Chinese remembered Fu-Hsi and his "sister-wife" Nu Kua Shih as the world first two human beings. They are, of course, the same persons as Adam and Eve the first two human beings and husband and wife to each other! Nu-Kua Shih was Eve. Nu-Kua Shih the first female Goddess is also known as Tou Mu the Mother Goddess and Hsi Wang Mu the Western Queen Mother. Fu-Hsi and Nu-Kua were supposed to be created in the legendary Kun-Lun Mountains.

Surprisingly, the geographical landmarks of the Kun-Lun Mountains, where the first man and woman Fu-Hsi and Nu-Kua were created, are known to ancient Chinese for the landmarks were given in the Shan Hai Ching (Waterbury, 1952):

2,700 miles west of China

South of the Western Sea

On the shores of shifting sands (desert)

North of the Salt Lake (Dead Sea)

North of the Red River (Red Sea)

Such landmarks identified the place of creation of Fu-Hsi and Nu-Hwa right in ancient Mesopotamia, the Biblical location of the Garden of Eden where Adam and Eve were created!

Figure 10.1 *Fu-Hsi and his sister-consort Nu-Kua — Wu Liang tomb-shrine relief (2nd century AD). Fu-Hsi is holding a carpenter's square, while the quipu (knotted cords) is personified. The inscription says: Lung Fu-Hsi first started kingly rule, trace the trigrams, the quipu, in order to rule within the seas.*

CHAPTER 10 EMPEROR FU-HSI, ORGINATOR

It is a mistake to assume that the watery waste before the creation of Fu-Hsi and Nu-Hwa was the Biblical Flood which drowned the whole world and through which only eight human beings of the family of Noah survived in an ark. According to the Bible the earth was also a watery waste before the creation of Adam and Eve the first two human beings:

> And the earth was without form and void; and darkness was upon the face of the deep. And the Spirit of God moved upon the face of the waters. And God said, Let there be light and there was light ... (Genesis 1:2-3)

These astonishing details show that the ancient Chinese know the Middle East legend of the Garden of Eden. Such a remembrance should not be surprising if the human race did migrate and radiate from Mesopotamia where the oldest civilisations were found.

The Bible credited Adam with naming birds and animals. Is this not what Fu-Hsi did?:

> (Wilhelm, 1951. pp.328-329) Chapter II. History of Civilisation : 1. When in early antiquity Pao Hsi [same as Fu-Hsi] ruled the world he looked upward and contemplated the images in the heavens; he looked downward and contemplated the patterns on earth. He contemplated the markings of birds and beasts and the adaptations to the regions. He proceeded directly from himself and indirectly from objects. Thus he invented the eight trigrams in order to enter into connection with the virtues of the light of the gods and to regulate the conditions of all beings.

Adam did many things done by Fu-Hsi himself:

> Baleus says: "From Adam all good arts and human wisdom flowed, as from their fountain. He was the first that discovered the motions of the celestial bodies and all other creatures. From his school proceeded whatever good arts and wisdom afterward propagated by our fathers unto

mankind; so that whatever astronomy, geometry and other arts contain in them he knew the whole thereof." Keckerman doubts not that "our first parents delivered over to their posterity together with other sciences, even logic also; specially seeing they are the nearest the origin of all things has an intellect so much the more excellent than ours by how much they excelled us in length of life, formitude of health and in air and food. ... From Adam sprang Seth, who, according to Josephus and more ancient records, followed his father in the pursuit of wisdom, as did his own descendents. It is said in so many words that "they were the inventors of that perculiar sort of wisdom which is concerned with the heavenly bodies and their conditions and indications." Hornius says: "The first mention of letters falls upon Seth's times; who, being mindful of his father's prophecy foretelling the universal dissolution of things, the one by the Deluge and the other by fire, being not unwilling to extinguish his famous inventions concerning the stars, he thought of some monument to which he might concredit these mysteries ... (Seiss, 1972. p.150).

■ Emperor Fu-Hsi, The Azure "Lung" at The East

In the "Five Emperor Gods" Pakua, "Lung" at the East is also the symbol of the world first Emperor Fu-Hsi. Why was Fu-Hsi called the "Azure Lung" and the Emperor of the East? Why is "Lung" the Heraldic Animal at the East?

Remember the associations of the Chinese Five Emperors with the Four Heraldic Animals and also that in the worship of the Nine Emperor Gods, the East, West, South, North and Centre are guarded by the Green, White, Red, Black and Yellow Dragons or Generals (Cheu, 1988). Note the implication:

> The Heraldic Animals of Phoenix, Snake and Tiger are interchangeable with "Lungs"! That is, the Five Emperors are equivalent to Five "Lungs"! As the whole Chinese race

particularly claim descendency from Fu-Hsi and Huang-Ti and these emperors are regarded as "Lungs" the Chinese race would therefore even referred to themselves as descendents of the "Lung."

The Chinese honour Fu-Hsi as the world first Emperor. Hence, it is natural for the Chinese people to claim descendency from "Lung" as the "Azure Lung" is Adam! While Huang-Ti, the other "Lung", is also the ancestor of the Chinese people.

There must be some essential links between the claim of the Chinese descending from "Lung" and the position of "Lung" at the East! Of course, the Chinese people are at the East. But the ancient secrets tell more than that! In the Pakua symbolism of the Five Emperors (and, as we shall see, the Nine Emperor Gods), the Chinese keep on stressing that "Lung" is the Emperor. The I Ching also emphasises the symbol of "Lung" as the "Great or Superior Man or Ruler"

"Lung" is the Emperor! Such a significance indicates that "Lung" is the ancient Chinese memory of a great ancient master! Someone in ancient times, someone linked to the Imperial line of ancient China, whose exploits affected significantly the fabrics of the ancient Chinese culture ... and gave rise to the legend of "Lung."

Original "Lung" Is Half-fish Half Man

In order to determine further the secret of Fu-Hsi as the "Azure Lung" at the East, it is necessary to examine other versions of this tale.

In the Pakua Four Heraldic Animals, the Chinese "Lung" is equivalent to the Ox in the Biblical-Kabalic knowledge and the Kabalic "Kerub" a bull-horned bearded man with limbed forefront and a fish backbody and tail (Figure 4.3). This bull-headed sphinx is featured in Assyrian, Egyptian and Indian hieroglyphs. It is the Greek

150 THE CHINESE PAKUA

god of the sea, Neptune! The bearded crowned god with a man upper torso and fish bottom holding a trident.

The double horns bearded head fish-tail lower torso is also characteristic of ancient versions of the world first Emperor Fu-Hsi! (Figure 10.2) It is clear that Emperor Fu-Hsi is the Kabalic Kerub with double horns, bearded head and fish-tail lower torso and the equivalent of the Greek God Neptune (or Zeus) and the Roman Jupiter.

The half-fish-half-man Angel or Animal of the East is always linked to Fu-Hsi who is Adam. The Pakua significance of Fu-Hsi as the two-horned bearded half man with a fish-tail lower torso is a universal symbol among many cultures besides that of ancient China. It is evidence that there is a diffusion of cultural symbolism from the older Middle East into the newer Chinese civilisation.

The Kabalic tradition is that the Bull-Headed Kerub at the East gate of Eden prevented Adam and Eve from reentering. Where did Adam go? He went East! Which is why Oriental traditions claim he visited Ceylon. He was also in China!

The "Five Emperors" arrangement of the Pakua is not only a memorial of that ancient great separation of the races to the Four Directions. Linked to this "Five Emperors" event is that the Chinese went to the position designated and visited by "Azure Lung" at the East.

Fu-Hsi is Adam, the Kabalic half-fish-half-man "Azure Lung" at east and the Greek Neptune or Roman Jupiter! "Lung" is not only the emperor, but Fu-Hsi is also the first "Lung"!

Hence, "Lung" became the symbol of the ancient Chinese when they arrived in China.

CHAPTER 10 **EMPEROR FU-HSI, ORGINATOR** 151

Fu-Hsi and Nu-Hua on an Eastern Han stone relief

Drawings from Han Tomb

Fu-Hsi and Nu-Hua on silk (T'ang Dynasty)

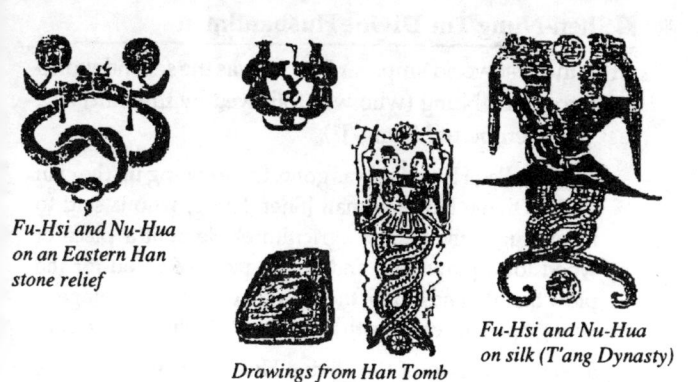

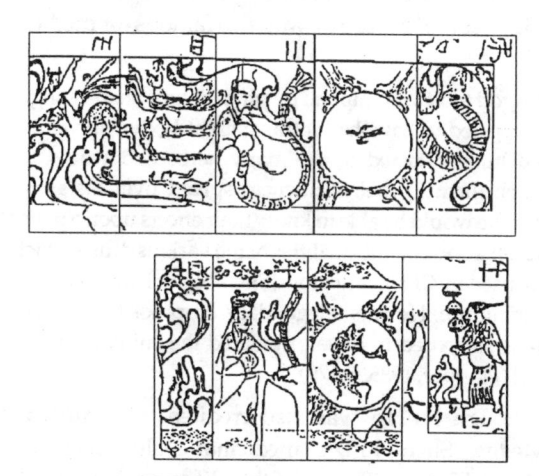

Fu-Hsi and Nu-Hua on a Western stone relief

Figure 10.2 Emperor Fu-Hsi with long fish-tail — The long fish-tail is actually the priest sash.

Shen-Nung The Divine Husbandman

After the first world emperor Fu-Hsi was the second world emperor Shen-Nung (who was followed by the third and last world emperor Huang-Ti):

> 3. When Pao Hsi's clan was gone, there sprang up the clan of the Divine Husbandman [Shen-Nung, who is said to have taught the people agriculture] He split a piece of wood for a plowshare and bent a piece of wood for the plow handle, and taught the whole world the advantage of laying open the earth with a plow... (Wilhelm, 1951. p.330)

> 5. When the clan of the Divine Husbandman was gone, there sprang up the clans of the Yellow Emperor, of Yao, and of Shun ... (Wilhelm, 1951. p.331)

Shen-Nung was credited with the invention of agriculture. Besides agriculture he was also famous for medicinal skills:

> The god most worshipped by physicians is Shen-Nung. He is reported to have had a transparent body. He went out and himself tasted of the many herbs and would then watch them as their influences spread over his system. Thus he would be able to know their effects upon a patient. He left a book on the qualities of the various drugs which is still used by Chinese doctors [Shen-Nung is also the God of Agriculture. He was a legendary Emperor living 2838BC He is supposed to have originated the cultivation of the soil] (Plopper, 1935. p.179)

Although Fu-Hsi was also credited with medicinal knowledge, Shen-Nung's medicinal skills were more prominent. The significance of the difference is akin to the observation that Shen-Nung introduced agriculture. Shen-Nung was reputed to come a number of generations after Fu-Hsi (Hirth, 1908. p.14) and some 1,260 years after Fu-Hsi (Li, 1914. p.3).

CHAPTER 10 **EMPEROR FU-HSI, ORGINATOR** 153

World climatic and physical conditions must have changed so much not only to warrant the introduction of agriculture, but also the changes were accompanied by greater appearance of sicknesses among mankind. Also:

> In the time of Yao there were ten suns, but they burnt up the trees and grasses, and were more than man could endure. The life of each sun was bound up in a large crow. Hou I took his bow and arrows and killed nine of these crows, whereupon their respective suns disappeared, leaving only the present one to bless mankind (Plopper, 1953. p.37)

The time of the "ten suns" was a testimony of the changed weather after Shen-Nung. It was apparent that something happened leading to the weather becoming terribly hot as if equivalent to "ten suns.". It took some time for the weather to stabilise back to the condition of a "one sun.".

This could be why Shen-Nung's position in the "Five Emperors Gods" is that of the South and of the Sun or Fire. Shen-Nung is also the Fire Emperor. It was in his time that the world climate became very hot.

A significant world event which could cause such drastic changes could be the Great Flood. If so, Shen-Nung was really Noah! Shen-Nung was Noah!

Gorn (1904, p.28) tries to show that the Great Flood occurred during the days of Yao and Shun: "It is worthy of note that the Chinese deluge took place in the time of Yaou and Shun, 2348BC and it was not the great deluge with which Yu was concerned... The curious agreement of both the Chinese and the Hebrew records in assigning the great flood to the year 2348BC is strong evidence of something in the nature of a vast, if not, indeed, an universal catastrophe. The Hebrew record from Genesis v. and vii. is as follows:

154 THE CHINESE PAKUA

	Years
Age of Adam at birth of Seth	130
Age of Seth at birth of Enos	105
Age of Enos at birth of Cainan	90
Age of Cainan at birth of Mahalaleel	70
Age of Mahalaleel at birth of Jared	65
Age of Jared at birth of Enoch	162
Age of Enoch at birth of Methusaleh	65
Age of Methusaleh at birth of Lamech	187
Age of Lamech at birth of Noah	182
Age of Noah at the Flood	600
Years to the Flood	1656
Beginning of record,	4004BC
Date of Flood	2348

However, the floods of Yao and Shun are not the size of the legendary Great Flood which drowned the whole world. Bearing in mind the varying dates given for the ancient Chinese emperors, the apparent agreement in dates claimed by Gorn is likely coincidental, due to a subjective selection of dates which led to the so-called agreement of dates at 2348BC

What is significant about Shen-Nung is that the legends all point to vast drastic changes in world climate at his time. The "Five Emperors Gods" Pakua even points to a transition from the peaceful "cool" green-wooded world of Fu-Hsi to the fiery hot world of Shen-Nung.

11

BASIS OF THE CHINESE IDEOGRAMS

■ Tradition Of Pakua As Origin Of Writing

Some believe Emperor Huang-Ti and his minister Ts'ang Chieh (circa 2700BC) invented the Chinese script (Kang and Nelson, 1979). However, though Huang-Ti and Ts'ang Chieh probably influenced the Chinese characters, there is an earlier tradition that it is the first world Emperor Fu-Hsi who invented the Chinese characters:

> **Written Characters**: The origin of the written language of China is of great antiquity. After events had been recorded by knotted cords (not unlike the Peruvian quipos) and notched sticks, a writing proper began, like the Egyptian, with 'wen' images, forms of visible objects, or ornaments; the first legendary Emperor Fu Hsi, 2953BC, the third Emperor Huang-Ti, 2698BC and the Statesman Ts'ang Chieh, 2700BC, are the traditional inventors of the k'o t'ou tzu, or "tadpole characters," and the niao chi wen, or "bird'tract script," consisting of undulating marks. The historic ku wen or ancient writings, imitative of natural forms, are found on stones and metallic vases, and are the prototypes of the subsequent sinograms (Williams, 1931. p.410).

The tradition of Chinese language goes back to 2943BC, long before Chinese civilisation emerged in China around 1400BC There is also a tradition that the invention of Chinese writings had something to do with the Eight Diagrams or Pakua:

> "History relates that, at the moment Fu Hsi was seeking to combine the characters proper to express the various forms of matter and the relation between things physical and intellectual, a wonderful horse came out of the river, bearing on his back certain signs of which the philosophic legislator formed the Eight Diagrams which have preserved his name." While the Great Emperor Yu, 2205BC, was engaged in drawing off the floods, a "divine tortoise" is said to have presented to his gaze a scroll of writing on its back, whence he deciphered the basis of his moral teaching and the secrets of the unseen. – (Williams, 1931. p.410)

How is the Pakua involved in the origin of the Chinese language – and for the matter, is the Pakua involved in the origin of all languages as indicated by the Chinese tradition?

Archaeological evidence indicate that urban Chinese civilisation started in China only around 1400BC with the Shang dynasty (Creel, 1938; Farmer et al, 1977). Similarly, archaeological evi-dence show that Chinese writings existed in Shang relics in an already advance form, but none are found in more ancient Chinese relics (Creel, 1938). Where are the evidence of the necessary earlier development? Is the Chinese language an import from elsewhere rather than the result of internal development?

Chinese documents already were produced during the Shang dynasty period (ca 1400–1122BC) (Creel, 1938. p.21). Creel (1938, p.35) notes that many have believed that the Chinese system of writing is an importation from elsewhere. Many books and articles have been written purporting to demonstrate that the basis of Chinese came from Egypt, Babylon or elsewhere.

In Chapter 3 on the Chinese Ganzhi-Pakua system, there are evidence that the twenty-two alphabets of the Hebrew language originated from the twenty-two symbols of the Ganzhi-Pakua system. This is not only evidence

BASIS OF CHINESE IDEOGRAMS

that alphabetic languages arose from astrological pictorial symbols but also that the Chinese language is rooted in the ancient Middle East.

There are also other evidence of the kinship between the Chinese and Middle East writings.

■ Alphabetic Languages Arose After Pictorial-ideographic Languages

According to Buttrick (1954, p.220, Volume 1) the oldest Semitic language was the Akkadian cuneiform script which is syllabic and ideographic. It was later that a consonantal-alphabetic script appeared, called the Ugarite cuneiform from Ras Shamra on the Syrian sea coast. Others (like Peloubet, 1947) also attribute the invention of the alphabets to the Phoenicians who lived along the Syrian coast. The Hebrew language, an alphabetic language, is built, like all Semitic languages, on a three-consonant verbal root system and receives several words from Assyrian, probably through the Babylonian exile around 500-700BC The Chinese language has remained ideographic with many added phonetic words based on the original ideograms.

The Akkadian dynasty of Mesopotamia existed between 2334-2154 B.C. (Farmer et al, 1977) which was after the Great Flood. Pictorial-ideographic languages were thus the original forms of language(s) before and just after the Great Flood.

De Francis (1984, p.139) writes: "In human history it seems that the idea of using a pictograph in the new function of representing sound may have occurred only three times: once in Mesopotamia, perhaps by the Sumerians [passing to the Egyptians], once by in China, apparently by the Chinese themselves [spreading to Korea, Japan and Vietnam], and once in Central American, by the Mayas ... Conceivably it was invented only once, but there is no evidence that the Chinese or the Mayas acquired the idea from elsewhere."

Similarities In Structures Of Chinese And Sumerian-Egyptian Characters

The Chinese characters are not arbitrary but adopt certain objective principles in usage of each character to convey its meaning(s) in the Chinese language. Basically, the Chinese characters could be grouped into two broad classes, semantics and phonetics:

1. Semantics. These are themselves of two types:
    a. **Imitative or Pictorial**
    These characters are practically pictures of the things they conveyed in meanings. The strokes have been polished through the ages but nevertheless still bear resemblance to the objects they are meant to represent.

    These imitative semantic characters include such as those for water, mountain, bird, horse, eye. These characters are essentially pictorial symbols.

    b. **Indicative, Associative or Ideographic**
    Such characters are formed through associations of two or more semantic subcharacters.

    The word for "talk" is formed from the words for "words" and "mouth". The word "talk" is therefore a simple indicative. A more complicated indicative is the word "kou" for "ancient" which is formed from the words for "ten" over a "mouth" – indicative of "ten generations" and therefore very old.

    The simple indicative is easily derived almost at once from the imitative meanings of the subcharacters. But the complicated indicative is derived from

CHAPTER 11 BASIS OF CHINESE IDEOGRAMS 159

association with more abstract things like the event of "ten generations."

The meaning of each indicative semantic character is thus linked to the individual meanings of the component subcharacters. A set of symbols combine to give the overall meaning.

2. Phonetics. The phonetics compose well over 90% of the total number of Chinese characters. Phonetics are said to arise owing to new things coming into the Chinese society and new words have to be coined to describe them. They are also of two basic types:

    a. In general the phonetics are formed through pairing two different sets of subcharacters. The phonetic or sound is given by the right set of character(s).

      The left character, however, usually indicates a general idea of what the overall phonetic character is related to. The left character is therefore a classifier or radical. For example, words related to watery things have the classifier "shui" for "water" as the left character. Sometimes the right character not only provides the sound but its semantic meaning may also be used in forming the overall meaning.

    b. However, several new modern phonetics characters have meanings unrelated to the subcharacters. For example, the word "Malaysia" is formed from a phrase of three words for "Ma" "Lei" and "Sia." This kind is often used to convey the sounds of names of non-Chinese.

Creation of Chinese semantic pictograms and ideograms words appears to end around 800BC (Kang and Nelson, 1979. p.33).

The ancient Chinese characters, including phonetics, will thus convey meanings related to the semantics of either the whole word or the subcharacters of the word. Exceptions would be rogue words which have come through copyist mistakes. It is important to realise that except for case (2. b) above, Chinese words often have overall meanings related to associations of the meanings of the sub-characters.

De Francis (1984) notes a number of similarities between the Chinese and Egyptian-Sumerian languages:

- From the Latin version of Ricci's observations, European readers learned that the Chinese have a system of writing "similar to the Egyptians hieroglyphics" and that they "express their concepts not by writing, like most of the world, with a few alphabetic signs, but by as many symbols as there are words" (p.134)

- Champollion, who deciphered the Egyptian hieroglyphic through a recognition of the phonetic hieroglyphics, recognised that both Egyptian and Chinese are basically ideographic but used phonetic hieroglyphics to transcribe new and foreign things. (p.136)

- The Chinese procedure of adding different radicals to a common phonetic is similar to the procedure adopted in both Mesopotamia and Egypt of using "determinatives" to suggest the semantic category of homophous words. (p.122)

- De Francis (1984) shows that the bulk of the characters in the Chinese, Sumerian and Egyptian languages are phonetics while only a small core are semantics.

There are similarities in the structures of the ancient hieroglyphic forms of the Sumerian, Egyptian and Chinese languages. The Sumerian and Egyptian civilisations were older than the Chinese civilisation. Hence, it is speculated that the Chinese language originated from the Middle East.

Ideographs As Memorials Of Ancient Events

The basis of pictorial characters are obvious – they represent what they look like! But the ideographs – their meanings come from associations. The association may involve common pictures and actions in everyday life.

Another way of creating meanings would be to base the association on a famous event or person. It is this class of ideograms which prove difficult today to decipher – for the events occurred so long ago and are now difficult to trace, many of which have become legends. Likely, those more complicated Chinese ideograms would have subcharacters which must in association represent some famous ancient event(s).

It would go a long way to decipher the origin of the Chinese language if we recognise the role of hyperbolism in ancient language. For example, the Bible utilise such hyperbolic associations of symbols with everyday things. Let us examine the example of Joseph's dream:

> Behold I have dreamed yet a dream: and behold, the Sun and Moon and eleven stars bowed down unto me." And he told it to his father and to his brethren; and his father rebuked him and said unto him: "What is this dream that thou hast dreamed? Shall I and thy mother and thy brethren come to bow down before thee to the earth?" (Genesis 37:9-10)

Joseph's dream was to come true. Jacob the father of Joseph was quick to realise the meanings of Joseph's dream in which Jacob knew the "Sun and Moon" refered to him and his wife as the father and mother of Joseph. How did Jacob associate the symbols of the Sun and Moon for father and mother? Would that not be pure conjecture? Of course, it was not conjecture! Jacob knew the meanings because in the language of his times the Sun and Moon were common hyperbolic symbols for father and mother! Meanings

162 THE CHINESE PAKUA

derived from hyperbolic symbolism existed in the times of the patriarchs of around 2000 to 1500BC!

Do Chinese characters preserve memory of very ancient events?

Indeed, of recent, there are writers who show that the Chinese words do contain remarkable revelations of Middle East legends such as the ancient Biblical story of Creation! Kang and Nelson (1979) note in their book "The Discovery of Genesis, How the Truths of Genesis were found hidden in the Chinese language" that many basic Chinese ideograms seem centred around two great events known in Middle East legends – that of the Edenic Creation (ca 4004BC) and the Great Flood-Deluge (ca 2348BC)

There were Jesuits writers in China who, as far back as the early 17th century, wrote that the Chinese characters contain Biblical incidents and truths (Rule, 1986).

■ Similarities Of Sumerian And Chinese Words

The oldest Chinese writings are those of the Shang oracle bones (circa 1400BC), of which over a hundred thousands have been found. These ancient oracle bones scripts contain at least a thousand different words.

To examine further the possible link between the Chinese and the ancient Middle East languages, the Sumerian and Chinese oracle bones characters for 18 basic words could be studied (Table 11.1). The Table shows that there are close similarities among the Sumerian and Chinese for 13 out of the 18 words:

Close similarities:
god	dingir	ti
earth	ki	tu
man	lu	jen
mountain	kur	shan
eat	ku	shih

CHAPTER 11 BASIS OF CHINESE IDEOGRAMS 163

water	a	shui
bird	mushen	niao
fish	ha	yu
barley	she	
wheat	lai	

Some similarities:

head	sag	shou
a mouth	ka	k'ou
ox	gud	mou
cow	ab	p'in

Among the 18 basic words, 13 have various degrees of similarities, including 9 close similarities. The ancient Chinese and Sumerian languages are closely related.

Ho's (1975, p.252) argues that the pronunciations are dissimilar and that the Chinese characters are less pictorial. Therefore, he claimed that the Sumerian and Chinese languages have no common links. However, dissimilarities of pronunciations prove little, as it is known that the Chinese dialects using the same Chinese characters can be very different. The argument that the Chinese characters are less pictorial and more calligraphic still means that there are recognisable similarities – only that the Chinese scripts have developed a little further.

The Chinese oracle bones characters, being less pictorial and more calligraphic, is evidently a more advance development than the Sumerian script. The Chinese language must have developed from an older language form that once exist in the Middle East. For all the evidence, it is likely that the Chinese oracle bones characters could have even evolved from the more ancient Sumerian script!

Among these 18 sets Sumerian-Chinese characters, it is curious to note that the first set, for "god", are eight points symbols in the Sumerian as well as Chinese scripts! These

164 THE CHINESE PAKUA

A Comparison of Sumerian Words with Chinese Oracle-Bone Characters

	Sumerian		Shang oracle inscription		Modern Chinese
1. a. heaven	an	※	t'ien	[pictographs]	天
b. god	dingir		ti	[pictographs]	帝
2. earth	ki	[pictograph]	t'u	[pictographs]	土
3. man	lu	[pictograph]	jen	[pictographs]	人
4. woman	munus	▽	nü	[pictographs]	女
5. mountain	kur	[pictograph]	shan	[pictographs]	山
6. slave-girl	geme	[pictograph]	pei	[pictograph]	婢
7. head	sag	[pictograph]	shou	[pictographs]	首
8. a. mouth	ka	[pictograph]	k'ou	[pictographs]	口
b. speak	dug		yüeh	[pictographs]	曰
9. food	ninda	▽	shih	[pictographs]	食
			ssu	[pictograph]	飤
10. eat	ku	[pictograph]	shih	(same as in no. 9)	食
			hsiang	[pictographs]	饗
11. water	a	≈	shui	[pictograph]	水
12. drink	nag	[pictograph]	yin	[pictographs]	飲
13. a. to go	du	[pictograph]	chih	[pictographs]	之
			wang	[pictographs]	往
b. to stand	gub		li	[pictographs]	立
14. bird	mushen	[pictograph]	chui	[pictographs]	隹
			niao	[pictographs]	鳥
15. fish	ha	[pictograph]	yü	[pictographs]	魚
16. ox	gud	[pictograph]	mou	[pictograph]	牡
17. cow	ab	[pictograph]	p'in	[pictographs]	牝
18. barley	she	[pictograph]	mou*		牟、麰
wheat**			lai	[pictographs]	來
			mai	[pictographs]	麥

* The character for "barley" is missing in both Shang oracle texts and the Chou bronze inscriptions.

** The Sumerian word *"she"* may also mean grains including wheat; hence I have added two late-Shang characters for wheat for further comparison.

SOURCES: The eighteen Sumerian words are given in S. N. Kramer, *The Sumerians*, pp. 302–306. The oracle-bone characters are taken from Li Hsiao-ting, *Chia-ku wen-tzu chi-shih* (Academia Sinica, 1955), 16 vols.

Table 11.1

eight points symbols are really the Eight Diagrams or Pakua!

For 13 out of 18 words to show similarities is too much a coincident and can only indicate a strong closeness between the Sumerian and Chinese characters and that both sets of characters have common origin(s). These common origin(s) can only be in the Middle East.

12

MIDDLE EAST LEGENDS IN CHINESE IDEOGRAMS

■ Middle East Legends In Chinese Ideograms?

Writers, like Kang and Nelson (1979), believe that the Chinese words contain remarkable revelations of Middle East legends such as the Edenic Creation (ca 4004BC) and the Great Flood-Deluge (ca 2348BC). There were Jesuits writers in China who, as far back as the early 17th century, wrote that the Chinese characters contain Biblical incidents and truths (Rule, 1986). Their contentions, if correct, imply that the Chinese language must have a Middle East basis.

This section examines several ideograms believed to contain stories of common Middle East legends.

In interpreting subcharacters of a Chinese ideogram, it is easy to conjecture meanings. However, as already discussed, the Chinese characters are not arbitrary but adopt objective principles to convey their meanings. The association of ideas indicated by the subcharacters often provides the overall meaning of the ideogram.

Now, where the ideas involve major ancient events, the ancient Chinese ideograms, unwittingly or purposefully, would have become devices to preserve ancient history!

There are many Middle East legends. One of the clearest versions would be the Biblical version. Many ancient Middle East or Biblical events could have been witnessed by the ancient Chinese and form parts of the ancient history of the Chinese people.

■ The Creation Ideograms

Many cultures tell of a legend of creation. The Bible records:

> In the beginning God created the heaven and the earth. And the earth became without form and void and darkness was upon the face of the deep. And the Spirit of God moved upon the face of the waters (Genesis 1:1-2)

The first chapter of the Biblical book of Genesis records that God took "seven days" to re-create the world of living things including the race of man (Genesis 1). Genesis 1:1-2 actually show that before the "seven days" re-creation the heaven and worlds already existed in a chaotic form. This was what the ancient Chinese believe – that the original stage before creation was chaos covered with water! (Werner, 1922).

It was in the midst of this original chaos that the first two human beings were created – Fu-Hsi (also the first world human emperor) and his sister Nu Kua Shih (Werner, 1922). Fu-Hsi and Nu-Kua were not only brother and sister but they were also husband and wife and gave rise to the rest of mankind (Walls and Walls, 1984) – they were the Biblical Adam and Eve.. The legend was that the Goddess Nu Kua Shih repaired the heaven and earth from the waters (Werner, 1922).

The Chinese language actually preserved various ideograms describing the legend of an original Genesis creation!

Ling For Spirit

The word "Ling" for "spirit" (Table 12.1) composes of three sets of subcharacters:

> The first set has the words 1. heaven 2. cover and 3. water (ancient form). This first set meaning "cover with water" is also the word for "rain."

The next set is the word for "mouth" in triplet. It denotes three persons and indicates the inherent triple form of the "Spirit."

The last third set has the words for 1. man and 2. work. The third word actually means "worker of magic." This is a Gammadion ideogram (Table 13.1).

"Ling" is a very complicated ideogram. Such a word should immediately indicate that the overall meaning of "ling" is a composite of the individual meanings of the subcharacters.

As "Ling" means "spirit", some of the subcharacters must refer to "spirit things". The subcharacters of "two men and work" whose combination mean a "magician" could convey the sense of "supernatural." So would the common symbol of "one" for "Heaven." These subcharacters would have natural places in the overall meaning of "Ling" for "spirit".

But what of "three mouths" and "water or rain"? What kind of famous event would connect all these subcharacters? An event like the Biblical story of the Spirit of God coming down from Heaven hovering over the water to initiate creation:

> In the beginning God created the heaven and earth ... And the Spirit of God moved upon the face of the waters (Genesis 1:1-2)

The "three mouths" are indicative of the Triune character of God, a common motif in many cultures! The ancient Chinese thus know the legend of the role of the Spirit in creation and hence associate major features of that creation to derive the meaning of "Ling" for "spirit".

CHAPTER 12 MIDDLE EAST LEGENDS

Table 12.1

CHINESE CHARACTERS DESCRIBING CREATION EVENTS

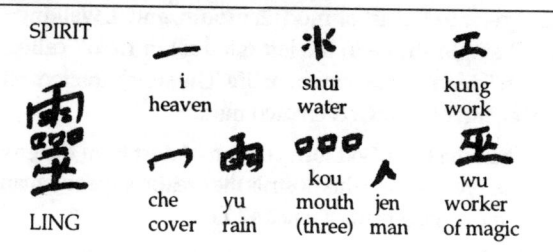

SPIRIT

靈 LING = 一 (i, heaven) + 氺 (shui, water) + 工 (kung, work) + 冖 (che, cover) + 兩 (yu, rain) + ooo (kou, mouth, three) + 人 (jen, man) + 巫 (wu, worker of magic)

Coming from heaven, covering the waters, the three mouths (beings of Trinity) work magic (Gen. 1:2)

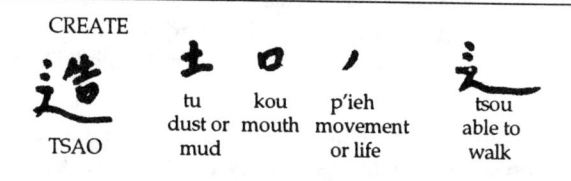

CREATE

造 TSAO = 土 (tu, dust or mud) + 口 (kou, mouth) + 丿 (p'ieh, movement or life) + 辶 (tsou, able to walk)

God formed man from dust of ground and breathed from mount life and man became a living thing able to walk (Gen 2:7)

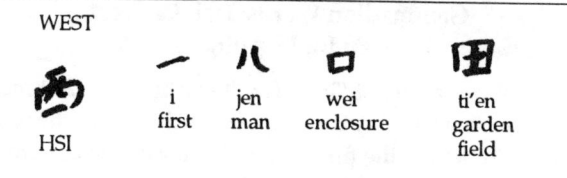

WEST

西 HSI = 一 (i, first) + 八 (jen, man) + 口 (wei, enclosure) + 田 (ti'en, garden field)

The first man in the enclosure (Garden of Eden) - Chinese remembered they came from Eden in west

HAPPINESS, BLESSING

福 FU = 礻 (Ti, God) + 一 (i, first) + 口 (kou, mouth) + 田 (ti'en, garden field)

Happiness is when Adam the first man was in the garden with God (Gen 1-2)

Tsao For Create

The subcharacters of the word "Tsao" for "Create" (Table 12.1) refer to 1. dust or mud; 2. mouth; and 3. walking. The small single stroke to the left of "dust or mud" called the "p'ieh" denotes movement or life. The subcharacters reflect the legend of how God created man:

> Then the Lord God formed man of dust from the ground and breathed into his nostrils the breath of life and man became a living being (Genesis 2:7)

God must have breathed with His mouth (qv Psalm 33:6-9, below) into man and the man became a living being able to walk. When the subcharacters for "dust or mud" is combined with "mouth" it is the word for "to speak or talk." It indicates God create through "speaking"! Did not the Bible state:

> By the word of the Lord were the heavens made; and all the host of them by the breath of his mouth ... he spake and it was done; he commanded and it stood fast (Psalm 33:6-9)

Gammadion Words: Hsi For West, Fu for Happiness

The subcharacters of "Hsi" for "West" (Table 12.1) mean 1. first; 2. man; and 3. enclosure or garden. Thus the word "West" refers to the first man in the enclosure or garden. The oracle bone script for the "enclosure" part is alike to "T'ien" for field or garden (Table 13.1). It preserves the meaning of the origin of the first man in the garden to the west! That is, the Chinese remember they came from the west! The "west" is the place of the first man in the garden.

That this western place is the Garden of Eden is denoted further by the Chinese word "Fu" for "Happiness" (Table 12.1). The subcharacters mean 1. God; 2. first; 3. mouth or person; and 4. garden. The word, which also contains the subcharacters for the first man, thus indicates that "happiness" is equated with the conditions the first man had with God in the Garden of Eden.

■ The Fall Of Man Ideograms

The Biblical legend tells that the Devil, through the form of the shining fiery serpent, came to the original two human beings in the Garden of Eden (Genesis 3). God had planted two special trees, the tree of life and the tree of knowledge of good and evil. Through a series of lies, Satan deceived Eve, the first woman, to eat the forbidden fruit from the tree of knowledge of good and evil. For this disobedience, to prevent them from eating of the tree of life, the first two human beings were driven from the Garden of Eden into the harsher world outside.

Gammadion Words: Kui For Devil, Mo For Tempter

Look at the word for "Kui" for "Devil" (Table 12.2). This word has three subcharacters meaning 1. man, son; 2. garden, field; and 3. secret, private. Actually the subcharacter for "man or son" is really the humanoid form of the devil. The subcharacters together indicate that the one who came secretly into the Garden of Eden. The "p'ieh" again denotes the "living" and hence the word refers to the devil.

Table 13.1 (in next Chapter) indicates that the humanoid is at the bottom or North of the garden. Is not the North creature the "Snake"? It is the Chinese version of "Old Serpent the Devil"!

From this word for "devil" we also get the word "Mo" for "Tempter" (Table 12.2.) This word contains the word for "devil" plus two other subcharacters for 1. cover and 2. tree. This is interesting as it denotes the devil hiding among the trees – is this not what Satan did when he hid among the trees to tempt Eve?

A number of other Chinese characters are associated with the subcharacters for devil and trees:

The word for "desire or covet" composes of the subcharacters for 1. two trees; and 2. woman. It denotes the origin of the feeling through Eve desiring the forbidden fruit of the "tree" in the Garden of Eden. The two trees represent one the tree of life and two the second tree of knowledge of good and evil whose fruit was forbidden to our first parents.

In fact, the Chinese word for "forbidden" has the subcharacters 1. two trees above; and 2. God. It refers to the original command of God concerning the two trees.

One of the Chinese words for "naked" is shown in Table 12.2. "Garden and tree" together is "fruit" and this word is the common element in three Chinese words for "naked". It denotes our first parents trying to use the products of the trees as clothings to cover their nakedness (Genesis 3:7). It is a Gammadion symbol with the tree at the North.

"Pain" or "sorrow" is denoted by the subcharacters for 1. two trees; and 2. a piece (from one man and his stretching arm). The word signifies the woman having to bear child in pains as a result of eating the forbidden fruit (Genesis 3:16). Another word for "sorrow" ("Bitter") is denoted by the act of eating among old weeds – i.e. man had to combat weeds in order to obtain food for living (Genesis 3:18-19).

The ideograms preserve the evil consequences of the action of our first mother Eve when she was tempted by the devil to eat of the fruit of the tree of knowledge and good and evil.

■ Original And Future States Of Man

The Chinese words also preserve indications of the original nature of man (Table 12.3.)

CHAPTER 12 MIDDLE EAST LEGENDS 173

Table 12.2
CHINESE CHARACTERS DESCRIBING EDENIC FALL OF MAN EVENTS

DEVIL 鬼 KUI	*Into the Garden came a being with a secret thing (Gen 3:1-7)*	ノ p'ieh — movement or life 田 ti'en — garden field 儿 jen — man ム ssu — privately
TEMPTER 魔 MO	*From the covering of the trees the being with the secret tempt Eve = tempter (Gen 3:1-7)*	广 kuan — cover 木 mu — trees 鬼 kui — devil
COVET, DESIRE 婪 LAN	*The fruit of the tree was coveted by the woman (Gen 3:6)*	木 mu — trees 林 lin — forest 女 nui — woman
FORBIDDEN 禁 CH'IN	*There were two trees and God forbided the fruit of one tree (Gen 2:16-17)*	木 mu — trees 示 Ti — God
NAKED 裸 LOU	*Adam tried to use products of tree in the Garden as aprons of clothing (Gen 3:7)*	木 mu — trees 田 ti'en — garden field 果 kuo — fruit 衣 i — clothing
PAIN, SORROW 楚 CH'U	*As result of eating the forbidden piece of fruit, Eve would deliver in pain (Gen 3:16)*	木 mu — trees 疋 ch'u — a piece
BITTER, SORROW 苦 K'U	"Ten" and "mouth" means "eating." To eat man must deal with old weeds tough life and sorrow (Gen 3:17-19)	十 shih — ten 口 kou — mouth 古 ku — ancient 艸 ts'ao — grasss

"Fire" is really "man" with tongues of flames from his side. This indicates the original shining nature of man before Adam and Eve fell. This meaning is supported by the word for "light" which shows 1. rays emerging from the; 2. first; and 3. man.

"Light" also has "three tongues of fire" above the "man". Like the "three mouths" in the character "ling" for "spirit", the "three tongues of fire" indicates the Triune character of God.

"Ancestor" is broken into 1. God; and 2. also, moreover. Thus the word for "ancestor" really indicates that man is "God also", that is, man is in the image of God:

And God said, Let us make man in our image, after our likeness ... (Genesis 1:26)

The word "First" really indicates Adam as the living man of the dust! In fact, the word "tu" for "dust" is actually a merging of the characters for "one" and "man"

According to the Jesuit Foucquet who was in China from 1699, the character "t'ien" for "heaven" is composed of symbols for "two" and "man" and must be read as a prophecy of the second Adam (Rule, 1986. p.173)

Rule (1986, p.173) also notes that the "Confucians called themselves "Ju" the character for which comes from "Jen" for "man" and "Hsu" for "expect or hope." Both the ancient form of the character Hsu and the canonical definition of the Hsu hexagram of the I-Ching are explained as "clouds ascending above the heavens". Who ascended above the heavens in a cloud of glory but the Lord Jesus Christ?

What is most significant of the Chinese characters' revelations of the original events surrounding that ancient creation is the original stage of man. Man actually descended from God not just symbolically but in some real material way. Man was originally a radiant being covered with some form of light energy and thus at that time did not require clothings – God is also covered with this kind of light:

> ... O Lord, my God ... thou art clothed with honour and majesty. Who coverest thyself with light as with a garment ... (Psalms 104:1-2)

■ The Flood Ideograms

The Biblical legend states that after the Edenic re-creation, mankind grew so wicked that around 2348BC God sent a Flood to drown the whole world (Genesis 7). Only eight persons, namely Noah, his wife, his three sons and three daughters-in-laws were saved through the ark built on God's instructions. Some Chinese ideograms appear to preserve the Flood story.

Ch'uan For Boat

The Chinese ideogram "Ch'uan" for "boat" (Table 12.4). has three basic sub-characters viz : "Chou", "Pa" and "Kou" which mean respectively "vessel", "eight" and "mouth". This is a ideogram as the sound is independent of any of the subcharacters. It is not produced by the imitative meanings of the subcharacters – an association with some event must be meant.

The meaning "boat" is already indicated in an imitative way to some extent by the subcharacter "Chou" for a small boat. The meaning of "Ch'uan" as a "big boat" could have been conveyed through an association between "Chou" and, say, the word "Ta" for "big" – such an association would have made the word imitative indicative. But behold, it was not written "Chou" with "Ta" but "Chou" with "eight" and "mouth". There must be some reasons why "Ch'uan" was not written with "Ta" and "Chou". Something more important than "Ta" is used to associate "Chou" to give "Ch'uan."

176 THE CHINESE PAKUA

Table 12.3
CHINESE CHARACTERS DESCRIBING STATE OF MAN

FIRE — *Man orginally had shining flames covering his body - covering flames lost after Fall (Gen. 3)*

火　　人　ヾ

HUI　　jen　hui
　　　　man　flames

LIGHT — Oirginally man has a halo around his head

光　　 尝　　 丷　　 儿

　　　　　　　hui
　　oracle　3-tongues
KUAN　bone (11.29)　fire　jen
　　　　　　　　　　　　man

ANCESTOR — *Our ancestor is also God - i.e. we were made in image of God (Gen 1:26-27)*

祖　　 ネ　　 且

　　　　　　kei
TSU　Ti = God　also

FIRST — *Adam the first man is of the dust (Gen 2:7)*

先　　 ノ　　 土　　 儿

　　　p'ieh　　tu　　jen
HSIEN　movement　dust　man

Why then is the subcharacter "Chou" associated with the subcharacters for "eight" and "mouth" to convey the overall meaning of "boat"?

The "mouth" is also a reference to "person", for the appearance of the subcharacter for "mouth" in several Chinese characters is meant to denote "person" or "people" or even "generation". So we know that "Ch'uan" for "boat" is associated with "eight persons and a boat". "Ch'uan" must thus be associated with some famous event where eight persons and a boat were involved. Looking through conventional Chinese history we may not realise what sort of famous event this could be. However, if Biblical history is reflected in Chinese memory in some way, then the Biblical Flood is a logical basis for that famous ancient event of "eight persons and a boat" giving rise to the actual meaning of the word "Ch'uan" for "boat".

So, the meanings of the subcharacters of the word "Ch'uan" would be objectively deciphered as coming from the eight persons escaping the Biblical Flood in the ark. "Ch'uan" would therefore be for a "large boat" while "Chou" is for a "small boat".

If we talk about the Biblical Flood a host of images would flash through our mind. The images would include terrible flood waters covering everything, the famous ark within which are the eight in Noah's family and the host of animals within, the forty days and forty nights of rains and storms, the power of God manifested through His anger at humanity as well as His grace to Noah. Hence, it is logical and more dramatic to picture a boat like the ark as "Chou" with "eight" and "mouth" rather than "Chou" with "Ta".

Tao For Island

"Tao" for "island" composes of the subcharacter for "bird" over the "mountain." It is odd to use this to depict an island. It would be more appropriate to use combinations like

178 THE CHINESE PAKUA

Table 12.4
CHINESE CHARACTERS DESCRIBING GREAT FLOOD EVENTS

BOAT 船 CH'UAN	The eight persons on the boat = Noah's family of 8 in the ark escaping the Flood (Gen 7-8)	舟 chou vessel / 八 pa eight / 口 kou mouth
ISLAND 島 TAO	Bird high above mountain = bird sent by Noah as Flood went down (Gen 8:6-12)	鳥 niao bird / 山 shan mountain
DROWN 溣 S'NG	"United" contains eight under one cover with "water" means great drowning of mankind. (Gen 7-8)	合 he'h united / ch'ing together / s'ng cover over / 氵 shui water
CONTINUE, HAND DOWN 沿 WO	Eight persons floating on water told to continue human race after Flood (Gen 9:1)	氵 shui water / 八 pa eight / 口 kou mouth
CAVE 穴 SIEH	The home of the eight after the Flood was a cave	宀 che cover / 八 pa eight
DIVISION 分 FEN	Using the knife to divide for eight persons	八 pa eight / 刀 li knife
SPEAK 說 SHOU	means spokeman who is elder brother. "Eight" over brother means exchange - therefore with words = speak	口 kou mouth / 儿 jen man / 兄 hsiung elder brother / 八 pa eight / 言 hua words

CHAPTER 12 **MIDDLE EAST LEGENDS** 179

"earth" over "water." So why use "bird" over "mountain" to depict an "island"? The character actually reflects the Genesis story of Noah sending forth the raven and dove:

> And he send forth a raven which went to and fro until the waters were dried from off the earth. Also he sent forth a dove from him to see if the waters were abated from off the face of the ground; But the dove found no rest for the sole of her foot and she returned unto him in the ark for the waters were on the face of the earth ... And he stayed yet another seven days; and again he sent forth the dove out of the ark; And the dove came in to him in the evening; and lo, in her mouth was an olive leaf pluckt off; so Noah knew that the waters were abated from off the earth (Genesis 8:7-11)

"Tao" for "island" thus is this Genesis record of the time when Noah sent out the raven and dove to search for habitable dry land above the Flood. It was the dove which returned with the olive twig showing habitable land had emerged from the Flood. At this time when the dove was first flying away from the ark, the waters were still around the mountain tops – These mountain tops were the first islands!

It appears that before the Flood there were no such thing as islands! The waters around the mountain tops was a sight never seen before! This indicates that the pre-Flood land was relatively flat and no islands existed in antediluvan times. Physical conditions changed with the Flood and for the first time islands appeared. Noah remembered the waters around the mountain tops and used the memory of the bird hovering over the mountain tops to depict "Tao" for "island".

S'ng For Drown, Wo For Continue, and others

"S'ng" for "drown" (Table 12.4) has the character for all united whose subcharacters are 1. man; 2. one; and 3. mouth. The second character denotes hands joined

180 THE CHINESE PAKUA

Table 12.5
CHINESE CHARACTERS DESCRIBING TOWER OF BABEL EVENTS

TOWER — *Ts'ao" and "he'h" indicate undertaking of bitter nature. The tower was made of clay bricks. Chinese remembered Tower of Babel. (Gen 11:19)*

塔	合	艹	土
T'A	he'h	ts'ao	tu
	united	grass	dust or clay

REBELLION, CONFUSION — *The speaking is of one leg only i.e. other leg is doing a different thing from what is said. Therefore confusion and rebellion from insincerity.*

乱	舌	乚
SZE	she	li
	tongue	right leg

MIGRATE — *In the west there was a great separation. This cause walking, i.e. migration (Gen 11:89)*

遷	西	大	巴	之
CHIEN	hsi	ta	sze	tsou
	west	great	separate	walking

SCATTER — *All families (or flesh) follow (Gen 11:89)*

散	丗	月	攵
SAN	sze	shen	fu
	all	flesh	follow

CHAPTER 12 MIDDLE EAST LEGENDS 181

together. The fusion of these two characters have the same essential meanings of unity as the Chinese character for "cover over". The classifer left character indicates that the word is related to watery things – one could drown only in water!

Why the "united and together" as the right subcharacters? It is not a phonetic and is another ideogram. The imitative meanings of the right subcharacters do not reflect the meaning of "drowning." Perhaps a right subcharacter for "struggling" of "submerge" would have more easily convey the overall meaning of "drowning". So again, some famous event involving "united together" must have occurred which connect the right subcharacters to the left classifier to give the overall meaning of "drowning". Such an event could be the united drowning of mankind during a Biblical Flood of Genesis 7.

Thus when the character for "water" is appended to the words with underlying meanings of unity and totality they indicate the phenomenon of drowning in the vast flood. It is the Chinese way to remember the total effects of the Great Flood in destroying all mankind except Noah and his family.

In "Wo" for "continue" (Table 12.4), the left classifier for "water" should puzzle about its contribution to the overall meaning – for what has "water" got to do with "continue"? Also, what have "eight mouths" got to do with "continue"?

The subcharacters have no phonetic contribution to the word. Unlike "S'ng" where the classifier for "Shui or water" alert one to its nature, the same classifier for "Wo" appears superflous – unless "Wo" is connected to some watery event! And "eight mouths" are involved.

The connection is more indirect. An event like the "eight persons surviving through the Biblical Flood" is a logical event as the basis for "Wo". Certainly the "eight persons surviving through the Biblical Flood" would have to "continue" the human race – hence the indirect meaning!

After the floodwaters receded, Noah's family left the ark to settle on the earth. Their subsequent home appeared to be a large cave. For the Chinese character for "cave" denotes 1. a cover over; 2. eight.

A number of Chinese characters incorporate the character for "eight" and may indicates activities which began just after the Flood:

Cave: with subcharacters 1. cover over; and 2. eight.

Elder Brother: with subcharacters 1. mouth over; and 2. man – indicating the man who become the spokesman.

Division: with the subcharacters for 1. eight over; and 2. knife.

Exchange: with the subcharacters 1. eight; and 2. elder brother.

Speak: with the subcharacters 1. words side by side with; and 2. exchange

The appearance of "eight mouths" is a common combination of subcharacters for Chinese words. They often indicate association with events related to the Flood legend.

■ Tower Of Babel Ideograms

The next famous Biblical legend is the Nimrodic rebellion at the Tower of Babel (Genesis 11:1-9). Something happened there which the modern world is not fully aware as yet. The result was that the human races were separated – hence the ancient origin of the world ancient civilisations.

"T'a" for "tower" (Table 12.5) has the character for "united, joined together" as already noted earlier. This word for "united" becomes "undertake" when covered with the subcharacter for "grass" – as the grass denotes bitterness the word for tower also indicate an undertaking of a bitter nature. When appended with the subcharacter for

CHAPTER 12 **MIDDLE EAST LEGENDS** 183

"earth" the combination denotes "tower." The pictogram shows that the first tower would be those built with clay. The Chinese remembered this unpleasant Tower of Babel (Genesis 11:1-9).

The Bible shows that soon after the Flood, Nimrod tried to get mankind to build a huge tower and that God in His displeasure stopped this ambitious project and scattered mankind through confusing their tongues:

> And the Lord said, Behold they are one people and they all have one language ... Come let us go down there and confuse their language that they may not understand one another's speech (Genesis 11:6-7)

The Chinese word for "rebellion" which also means "confusion" is shown in Table 12.5. It contains the subcharacters for 1. tongues; and 2. right leg. It shows that only one leg is associated with what is spoken – i.e. the other leg is doing a different thing. Confusion and a rebellion arising out of insincerity. The "right leg" really indicates the extended meaning of walking. The word means to walk off as a results of tongues and the resulting confusion:

> Therefore its name was called Babel, because there the Lord confused the language of all the earth; and from there the Lord scattered them abroad over the face of all the earth (Genesis 11:9)

In fact the Chinese word "Fen" for "division" (Table 12.5) has the subcharacters for 1. eight; and 2. knife. This signifies the division of the people who descended from the original eight persons. It also indicates that the Tower of Babel incident was not very long after the Flood.

The Chinese remembered how they had to leave as a result of this Babel rebellion and confusion! They preserved this incident in the word for "Migrate". (Table 12.5.) This word has the subcharacters 1. west; 2. great; 3. divisions; and 4. walking. This word for "migrate" indicates the ac-

184 THE CHINESE PAKUA

tion of walking as a result of "great divisions" in the west. The word even preserves the original location of their homeland in the west, in Mesopotamia! The Chinese came from Mesopotamia!

13

THE GAMMADION-PAKUA IDEOGRAMS

■ What Is the Gammadion?

According to MacKenzie (1926, p.2), the Gammadion, which is the symbol of the Cross and its variant the Swastika, is of considerable antiquity in Elam, Asia Minor, Central-Western-Northern Europe, India, China and Japan. He also notes that the Gammadion is basically the representation of the Four Cardinal Directions of South-East-North-West and that these Four Directions are often symbolised by certain animals.

The Chinese Eight Diagrams or Pakua system is very much a Gammadion. In the ancient Chinese culture, the Pakua's Four Directions are symbolised by the Phoenix (South), "Lung" (East), Snake-Tortoise (North) and Tiger (West). These animals representations have much similar equivalent with those of the Babylon-Assyria-Hebrew cultures. These Four Animals are also described in the Bible in Revelation 4:6-8 as well as Ezekial 1:10.

It is the premise here that the universal Gammadion is Mankind's memory of the four rivers in the Garden of Eden described in the Bible:

> And a river went out of Eden to water the garden and from thence it was parted, and became into four heads. The name of the first is Pison; that is it which encompasseth the whole land of Havilah where there is gold; And the gold of that land is good; there is bdellium and the onyx stone. And the name of the second river is Gihon; the same is it that compasseth the whole land of Ethiopia. And the name

of the third river is Hiddekel: that is it which goeth toward the east of Assyria. And the fourth river is Euphrates (Genesis 2:10-14).

It is for this reason that the ancient Chinese associate Fu-Hsi the first man as the East "Azure lung" in the Four Heraldic Animals. Fu-Hsi the first man is Adam and the Bible notes that Adam and Eve were driven from the Garden of Eden through the East:

So he drove out the man; and he placed at the east of the garden of Eden Cherubims and a flaming sword which turned every way to keep the way of the tree of life (Genesis 3:24)

The ancient Chinese depicts Fu-Hsi as a bearded man with two horns and a long fish-tail lower torso. This is not unlike the "Kerub", the East animal of the Babylon-Assyria-Jewish Cabalic Four Animals – the "Kerub" is also bearded with two horns and a fish-tail – better known as Neptune the Sea God.

The Gammadion is universal symbol of the Garden of Eden. The Gammadion or Pakua features significantly in certain Chinese ideograms. Chinese ideograms connected with this Gammadion-Pakua are shown in Table 13.1

■ Chinese Words With Gammadion

The ancient Chinese graph "T'ien", the word for "field" and also "garden" contains this Four Directions cross. Hence, the ancient Chinese remember the Garden of Eden with its four rivers as "T'ien" the garden with four rivers – this is the basic Gammadion.

The Gammadion is also found in the word "Yu" for "from, before, origin, cause, beginning." This is further evidence of Chinese belief that Mankind originated from the Garden of Eden.

CHAPTER 13 **GAMMADION-PAKUA IDEOGRAMS** 187

The Gammadion is seen in the oracle bone script for "Ti" or "God", which is a eight points star alike to the Sumerian eight points star for "God" (Table 11.1).

Other Gammadion words discussed earlier which have connection to the very origins of Mankind are:

- The words "Tung" for "East" and "Hsi" for "West" originally include the Gammadion.
- A Gammadion word discussed earlier is "Fu" for "Happiness." The word basically means "One or First Man with God in a Garden." It is the memory of the bliss when Adam was with God in Eden.

The Four Heraldic Animals of the Four Directions are known to compose the Ten Celestial Stems in the Ganzhi system of chronology and direction. The Chinese word for the first of these Ten Celestial Stems "Chia" has the Gammadion.

The Chinese ideogram for "Kuei" (Devil) shows a man at the North. The North is the heraldic position of the Serpent. Hence, this Chinese word for "Devil" remember the legend of the "Old Serpent the Devil" at the Garden of Eden.

The Gammadion is a very powerful symbol, for it is the basis of the word for "Wu" for "worker of magic". It also appears that thunder and lightning were first known to Mankind in the Garden of Eden! For the words "Lei" for "Thunder" and "T'ien" for "Lightning" contain the Gammadion. It is for this reason that the most powerful Taoist magic ritual is known as "Thunder Magic" which is connected to the summoning of the Four Heraldic Angels of the Four Cardinal Directions.

Many of the Gammadion words are linked to legends of the very origins of Mankind. The earliest forms of the language of Man incorporate the Gammadion-Pakua symbol. This is the reason why the ancient Chinese tradition links

188 THE CHINESE PAKUA

Table 13.1a
CHINESE CHARACTERS WITH GAMMADION

FIELD	Garden of Eden with its four rivers		
田 T'IEN	⊕ oracle bone (3.8)	口 Enclosure	+ Four rivers

FROM, ORIGIN — *Origin is from Garden of Eden at South, i.e. from Phoenix (Bird of South & symbol of Holy Spirit) = Origin from Holy Spirit of God*

由 YU	田 Tien Garden of Eden	! from South

WEST — *The first man in the enclosure (Garden of Eden). Chinese remembered they came from Eden in west*

西 HSI	田 Oracle bone (20.2)	一 i first
	八 jen man	口 wei enclosure	田 ti'en garden field

EAST	*This word is not easy to decipher*	
東 TUNG	田 Oracle bone (20.1)	

HAPPINESS, BLESSING — *Happiness is when Adam the first man was in the garden with God (Gen 1-2)*

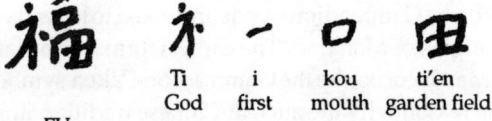

福 FU	礻 Ti God	一 i first	口 kou mouth	田 ti'en garden field

CHAPTER 13 **GAMMADION-PAKUA IDEOGRAMS** 189
Table 13.1b
CHINESE CHARACTERS WITH GAMMADION (cont)

GOD 帝 TI	*In the modern form the PAKUA is not seen. However, the oracle bone script shows Ti" is a 8-points star the Pakua.* Oracle bone (2.2)
THUNDER 雷 LEI	*Thunder first known in Garden of Eden* Oracle bone (19.28)
LIGHTNING 電 T'IAN	Lightning first know in Garden of Eden Oracle bone (19.29)
1ST CELESTIAL 甲 CHIA	The first is Heaven at the North. Oracle bone (17.19) Tien Garden of Eden from North
DIVINE 神 SHEN	*The God who is the Phoenix fighting the Serpent = meaning of constellation of Scorpio or "Fire Star"* Ti shen = time when south fights north God Phoenix fights Serpent

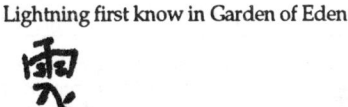

Table 13.1c
CHINESE CHARACTERS WITH GAMMADION (cont)

WORKER OF MAGIC	*Pakua is source of magic power*		
巫 WU	十 Oracle bone (16.7)	=	Four Directions

DEVIL

Into the Garden came a being with a secret thing (Gen 3:1-7). Man at North is "Serpent" therefore is Devil the Serpent.

鬼
KUI

甼 Oracle bone (18.10)		ノ p'ieh movement or life	
田 ti'en garden field	八 jen man at South	ム ssu privately	

TEMPTER — *From the covering of the trees the being with the secret tempt Eve = tempter (Gen 3:1-7)*

魔
MO

广 kuan cover	木 mu trees	鬼 kui devil

MIGRATE — *In the west there was a great separation. This cause walking, i.e. migration (Gen 11:8-9)*

遷
CHIEN

西 hsi west	大 ta great	巳 sze separate	辶 tsou walking

CHARIOT — *Legend of Huang-Ti separating the races to Four Directions from the chariot = Five Emperors Gods Pakua symbol.*

車
CHE

Oracle bone (12.14)	=	chariot carrying Four Directions

Fu-Hsi's creation of Chinese writings to the Eight Diagrams or Pakua.

Another Gammadion word of a later era is "Che" for "Chariot." The oracle graph shows a line connected to two crossed-circles with a crossed-square on the line. Is this connected to the legend of Emperor Huang-Ti riding a chariot assigning the races to the Four Cardinal Points of the world? Possibly Huang-Ti was the inventor of the chariot! He might have used it in his successful battles against Chih You for mastery of the world.

■ Pakua Has Roles In The Origin Of Languages

The Gammadion, universally known in so many ancient cultures in the Middle East, is the same as the Pakua. The relationship of the Chinese writings to the Pakua and hence the Gammadion means that Chinese writings originated in the Gammadion region where the Garden of Eden was – the Middle East.

The Pakua, through the 22-symbols Ganzhi system, is the source of origin of the alphabetic languages. The Pakua, through the symbol of "t'ien", the garden with the four rivers, is also obviously involved with the early development of ancient Chinese writings.

Hence, the significance of the Chinese tradition that the first man, Fu-Hsi alias Adam, invented writings in connection with the Eight Diagrams or Pakua:

> The Pakua could be the source and origin, not only of the Chinese writings, but also of the languages of Mankind.

■ Path Of Righteousness In Chinese Ideograms

The Chinese ideograms not only preserve certain important ancient Middle East Biblical legends but they also preserve a way of righteousness of God similar to that given to the ancient Hebrews!

Have you ever wondered at the signboards and tablets the Chinese used to hang over and by their household doors? Especially the Spring couplets. These signs and tablets, which may be on wood, bamboo and silk cloth, contain certain auspicious words which are actually religious instructions. Such a practice of putting up signs with religious instructions is actually an ancient Middle East-Biblical practice!:

> Therefore shall ye lay up these my words in your heart and in your soul and bind them for a sign upon your hand that they may be as frontlets between your eyes. And ye shall teach them your children, speaking of them when thou sittest in thine house and when thou hast liest down and when thou risest up. And thou shalt write them upon the door posts of thine house and upon thy gates. That your days may be multiplied and the days of your children ... (Deuteronomy 11:18-21)

One common highly esteemed phrase has four words "Jen Yi Tao T'ieh" mean "Benevolence or Love, Righteousness, Truth and Virtue or Good Works" (Table 13.2) This phrase existed before Confucius's time (Goh et al, 1983) and features in a number of sayings (Plopper, 1935). "Tao-T'ieh" is also the term for "civics" as taught in Chinese schools. The phrase, however, reflects ancient Chinese practices familiar to the ancient Hebrew culture.

Jen For Benevolence

"Jen", the Chinese word for Benevolence, love or perfect in loving harmony has two subcharacters 1. two or second; and 2. first man. The word represents the original sinless nature of the first two human beings whose relationship was full of loving harmony. Their "love" in that original unfallen stage was the most beautiful form of love known to man.

A far more arbitrary derivation was given by Vacarri and Vaccari (1950, p.65): "Were man living alone and isolated from the rest of the world he would be unable to express any of his tender feelings and that is only when he is or associates with another or more of his kind that he can show kindness and sympathy."

Prophetically, the word could also foreshadow the "second man." If the subcharacters were merged as in Table 13.1, they mean "T'ien" or "Heaven". (If the subcharacter for the man is merged with the subcharacter for "one" we get the word "Tu" for "Earth"). Goh et al (1983) maintains that the word for "benevolence" contains an intrinsic prophecy: Adam the first man is of the earth. But the second man who would bring true lasting benevolence is from Heaven – the Middle East-Biblical legend of the Saviour from Heaven, like the Christian Lord Jesus Christ!

Yi For Righteousness

An important word would be the Chinese word "Yi" for "Righteousness" (Table 13.2) This word has two basic words – characters viz a "sheep" over "I or me." The character "Wo" for "I or me" is a composite of the subcharacters for "hand" and "spear" – it really signifies the warrior man stabbing or striking with a spear or blade.

Hence the Chinese word for "Righteousness" is a picture of a man using a blade to strike or stab a sheep. This Chinese word thus signifies that "righteousness" is the result of this sacrifice of the sheep. Is this not the Biblical concept of the sacrificial sheep? That "Righteousness" would come through the Sacrifice of the Unblemish Lamb (i.e. Christ-type)? It is evident that the Chinese preserve the prophetic promise God gave in Eden:

And I will put enmity between thee and the woman, and between thy seed and her seed; it shall bruise thy head and thou shalt bruise his heel (Genesis 3:15)

The sheep is an important sacrificial animal for the Hebrews as this animal was used as a sin offering to God to cleanse the person from sin. Christians take this sheep to be a symbol for the Son of God who would have to die to redeem for the sins of the whole world so that mankind would have the chance to become righteous! The sheep was also an important sacrificial animal in the early Chinese worship of Shang-Ti (Bilsky, 1975; Creel, 1938). Hence, both the Chinese and Hebrews preserve the same ancient practice of sacrificing the sheep to God. Both ancient Chinese and Hebrews know the sheep sacrifice was necessary for the righteousness of the person. The ancient Chinese preserve this significance into the word "Yi" for "Righteousness."

Interesting enough, if a Hebrew could not afford a sheep a bird like the dove could be used. Is this not the forerunner of the Chinese practice of birds sacrifices?

Tao For Truth

The third word "Tao" means the Way or Truth. This word is more complicated as the subcharacters have been abbreviated. According to Vaccari and Vaccari (1950, p.144) the combination of symbols is "Shou" for "head" and "Tsou" for "walking" and means that "A road is the place for men to walk (forward movement)". But a more logical meaning, involving breaking the character into more than two subcharacters is given below.

Basically, there are three subcharacters viz the more recognisable one 1. walking; then 2. see; and overtopped by 3. fire. The subcharacters for 1. walking and 2. see represent

CHAPTER 13 GAMMADION-PAKUA IDEOGRAMS 195
Table 13.2
THE JEN-YI-TAO-TI'EH CHINESE CHARACTERS

LOVE — *The relations of two persons = love. The role of the second man to bring love (Christ)*

JEN

	jen	erh
	man	two or second

RIGHTEOUSNESS — *The hand using a spear to sacrifice the lamb result is righteousness. Chinese knew righteousness will come from slain lamb*

YI

ya	mou	ke	wo
sheep	hand	blade	I

TRUTH — *"Yen" and "tsou" indicates ability to see and walk. This is result of is result of "fire" from above heaven. "Fire" above the "one" indicates "Holy Spirit"*

TAO

i	yen
one	eye

p'ieh	shou		tsou
movement of life	classifier of songs, poems	fire	walking

VIRTUE, GOOD WORKS — *To all men and in all things in four directions be of one heart i.e. wholehearted sincere efforts.*

TI'EH

jen	shih	ssu	i	hsin
all men	ten	four	one	heart

the ability to see and walk – but according to what? According to the influence of the third subcharacter! – fire.

The Chinese character for "fire" is a memory of the original form of man which was clothed with the shining glory from God. The shining glory was lost in the Fall. This "fire" represents the Holy Spirit.

"Tao" is the ancient Chinese recognition that man needs something from God or Heaven above in order to live the Way of Truth. That is, one must receive from above the "fire of God" in order to live a truthful life. The Chinese knew it is very difficult and very rare and near impossible for a man to be perfect in following "Tao". The person who could walk the Way of Truth would be almost a divine being! Confucius often lamented that he could not find any who really walked according to "Tao" (Lau, 1979) – well, of course, because man has no intrinsic ability to measure up to the standards of God and needs the Holy Spirit of God to do so!

This concept of man requiring some form of spiritual force to walk according to the Truth is not strange. After all the ancient sages of even many other religions often underwent various procedures to try to obtain that "magic" which could make the difference. This is really the ancient recognition that man needs the power from God to live the Way of Truth.

Hence the "Tao" denotes an ability to see and walk according to the influence of the "fire" of God – i.e. the Holy Spirit. The words is also a prophecy of the coming of the Holy Spirit from high to enable us to see and walk the Way of Truth!

T'ieh For Virtue

The last fourth word "T'ieh" means virtue, excellence or good works. It has three groups of subcharacters and their meanings are viz 1. all men (whole, total); 2. "ten" on top of "west" (everything in the four directions); and 3. "one" on top of "heart" (united or wholeheartedly). Although there are further hidden meanings to these groups of subcharacters, the combination denotes the spirit of wholeheartedness in two main aspects, one in doing everything and second in doing everything for all mankind. The word "T'ieh" is therefore a prophetic indication that the things man would do towards his fellow beings would come straight from his heart. The result is virtue or excellence.

Jen-Yi-Tao-T'ieh

This set of words "Jen-Yi-Tao-T'ieh" features in some Chinese sayings such as "Wisdom, and virtue, and benevolence, and rectitude, without politeness are imperfect" or "To have a mouth full of benevolence, righteousness, reason, and virtue; but in the heart a thief or whore." (later one meaning "Saint outside, devil inside") (Plopper, 1935).

Some Chinese recognise that the term "Tao T'ieh" signifies the rare ability to keep to the Way of Truth only through something from God. That is why the ancient sages went up the mountains to meditate, hoping that they would receive that divine spark which would make them the perfect being. In some way this concept recognises that man of himself is intrinsically unable to follow effectively the Way of Truth – until he receives that something, some divine spark from God. How to receive this divine spark from God?

To the Bible, this "divine spark" as the "Holy Spirit" and the Bible exhort:

> Repent and be baptised every one of you in the name of Jesus Christ and ye shall receive the gift of the Holy Spirit (Acts 2:38)

The "Jen-Yi-Tao-T'ieh" concept indicates that the Chinese ancient way of morals was similar to those of the Bible!

While each of the four words "Jen-Yi-Tao-T'ieh" has its remarkable noble signficance, the four words combined together have even more significant meanings! For one thing, the set represents the four main characters in the Plan of God!:

JEN	Benevolence	God the Father in His Eternal Love to the first two human beings who represent the whole human race
YI	Righteousness	God the Son of God in His Humble Sacrifice so that the whole human race would become righteous
TAO	Truth	God the Holy Spirit in His Agency of Knowledge to provide man with that missing intrinsic power to walk the Way of Truth
T'IEH	Virtue	the Completed New Man

The "Jen-Yi-Tao-T'ieh" thus indicates prophetically the merging of Man into the Family of God! The Chinese word "Tsu" for "Ancestor" already indicates that our original ancestor is God. While Man failed to attain full divinity in the Garden of Eden, God has a plan to ensure that Man would eventually enter into the Kingdom of God.

⊛ PART C ⊛
ROLE OF PAKUA IN RELIGION OF ANCIENT CHINA

The Pakua contains the secret of the original religion of ancient China.

The Pakua shows that the original religion of Mankind is a monotheistic worship of Shang-Ti the One Supreme God Who is surrounded by His four major angels. Ancient China kept to this monotheistic worship of Shang-Ti until around 500BC when deviations into polytheism occurred through corruption and political motivations.

The Emperor is a central figure in this monotheistic worship of Shang-Ti for he acts as the priest-king of Shang-Ti. The ancient title for "Priest-King" is "Lung", which has been misleadingly equated with the western "Dragon-Serpent."

"Lung" is the East Angel of the Pakua while the "Dragon-Serpent" is the North Angel of the Pakua.

14 Pakua Is Original Ancient Religion Of China
15 The Worship Of Shang-Ti, The Supreme God
16 Circumpolar Star System Of The Pakua
17 Pakua-Sigil Formations In Nine Emperor Gods
18 Chinese "Lung" At The East

14

PAKUA IS ORIGINAL ANCIENT RELIGION OF CHINA

■ Original Chinese Worship Had Very Few Gods

One of the most astonishing humbling secrets of the Pakua is that the Pakua is actually all that formed the original ancient religion of China!

It is not well known that the present Chinese polytheistic religion of mixed so-called Taoist-Buddhist-animist elements did not exist in ancient China before 500BC (Bilsky 1975; Wu, 1982. p.7). The concensus of Chinese historical documents is that Chinese religious culture was previously monotheistic, but a series of politically motivated events from around 500BC caused the appearance of polytheistic gods in the Chinese religious culture.

Wu (1982, p.7) writes: "There is no question that the ancient Chinese believed in one almighty God. All the records, from the earliest times, testify to this. They called Him di, "the Lord," or shangti, "the Lord Above." As God abides above, and above heaven, tian, so they also called Him tian, "Heaven". Unlike other people, however, they never endowed their God with human attributes or with any kind of physical image. From all records prior to the 2nd centuryBC there is no indication that they had ever worshipped idols. Idol worship appeared only in the reign of the brillant but superstitious wudi "the Martial Emperor" (144-88BC) of the Han dynasty ... In fact, idol worship was introduced to China only after the advent of Buddhism in the 1st century A.D."

202 THE CHINESE PAKUA

Idol worship appeared in ancient China only after 200BC

Werner (1922, p.67) notes the "crushing judgement of an over-zealous Christian missionary sinologist that, unlike the early western religions, including those of India, the Chinese religion appears chaotic as it lacks the kind of system conferred by a systematic hierachy of gods such as the Greek Olympian gods or the Sun God-Earth Mother Goddess cults". This difficulty in reconciling Chinese polytheism to Western polytheism is primarily due to that while Western polytheism have Middle East origins as far back as before 1500BC, the Chinese polytheism was a late development from around 500BC Development of Chinese polytheism is of an independent nature with very few parallels from Western polytheism.

Chinese Gods Are Canonised Human Beings

How then did the Chinese many gods arise? Werner (1922) also states that most of the Chinese gods were former human beings canonised to become gods from three main periods, being the first in the reign of Emperor Hsien Yuen (Huang Ti) around 2698BC, the second in the beginning of the Chou dynasty in 1122BC, and the third period in the Ming dynasty around A.D. 1400.

Table 14.1 indicates the more popular deities worshipped by the Chinese today. On the basis of their appearance in Chinese ancient history they could be grouped as follows:

1. Before Emperor Hsien Yuen (Huang-Ti) around 2688BC, the so-called early Chinese gods involved a few figures centred around Shang-Ti the Supreme God (alternate being "T'ien") and a surrounding small echelon of human beings who became stargods and deities like Tou-Mu, Hsi Wang Mu-Mu Kung, Fu Hsi.

Only Shang-Ti is imageless, while the four Chinkangs had no human origins and appeared to be "Lung-dragon spirits".

2. The second group of human beings canonised as gods were those human beings during Shen-Nung-Huang-Ti's time.

3. A small group of gods who were human beings of Chiang Tzu-ya's time; Chiang Tzu-ya being the prime minister who was chiefly responsible for the success of the Chou dynasty in overcoming the Shang dynasty around 1122BC

4. After that a host of human beings (as early as 1000BC to as late as the Sung dynasty in AD 1280) became gods.

A few famous gods were created through deliberate fraud but still remain in the Chinese echelon of gods to this day:

- The famous Jade Emperor God, Yu Huang is known to be the spurious invention of Emperor Cheng-Tsung of the Sung dynasty, 1005 AD and his crafty unreliable minister Wang Ch'in-jo. "This is the origin of Yu Huang. He was born of a fraud and came ready-made from the brain of an emperor." (Werner, 1922. p.131)

  Maspero (1945, p.90) acknowledges that several scholars regarded that Emperor Chen Tsung was a dissimulator and purely dreamt up his dreams to deceive the people and thereby invented Yu Huang.

- The Kitchen God, Tsao Chun, is an invention of the Taoist priest Li Shao-chun of Ch'i State in 140-86BC (Werner, 1922. p.167). This priest deceived the credulous monarch Emperor Hsiao Wu-ti into sacrificing to Tsao Chun. Eventually the Emperor discovered the trick and executed Li Shao-chun. But the worship of the false Kitchen God continued.

In the very dawn of Chinese cultural history there was thus only a small echelon of gods, involving the imageless

Supreme God Shang-Ti (or T'ien), the four Chinkangs and a small group of canonised human beings. So, except for Shang-Ti the Supreme God (alternate = T'ien or Heaven) and the Four Chinkangs, the other deities were actually all canonised human beings. How did the human gods arise?

The archeological evidence has indicated that actual civilisation started in China only around 1400BC, corresponding to the Shang dynasty. Before this period, so-called Chinese gods may be figures from non-Chinese races.

■ True Nature Of Original Ancestor Worships

There are evidence that great human beings were originally remembered in ancestral memorials of powerful families but due to political reasons became elevated to deities during the Eastern Chou era (Bilsky, 1975).

These original Chinese remembrance of ancestors was not through worship but memorials:

- Of the sacrifices offered to spirits in the Chou dynasty, Khung Ying-ta said that "the spirits were men, who, when alive, had done good services and were therefore sacrificed to when dead." (Legge, 1967. p.395).

- The Li Chi (Book of Rites compiled by Confucius) mentions an important reason for the offerings to the dead: When a man dies, there arise a feeling of disgust. Its impotency goes on to make us revolt from it. On this account, there is the wrapping it in the shroud, and there are the curtains, plumes to preserve men from that feeling of disgust. Immediately after death, the dried flesh and pickled meats are set out. When the interment is about to take place, there are the things sent and offered; and after the interment there is food presented. The dead have never been seen to partake of these things. But from the highest ages to the present they have never been neglected; – all to cause men not to revolt. This it is that what you blame in the rules of

CHAPTER 14 **ORIGINAL ANCIENT RELIGION** 205

Table 14.1

DATES OF ORIGINS OF CHINESE GODS
(after Werner, 1922; Plopper, 1935)

Three periods of creations of gods:		
Hsien Yang (Huang-Ti)	BC 2698	
Chiang Tzu-ya	BC 1200	
Ming dynasty	AD 1400	

Name	God of:	Date	Originator		
Mo-li(a) Ch'ing	Chinkang, a east	z		These four Chinkangs	120
Mo-li(b) Hung	Chinkang, b south	z		fought against Chou	120
Mo-li(c) Hai	Chinkang, c west	z		dynasty	120
Mo-li(d) Shou	Chinkang, d north	z			120
Hou-te Hsing-chun*	Fire Minister	z			236
Hsi Wang Mu	f:Golden Mother	z		Yu Huang's counterpart	136
Hsi Wang Mu,b	f:Golden Mother,b	z		nine sons, 24 daughters	136
Tou Mu*,b	f:North Pole Star Goddess	z			
Tou Mu*	f:h Queen of Heaven	z		mother of JuiHuang Ye	144
Mu Kung	Immortals, God	z			136
Kuei Hsing Lou*	Literature God, d	z		Northern Bushel	108
Shou Hsing*	Longevity God	z		Southern Bushel	171
T'ien	s:Heaven	z		not same as Shang-Ti	95
T'ien,b	s:Heaven,b	z		worshipped by people	95
Shang-Ti	s:Supreme Emperor	z		worshipped only by	94
Shang-Ti,b	s:Supreme Emperor,b	z		Chinese emperors	94
Nu Kua Shih	f:Creator	BC 2953-2838	Lieh Tzu, BC 500	y.sister of Fu Hsi	81
Fu Hsi	Medicine God	BC 2953-2838		Celestial Emperor	247
No-cha	Fire-wheel God	BC 2828#		T'ai Chen-jen's student	306
T'ai I	Great One	BC 2828#	Shu King	same time as Shen Nung	143
T'ai I,b	Great One,b	BC 2828#		T'ai Chen-jen, No-cha's master	305
Li Ching	Heaven's Prime Minister	BC 2828#		Pagoda-bearer, No-cha's father	305
Yu Shih	Rain Master	BC 2828#	Shen Nung	Ch'ih Sung-tzu	205
Chu Jung	Fire Emperor	BC 2698-2598	Emperor Hsien Yang	Huang-Ti ordered Chu Jung to fight	238
Chu Jung,b	Fire Emperor,b	BC 2698-2598		Hui Lu (qv Hui Lu)	238
Shen Shu	Door God, left	BC 2698#	Emperor Hsien Yang		
Yu Lu	Door God, right	BC 2698#	Emperor Hsien Yang		
Hui Lu	Fire God	BC 2436-2366	Ti-kao, Yao's father	Huang-Ti ordered Chu Jung to fight	238
Hui Lu,b	Fire God,b	BC 2436-2366		Hui Lu (qv Chu Jung)	
Ch'eng-huang	City God	BC 2357	Emperor Yao	Pa-cha, the 8 spirits	165
Shen-I*	Archer, Divine	BC 2346	Emperor Yao	Shot nine sons	180
Heng-o or Ch'ang O*	f:Moon Goddess	BC 2346		Wife of Shen-I	182
Ta'i-yin Huang-	f:Moon-queen	BC 2346		also called Yueh-fu	179

206 THE CHINESE PAKUA

chun*				Ch'ang O	
Ta'i-yang Ti-chun	Sun-king	BC 2346		Ch'ih-chiang Tzu-yu/ Shen-I	179 239
Shen Nung	Fire Emperor	BC 2338-2698			
Shen Nung,b	Medicine God	BC 2338-2698		also Fu Hsi, Huang-Ti	247
T'ung-t'ien Chiao-chu	1st Taoist Patriarch	BC 1122#		aided Emperor Chou	133
No-cha,b	Fire-wheel God,b	BC 1122#		aided Chou dynasty	153
Nan-chi Hsien-weng	South Pole Immortal	BC 1122#		aided Chian Tzu-ya	154
Lu Yuen	Sickness Minister	BC 1122	Chiang Tzu-ya		241
Wen Chung	Thunder Minister	BC 1122	Chiang Tzu-ya	Minister of Emperor Chou	193
Ts'ai Shen	Wealth God	BC 1122	Chiang Tzu-ya	Chao Kung-Ming, Shang patriot	170
Feng Po*	Wind God	BC 1122		FeiLien, Minister of Emperor Chou	204
Feng Po*,b	Wind God,b	BC 1122			
Sun Hou-tzu	Moneky God	BC 1000#	from Hinduism	master = P'u-t'i Tsu-shih	325
Yang Hou	Sea Spirit	BC 0300	Chin dynasty	Marquis of Yang, drowned	212
Kuan Yin	f:Mercy Goddess	BC 0200#	Buddhism		251
Tsao Chun	Kitchen God	BC 0140-86	Taoist Li Shao-chun	A trick on Emperor siao Wu-ti	166
Lei Kung	Thunder Duke	BC 0100		= Garuda	200
Wen Ch'ang	Literature God	AD 265-316	Chin dynasty	abode is Kuei in	104
T'ai Sui*	Year or Time God	AD 1280-1368		Jupiter, son of Emperor Chou	194 195
Ts'ao Kou-chiu	Immortal with tablet	AD 1023-64			300
Yu Huang	Jade Emperor	AD 1005	Emperor Cheng Tsung	created by fraud	130
Yu Huang,b	Jade Emperor,b	AD 1005		= Indra	132
Li T'ieh-kuai	Immortal with crutch	AD 1000#		instructed by Lao Tzu	
Pa Hsien Eight	Immortals	AD 0960-1280	Sung dynasty		288 304
Wen Ch'ang,c	Literature God, c	AD 0960-1280	Sung dynasty	stars of square	104
Chang Hsien*	Shooter of Heavenly Dog	AD 0935-964	Emperor Jen Tseng	Spirit of star Chang	177 178
Lu Tung-pin	Immortal with sword	AD 0798			298
Han hsiang Tzu	Immortal with basket	AD 0768-824			299
Chang Kou	Immortal riding mule	AD 0700-800			294
Li Kuei-tsu	Happiness God	AD 0697-781		Ministerof Wei dynasty	170
Ho Hsien Ku	Immortal with lotus	AD 0684-705			296
Chung K'uei	Exorcism Minister	AD 0618-627	Tang dynasty		248
Lan Ts'ai Ho	Immortal hermaphrodite	AD 0600#	Tang dynasty		293
Wen Ch'ang, b	Literature God, b	AD 0600#	Tang dynasty	Great Bear - four	104
Fu Shen*	Happiness God	AD 0502-550	Emperor Wu Ti		169
P'an Ku	Creator	AD 0400	Magistrate Ko Hung		79
Kuan Ti	War God	AD 0200			
Chung-li	Ch'uan Immortal	AD 0100	Han dynasty		291

propriety is really nothing that is wrong in them." (Legge, 1967. pp.177-178). Thus, Confucius did not regard these ancestral sacrifices as denoting worship of the dead – this is in accordance with the known view of Confucius against worship of spirits and gods.

- Even during the more recent Manchu dynasty, Emperor Kang-Hsi (reign 1662-1722) supported the declaration that "performance of the ceremony of sacrifice to the dead is a means of showing sincere affection for members of the family and thankful devotion to ancestors of the clan: that tablets of deceased ancestors were honoured as a remembrance of the dead rather than as the actual residence of their souls" (Rule, 1986. p.132).

Kung and Ching (1928, p.38) also records thus: " ... it proved futile for Emperor K'ang-hsi to issue an official affirmation that Kung Fu-tzu was only venerated as a teacher and not a god, and that the veneration of ancestors was a memorial and not a divine service ...

The corruption of ancestral memorials to famous human beings is the main factor leading to the proliferation of deities and emergence of Chinese polytheism.

■ Proliferation Of Deities During Eastern Chou Era

The historical evidence indicate that deviations from the original sole worship of Shang-Ti, the Supreme God, started around the Eastern Chou era (771-256BC) (Bilsky, 1975).

The Chinese ancient records were not sufficient to determine the nature of the sacrificial rites of the Shang dynasty. Looking at Western Chou records, Bilsky (1975, pp.58-59) writes:

- Ancestral spirits, foremost among them being the spirits of the Chou royal line, were the focal points for state worship both in ancestral temples and outdoor altars. With the exception of the supreme deities, Heaven and Shang-ti, the gods of nature had rather restricted areas of power ... " The Western Chou dynasty covered the period of 1122-771 BC and it is very evident that during this period, discounting the ancestral spirts, only Shang-Ti (and its other equivalent Heaven) was worshipped.

In the Eastern Chou era (771-256 BC) the Chou emperors became only figureheads, while the nation was split into groups of states whose groupings changed with the tide of affairs. The weakening of the Chou emperors led to the deterioration of ancestral worships and the worship of Shang-Ti (Bilsky, 1975. pp.141-152). The states, of course, would not like to honour these rites as that would mean recognition of the Chou emperors' sovereignty over them. The nature gods who were formerly little invoked in the Western Chou era became more prominent in the Eastern Chou era. Worship was given to nature gods such as the Mountain God, The Fire God. The Ch'in especially offered worship to the Four Heavenly Kings (or Chinkangs).

Thus, other gods besides Shang-Ti the Supreme God, began to be worshipped during this Eastern Chou era of 771-256 BC The slide away from the worship of the One True God worsened. There appeared to be a purposeful creation of a new series of gods from legendary figures to replace the former centralised worship (Bilsky, 1975. pp.169-174). Legendary figures like Shen-Nung, the fire gods Chu-yung and Hui-lu were created for worship. By the sixth century BC of the Eastern Chou, the natural gods had become a myriads of deities. However, from 500 BC onwards the worship of Shang-Ti regained prominence as the rulers realised they could not ignore the awesome powers of such a deity and there were even condemnations of the nature gods worship (Bilsky, 1975. pp.185-189).

In the Eastern Chou era, many ancestral worships were elevated to deities level (Bilsky, 1975). This indicates that ancestral worships were originally innocent memorials but through corruption and political reasons a number of deities worships were created from these ancestor worships. Ancestral memorials began to take the nature of spirit worships. Contending rulers of the warring states of the Eastern Chou era claimed ancestry to legendary figures before the Chou and even Shang to attempt to confer legitimacy on their rules and the legendary ancestors became elevated to deities.

■ The Mother Goddess

Note in Table 14.1. that before Emperor Hsien Yang in 2698BC there appear worshipped a number of female deities, namely Hsi Wang Mu, Tou Mu and Nu Kua Shih. The legends that Hsi Wang Mu and Tou Mu each had nine sons indicate they are actually the same female deity.

Nu Kua Shih, the first female and sister-wife of the world first Emperor Fu-Hsi is Eve, the Middle East Biblical first woman.

Plopper (1935) notes: The Yin and Yang principles have been deified as Tung Wang Kung, the Royal Father of the East and his consort Hsi Wang Mu the Royal Mother of the West. The Royal Father lives in a kind of Paradise in the Eastern Ocean. The Royal Mother rules in the K'un Lun mountains which are said to be the junction point between Heaven and Earth ... Once each year Hsi Wang Mu goes to her husband, crossing over the back of a gigantic bird which is said to overshadow them and they spend a short space of time in each others company ... p.23

Plopper (1935) also notes a few pertinent aspects of the early Chinese worship:

In the time of Yao there were ten suns, but they burnt up the trees and grasses, and were more than man could endure. The life of each sun was bound up in a large crow. Hou I took his bow and arrows and killed nine of these crows, whereupon their respective suns disappeared, leaving only the present one to bless mankind. p.37.

In the Li Ki we learn the worship of the Sun goes back to at least the Chou dynasty, 1122BC ... p.37.

Hoú-I (also called Shen-I the Divine Archer) is also the same person as Ch'ih-chiang Tzu-yu canonised as the Sun-God by Emperor Yao in 2346BC His wife was Chang-O the Moon Goddess. According to the legend (Werner, 1922; Plopper, 1935; Lai, 1984) Hou-I received a magic pearl of immortality from Hsi Wang Mu and this pearl was mistakenly swallowed by Chang-O. Chang-O fled from her husband Hou-I to the moon. These two new deities may be confused by some with the earlier Hsi Wang Mu and her husband, indicating the kind of misleading interchangeability and syncretism common in many pagan religions.

However, it should be noted that this legend indicates that the Hsi Wang Mu-Tou Mu Mother Goddess figures are not the same as the Sun God and Earth-Moon Goddess. Hsi Wang Mu and Tou Mu thus came from older traditions different from the Sun God-Earth Mother Goddess figures so prominent in the western religions. It is important to note at this juncture that these ancient female goddesses were nevertheless human beings.

The Mother Goddess Tou Mu is also the mother of the nine human kings deified as Nine Emperor Gods who are the stellar deities of the Great Bear or Dipper constellation (Cheu, 1988). Plopper (1935) writes of the Dipper gods:

Each day is governed by a constellation, but of them all, those most worshipped are the Northern and Southern Dipper. The Northern Dipper is supposed to control death,

CHAPTER 14 ORIGINAL ANCIENT RELIGION 211

and the Southern Dipper is suppposed to control life ... The Spirits of the Northern Dipper record men's actions ... Those most worshipped of this constellation are the "Three Stars" [The Three Stars shining together, i.e. May you have happiness, emoluments, and longevity]. Of these the Star of Longevity is the most important [The Hsou Hsing Lao...] ... [There are the Spirits of the Three Stars and of the Northern Dipper {The fourth, fifth and sixth Stars of the Northern Dipper are called the Three Tai. The fourth Star governs long life, the fifth Star governs the happy mean, and the sixth Star governs man's income}] ... pp.40-41

The Chinese Mother Goddess and her nine human king-sons were thus also ancestral human beings who were deified. Although the Mother Goddess and her nine sons came from a period long before Emperor Hsien Yang (Huang-Ti) of 2698BC they, like the other Chinese gods, came into worship only after 500BC If we carefully disregard the Mother Goddess and her Nine Emperor Gods sons, we will find that the original religion of China would be confined only to the worship of Shang-Ti, the Supreme God, or the alternate Tien, Heaven.

■ Original Ancient Chinese Religion Is Pakua

The Four Chinkangs are very old deities. They had no known human origins and appeared to be related to non-human origins such as "dragon spirits." They really represent four major angels as discussed in Chapter 3.

Once the canonised human gods are stripped away, all that would be left would be the Supreme God Shang-Ti and the Four Chinkangs. The Four Chinkangs, of course, form the Four Heraldic Animals of the Pakua ruling the four spheres of the universe. Right in the centre of the Four Chinkangs would be that spinning Yin-Yang symbol of the Supreme God Shang-Ti.

So, all which would be left is actually the Pakua symbolism of Shang-Ti and His Four Chinkangs. There were no human gods yet. Like what the Bible say: There is only God Who is surrounded by His four major angelic beasts.

In those very ancient times, the true worship of ancient world is symbolised by the Gammadion Pakua.

15

THE WORSHIP OF SHANG-TI, THE SUPREME GOD

■ Shang Ti And T'ien

"Shang-Ti" (Supreme God) and "Tien" (Heaven) are the two terms representing the highest forms of the Chinese worship. Werner (1922, pp.94-97) states that although "Shang-Ti" and "T'ien" are different, they have been confused and used interchangeably.

In ancient times the sacrifices to Shang-Ti could be offered only by the Emperor as Shang-Ti's High Priest on earth. The Chinese Emperor was a Priest-King not unlike the Biblical Priest-King Melchisedec. The common people were not allowed, on penalty of death, to worship Shang-Ti. The Emperor would be assisted in this worship by other members of his own family and clan. (The restriction of priesthood to families is also common in many ancient religious cultures).

But the people eventually began to want to worship. Shang-Ti, became synonymous with Tien. Even the Emperor eventually came to worship Heaven at the great altar at the Temple of Heaven (Tien-An-Mien) in Peking while the people, even to this day, worship Tien through placing an altar outside the house. This Shang-Ti worship spread to the people: "Heaven and Earth are known, appealed to and worshipped in practically every home in China. Early in the morning of the first day of the year the incense burner or tripod is taken out into the courtyard in front of the door and there under a clear sky incense is burned for the family ... The tablet to Heaven and Earth is found in nearly every household. It is worshipped on the first and fifteenth of every month and on every occasion of importance ... " (Plopper, 1933. p.29).

There are other names given to Heaven. The "Tao" of Lao Tzu has the same attributes and holds the same place as Heaven by the Chinese. Heaven is also regarded as the great King, the all powerful Sovereign of the universe.

■ Ancient China Worship Only Shang-Ti

Shang-Ti was worshipped by the Emperor as the ancestor of the royal house (Plopper, 1935. pp.59-76, also Bilsky, 1975). Shang-Ti is regarded as God the Father:

"Man might be, but the Heavenly Father could not be deceived" and "The Heavenly Father is unwilling to cause man to suffer loss." (Proverbs quoted by Plopper, 1935. pp.59-76)

Thou hast vouchsafed, O Ti, to hear us, for Thou regardest us as a Father. I, Thy child, dull and unenlightened, am unable to show forth my dutiful feelings ... Thy sovereign goodness is infinite. As a potter, Thou hast made all things. Thy sovereign goodness is infinite. Great and small are sheltered by Thy love. As engraven on the heart of Thy poor servant is the sense of Thy goodness, so that my feeling cannot be fully displayed. With great kindness our demerits dost grant us life and prosperity (quoted by Kang and Nelson, 1979. pp.15-16 – qv the similarity with Isaiah 64:8 KJV: But now O Lord Thou art our Father; we are the clay, and Thou our Potter and we all are the work of Thy hand)

The Imperial Shang-Ti worship is very old. According to the Shu King (Gorn, 1904), Emperor Shun (circa 2315-2255BC) sacrificed to Shang-Ti. These Imperial sacrifices were the "border sacrifices" of the summer and winter solstices, being respectively offered at the northern and southern borders of the country (Kang and Nelson, 1979. p.14).

Archaeological evidence show that among the Shang dynasty relics, the characters for the deities Tien, Ti and Shang-Ti appeared quite a number of times (Creel, 1938. pp.50-51). Names of other deities were not known.

This Shang-Ti worship is carried out on various occasions like Chinese New Year and the Summer-Winter Solstices. "It was customary under the Empire while the people were burning incense upon the Winter Solstice, for the Son of Heaven (the Emperor) to officially perform rites as High Priest for the people. After purification, fasting and prayer, he would go to the Round Altar very early in the morning. In the centre of it was placed the deep blue jade Tablet to Heaven. Twelve offerings of blue silk were made and three kinds of incense burned. A young ox was sacrificed. There were music and dancing. This service was supposed to reach the highest point of organised worship in China." "The Son of Heaven sacrifices to Heaven, then the feudal princes sacrifice to the Earth." "When he worships Heaven he wears robes of a blue colour, in allusion to the sky; and when he worships earth he puts on yellow to represent the clay of this earthly clod; so, likewise he wears red for the sun and pale white for the moon." "The ox has to be fattened and cleaned for ninety days before the sacrifice." (Plopper, 1935. pp.61-62)

Besides the oxen calves, other animals sacrificed include sheep: "During the Four Seasons and Eight Periods, leading sheep and bearing wine – sacrificing uninterruptedly. Used of temples where there is constant worship." (Plopper, 1935. pp.196). Oxen were expensive and often substituted with sheep (Bilsky, 1975).

The Chinese civilisation in China started with the Shang dynasty in 1400BC The domesticated animals in the earlier Neolithic cultures were commonly dogs and pigs;

cattles and sheep were rarer. The Shang dynasty also had cattle and sheep (Creel, 1938. pp.182-189) – this is evidence that these cattle and sheep were not indigenous to ancient China but were brought into China by the Shang.

The Chinese Emperor as the Priest-King has the same role as the Middle East priest-king, like the Biblical Abrahamic Priest-King Melchisedec (Hebrew 7; Genesis 14). When Moses set up the Levitical Priesthood for Israel, there was the Levitical High Priest who however was not the king. This Levitical High Priest retained the sole right to make the final offering to God. Like the Chinese Emperor, the Hebrew High Priest had to fast and purify himself before making the final sacrifice. Interestingly, the Hebrew High Priest also had to sacrifice an ox like the Chinese Emperor before he could proceed into the presence of God. The Hebrew High Priest offered for the whole nation, just as the Chinese Emperor offered for the whole Chinese nation!

Besides the ox, sheep were common sacrificial animals in the Hebrew worship of God. Hence the Hebrew worship of God has striking similarities with the Chinese Imperial worship of Shang-Ti. Both ancient nations worshipped the same God!

■ Initial Corruption Of The Shang-Ti Worship Extend To The Four Heraldic Animals

Evidence indicate that before the Eastern Chou era (771-256BC) that, excluding ancestral sacrifices, the worship of deities was almost confined to the worship of Shang-Ti, the Supreme God, and its manifestation Heaven (Bilsky, 1975). It was only during the middle of the Eastern Chou era that other deities like the Mountain God and the Fire Gods were worshipped and from that time other deities creeped in.

CHAPTER 15 **WORSHIP OF SHANG-TI** 217

Corruption of the worship of the One True God set in because the warring states in the Eastern Chou era wanted to deny the sole rights of the Chou emperors (as the legitimate Priest-Kings of Shang-Ti). Various excuses were introduced to justify variations of worship including those of other deities. During this time too, that many ancestral worships were also deified.

In the confusion, the original four major angels of Shang-Ti became worshipped, mixing the sole worship of Shang-Ti at Tien-An-Mien with the Four Heavenly Kings. Although, initially, only Shang-Ti, the Supreme God, was worshipped by the Chinese Emperors at Tien-An-Mien the worship apparently extended to other figures like the "Five Emperors":

" ... Five Emperors ... Their spirits, because they at times reside in the Five Stars are also called Gods of the Five Planetary Stars ... They were also worshipped yearly as the Five Planetary Stars, during the services on the Altar of Heaven." (Plopper, 1935. p.43)

These Five Planetary Star-Gods were a later addition. There are internal evidence in the very recitation of the annual Imperial border sacrifices:

Of old in the beginning, there was the great chaos, without form and dark. The five elements (planets) had not begun to revolve nor the sun and the moon to shine. In the midst thereof there exist neither forms nor sound. Thou, O spiritual Sovereign camest forth in Thy presidency and first didst divide the grosser parts from the purer. Thou madest heaven; Thou madest earth; Thou madest man. All things with their reproducing power got their being. (quoted by Kang and Nelson, 1979, p.15)

The recitation shows that the Five Planetary Star-Gods were not yet in existence at one time and were formed by Shang-Ti Himself. As the Tien-An-Mien was supposed to be the Temple of Heaven devoted only to the worship of Heaven (or Shang-Ti), the worship of the Five Planetary Star-Gods must be superfluous, supplementary and represents some eventual addition to and corruption of the original Shang-Ti worship.

■ Worship of Shang-Ti At Sacred Mountains

Chinese gods were often worshipped at various mountains. Shang-Ti was worshipped at certain sacred mountains. T'ai Shan (Eastern Peak) located in Shantung is the most noted and sacred of the Five Sacred Mountains. The worship on T'ai Shan is very old: "Shun came here in the first year of his reign 2255BC, presenting offerings to Heaven and sacrificed to the hills and rivers." (Plopper, 1935. p.189).

Confucius's mother prayed at Mount Ni for a son.

The worship of Heaven at Mount T'ai was the sole right of the Emperor. Confucius once made a disapproval of the attempt of the Chi family to worship at Mount T'ai:

> Book III. 6. The Chi Family were going to perform the sacrifice to Mount T'ai. The Master said to Jan Ch'iu, Can you not save the situation?

The prominence given to Mount T'ai indicates that the original form of worship at the mountains is most likely devoted to Shang-Ti at the sacred mountain Mount T'ai. It is in later times that corruption set in the mountains were used to worship other gods.

■ What Confucius Said About Gods

There is a confusion over the views of Confucius about God. Let us examine some of the statements attributed to him:

> Book VII. 21. The topics the Master did not speak of were prodigies, force, disorder and gods (Lau, 1979)

The Master said 'To give one's self earnestly to the duties due to men and while respecting spiritual beings, to keep aloof from them, may be called wisdom (Bilsky, 1975. p.197)

Tzu-lu asked how one should serve ghosts and spirits. The Master said, Till you have learnt to serve men, how can you serve ghosts? Tzu-lu then ventured upon a question about the dead. The Master said, Till you know about the living, how are you to know about the dead? (Bilsky, 1975. p.197)

It has been said that Confucius advocates a philosophical system without reference to any god or spirit. This view is not entirely correct for in the Lun Yu (Analects of Confucius) Confucius made respectful statements about certain aspects of the religious worship of his days (Lau, 1979):

Book II. 1. The Master said, The rule of virtue can be compared to the Pole Star which commands the homage of the multitude of stars without leaving its place.

4. The Master said, At fifteen I set my heart on learning; at thirty I took my stand; at forty I came to be free from doubts; at fifty I understood the Decree of Heaven; at sixty my ear was attuned; at seventy I followed my heart's desire without overstepping lines.

24. The Master said, To offer sacrifice to the spirit of an ancestor not one's own is obsequious.

Book III. 6. The Chi Family were going to perform the sacrifice to Mount T'ai. The Master said to Jan Ch'iu, Can you not save the situation?

17. Tzu-kung wanted to do away with the sacrificial sheep at the announcement of the new moon. The Master said, Ssu, you are loath to part with the price of the sheep, but I am loath to see the disappearance of the rite.

Book VII. 17. The Master said, Grant me a few more years so that I may study the Changes at the age of fifty and I shall be free from major errors

21. The topics the Master did not speak of were prodigies, force, disorder and gods

Book VIII. 2. The Master said, Unless a man has the spirit of the rites, in being respectful he will wear himself out, in being careful he will become timid, in having courage he will become unruly, and in being forthright he will become intolerant.

8. The Master said, Be stimulated by the Odes, take your stand on the rites and be perfected by music.

19. The Master said, Great indeed was Yao as a ruler! How lofty! It is Heaven that is great and it was Yao who modelled himself upon it ...

Book X. 21. When he went inside the Grand Temple, he asked questions about everything.

Book XI. 1. ... When it comes to putting the rites and music to use, I follow the former.

Book XIV. 35. The Master said ... If I am understood at all, it is, perhaps, by Heaven.

Book XVI. 8. Confucius said. The gentleman stands in awe of three things. He is in awe of the Decree of Heaven. He is in awe of great men. He is in awe of the words of sages. The small man, being ignorant of the decree of Heaven, does not stand in awe of it. he treats great men with insolence and the words of the sages with derisions.

Book XX.1. Yao said, Oh Shun, The succession, ordained by Heaven, has fallen on thy person ...

These statements indicate that Confucius subscribed to these features of worship:

1. Heaven or Shang Ti

CHAPTER 15 **WORSHIP OF SHANG-TI**

2. North Pole Star
3. The Book of Changes
4. Rites
5. Sacrifices for Ancestor worship
6. Sheep sacrifices
7. Sacrifice at Mount Ta'i
8. Grand Temple

It is true, however, that Confucius did not mention the myriads of gods and spirits so common today among the Chinese.

But Confucius subscribed to the worship of Heaven as indicated by his references to Heaven, the Grand Temple to worship Heaven and the sheep sacrifice which was made to Heaven. Mount T'ai was the Sacred Mountain where the Emperor worshipped Shang-Ti. Confucius refered to the North Pole Star which is the symbolic seat of Heaven. His reference to the Book of Changes (or the I Ching) also indicated his acceptance of the system of worship advocated in the I Ching. In fact, Confucius not only compiled the I Ching but also the Shu King and the Li Ching, indicating that Confucius respected if not followed the systems of worship contained therein.

The reason why Confucius may not have spoken about "gods and spirits" is that he regarded these "gods and spirits" as meriting less attention than ancestral worship Confucius did not see these "gods and spirits" meriting the kind of worship which should be given only to Shang-Ti.

That is, Confucius advocated the worship of Shang-Ti or Heaven but not the worships of "gods and spirits" or even ancestors.

Lao-Tzu Version Of Shang-Ti

Lao-Tzu, the attributed founder of Taoism and whom Confucius met and later described as an "Azure Lung", also did not advocate the worships of gods and spirits in his book the Tao-Teh-King (Goddard, 1938). This famous philospher, however, made various allusions to Tao and Heaven:

> The original state is eternal. To understand this eternality of emptiness is enlightenment: without this enlightenment one's mind is engrossed in confusing and evil activity. Understanding this truth of eternality makes one merciful; mercy leads one to be impartial; impartiality results in nobility of character; nobility is like Heaven. To be Heavenly means to have attained Taohood. To have attain Taohood is to be unified with eternity. One can never die even with the decay of his body (section 16)

> How Great is Tao! But so is Heaven Great; and so is earth Great; and so is the perfect Sage Great. On the earth there are these four Greatness and among them is the perfect Sage. Men act in conformity with the laws of earth; earth acts in conformity with the laws of Heaven; Heaven acts in conformity with the laws of Tao; Tao acts in accordance with its own self-nature (section 25)

> In governing people and worshipping Heaven, nothing surpasses the Teh of self-restraint ... (section 59)

Lao-Tzu regarded Heaven and Tao as the highest, the former being the manifestation of the later.

As section 59 indicates, Lao-Tzu advocated the worship of Heaven. In saying so he must evidently have in mind the Imperial practice of his days. Hence, like Confucius, his reflection on Heaven and his silence on the other gods and spirits, Lao-Tzu confirmed that in his days such philosophers as himself and Confucius regarded the Heaven worship as the only legitimate forms of worship.

Historical Evidence Of ChinKang Corruption Of Shang-Ti Worship

The worship of the Four Chinkangs appeared to be introduced by the Chin Emperor Shih Huang-Ti around 246BC This person was noted for unification of China and the building of the Great Wall. He also standardised the style of writing the Chinese characters. But, he is notorious for his massacre of Confucian scholars and the Great Burning of the books, destroying irrevocably several valuable ancient texts.

Kang and Nelson (1979, p.18) note that the Emperor fell under the influence of Taoism and in the ancient border sacrifices to Shang-Ti added four altars to the white, green, yellow and red "Tis" (heavenly rulers).

This worship of the four "Tis" was carried forth into the Han dynasty by the Taoist Sin Hwan-ping in Emperor Wan's times. The chief of censers accused Sin Hwan-ping of treason in this meddling of the ancient rites:

> I venture to say that nothing is more foolish than this new figment of the spirits ShangTi of which he says that there are five. It is indeed certain that from the most ancient times, all who have been wise and deemed masters of the nation on account of their reputation for distinguished wisdom have known but one ShangTi, eminent over all, on whom all things depend, from whom is to be sought whatever is for the advantage of the empire, and to whom it is the duty and custom of the emperors to sacrifice (Kang and Nelson, 1979. p.18)

The error was perpetuated for more than twelve centuries until during the Ming dynasty an investigation was carried out into the ancient imperial sacrificial system in 1369 A.D. Looking through the ancient records they discovered the deviation from the original sacrificial rites of the first three dynasties of Hsia, Shang and Chou. They abolished the additional Ti's and reverted back to the ritual of Chou by which the Emperor worshipped a solitary heavenly ruler Shang-Ti (Kang and Nelson, 1979. p.19)

The Three Dynasties of Hsia, Shang and Chou were thus recognised as worshipping only Shang-Ti, while the four guardian Chinkangs were not worthy of worship.

■ Conclusion: Only Shang-Ti Is To Be Worshipped

The ancient Chinese worshipped only Shang-Ti the Supreme God (or Heaven) until the middle of the Eastern Chou dynasty (771-256BC).

Around 550BC Confucius and Lao-Tzu also advocated the worship of Shang-Ti the Supreme God or Heaven and disapproved of the rising trend in the Eastern Chou era to worship other spirits. The Chin state was one of the earliest to deviate from the original worship of the One True God. When the Chin Emperor Shih Huang-Ti came to rule over all China he tried to contaminate the Shang-Ti worship with the Four Chinkangs. Emperor Shih Huang-Ti also reacted against the Confucian scholars by massacring them and burning their books.

That original ancient worship of Shang-Ti the Supreme God is what the Pakua signifies. The Four Heraldic Animals with the central spinning globe is Shang-Ti the Supreme God surrounded by His Four Guardian Chinkangs, the latter, however, should not be worshipped. The Pakua is the sacred reminder of One True God.

16
CIRCUMPOLAR STAR SYSTEM OF THE PAKUA

And God said, Let there by lights in the firmament of the heavens to divide the day from the night; and let them be for signs, and for seasons, and for days, and for years (Genesis 1:14)

■ Circumpolar Chinese Astrology

The Eight Diagrams-Pakua is intimately linked with Chinese astrology (Skinner, 1982; de Kermadec and Poulson, 1983). The term "astrology" should be better stated as "ancient astronomy" and refers to the study of the heavenly bodies of sun, moon, planets and stars. But because ancient astronomy is often mixed with mystical elements of forcasting of future fates and divination, "astrology" is the proper term. This is unfortunate as this term "astrology" leads to a tendency to regard ancient astrological lores as mythical.

Contrary to many Christians who misleadingly view astrology as demonic, a number of Christian writers (Fleming, 1981; Seiss, 1972; Bullinger, 1964; Adam, 1937) note that the Bible actually uses many astrological terms favourably. Jewish traditions noted Abraham wore an astrological symbol:

> The Midrash stated Terah, Abraham's father, was an astrologer and that both Midrash and Talmud described that Abraham wore a large astrological tablet on his breast. Each morning the kings of the East and West would gather before him to seek his advice. (Joel, 1977. p.150-158)

The astrological lores among ancient nations are remarkably similar. They have common features as the 365 days – 12 months year, the 7 days-week, the four seasons, the lunar cycle of 28 days, etc. From ancient times, they also agreed on the moon as differentiated from the seven planetary bodies and at that time they excluded the planets Uranus and Pluto which were not visible to naked eyes. These common features are also found in Chinese astrology (de Kermadec and Poulsen, 1983).

But there are two major types of ancient astronomy, the more ancient circumpolar one and the other elliptical system (Needham, 1959). The Chinese system of astronomy which is the more ancient circumpolar one reflected in Pakua is very ancient. Shu King calculations indicate it must be as old as BC 3000 (Needham, 1959. p.177). The antiquity of the system was confirmed by discoveries of the oracle-bones at Anyang which date from the Shang period of c. 1500 (Needham, 1959. p.242).

The Chinese astrological lore has remarkable similarities to the Jewish astrological lore. The Chinese month which is lunar has 30 days, which was also the duration of the ancient Jewish month until 300 years after Christ (Martin, 1977a). The Chinese and Jewish calendars also use intercalary months (compare de Kermadec and Poulson, 1983; with Martin, 1977a and Joel, 1977). Through a combination of the 12 animals years (Jupiter cycle) and the five elements, the Chinese calendar has a 60-years cycle. The Jewish astrological lore recognises that the conjunction of Saturn and Jupiter is an important feature (Joel, 1977. pp.33,36). This Saturn-Jupiter conjunction occurs every 20 years. Every 60 years, the conjunction changes its Earth-Air-Water-Fire triplicity and is known as the Great Conjunction (the conjunction occurring within the 60 years cycle is known as the Normal Conjunction, while the Magnificent Conjunction occurs every 2,160 years, which is also the Prophetic Age).

Seiss (1972. p.141) writes: Astronomers agree this Lunar Zodiac as containing the most ancient remains of the science of the stars. The Romans, Greeks and Egyptians knew little or nothing about it, but it is a matter of record in China that it was known and understood in that country as early as the reign of Yao, about twenty-three hundred years before the Christian era which was before the time of Abraham. In the Chinese astronomy it begins with Virgo which would seem to indicate that the Chinese table came from the antediluvian times.

■ Emphasis On Some Stars

The Chinese and the Hebrew have emphasis on similar major stars. The Bible states the heavenly bodies are to SIGNS:

> And God said, Let there by lights in the firmament of the heavens to divide the day from the night; and let them be for signs, and for seasons, and for days, and for years. (Genesis 1:14)

Note well that in addition to their use to demarcate times of seasons, days and years, the heavenly bodies would also be SIGNS. The Bible states that all the stars were named by God:

> He telleth the number of the stars; he calleth them all by names (Psalm 147:4)

> Lift up your eyes on high and behold who hath created these things that bringeth out their host by number: he calleth them all by names by the greatness of his might, for that he is strong in power; not one faileth (Isaiah 40:26)

> And he brought him[Abraham] forth abroad and said, Look now toward heaven and tell the stars if thou shalt be

228 THE CHINESE PAKUA

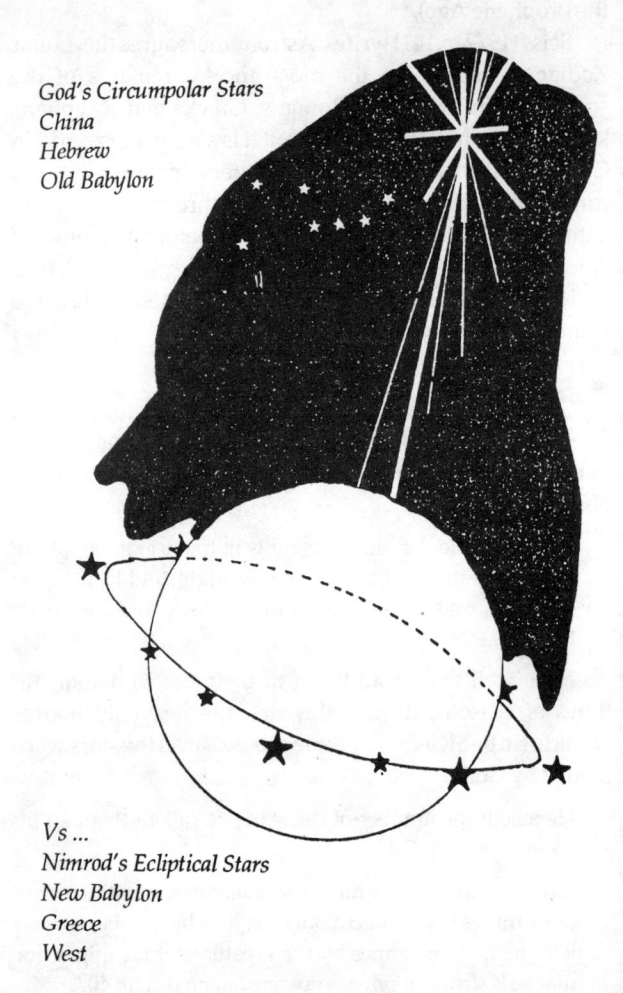

God's Circumpolar Stars
China
Hebrew
Old Babylon

Vs ...
Nimrod's Ecliptical Stars
New Babylon
Greece
West

Figure 16.1 Thie Chinese Circumpolar Stars System

able to number them and he said unto him, So shall thy seed be (Genesis 15:5)

Bullinger (1964) writes: "Most of these names have been lost; but over 100 are preserved through the Arabic and Hebrew and are used by astronomers today though their meaning is unknown to them ... These names and the twelve "signs" go back to the foundation of the world. Jewish tradition, preserved by Josephus, assures us, that this Bible astronomy was invented by Adam, Seth and Enoch ... We have to remember that our written Scriptures began with Moses, say in 1490BC, and thus, for more than 2,500 years, the revelation of the hope which God gave in Genesis 3 was preserved in the naming of the stars and their groupings in Signs and Constellations. These groupings are quite arbitrary. There is nothing in the positions of the stars to suggest the pictures originally drawn around them. The Signs and Constellations were first designed and named; then the pictures were drawn around them respectively" (Appendix 12, The Companion Bible).

The books of Amos and Job have interesting references to astrological signs including the twelve signs of the Zodiac:

Seek him that maketh the seven stars and Orion ... (Amos 5:8)

Canst thou bind the sweet influences of Pleiades [Cimah, the seven stars] or Orion [Cesil]? Canst thou bring forth Mazzaroth [the twelve signs] in his seasons? or canst thou guide Arcturus [Bear and her train] with his sons? (Job 38:31-32)

Which maketh Arcturus, Orion and Pleiades and the chambers of the south? (Job 9:9 – or Ash, Cesil and Cimah – according to Joel, 1977. Job 9:9 refers to the chambers of the South [Hebrew XDRY TYMNf] which covers the constellations of Capricorn, Aquarius and Pisces)

230 THE CHINESE PAKUA

Psalm 19 indicates that the ancient Hebrews were guided by two books of revelation. The second book of revelation is

> The law of the Lord ... (Psalm 19:7 onwards)

The first book is connected with

> The heavens declare the glory of God; and the firmament shewed forth his handywork. Day unto day uttereth speech and night unto night sheweth knowledge ... (Psalm 19:1-6)

It is speculated that Psalm 19:1-6 refers to a book on astrological knowledge! And that these astrological knowledge actually prophesised of the coming Christ (Bullinger, 1964. Appendix 12, Companion Bible)

That there was an eventual abuse of the astrological lores in the history of Israel the Bible also indicates:

> And he put down the idolatrous priests whom the kings of Judah had ordained to burn incense in the high places in the cities of Judah and in the place of Jerusalem them also that burn incense unto Baal, to the sun and to the moon and to the planets [constellations of the zodiac] and to all the host of heaven (2 Kings 23:5)

You will note that of the stars of heaven, the ones particularly and most prominently named are Arcturus, the Pleiades and Orion, besides the twelve signs. Of Arcturus, Seiss (1972) comments:

1. "Arcturus" (Ash), which nearly all the best commentators, Jewish and Christian, take as denoting the north polar constellation now known under the name of Ursa Major, the Great Bear. (Job 9:9, 38:32)

The Chinese also appear to give emphasis to more or less the same groups of stars! Besides the stars of the Great Bear (to which the Pakua is associated), the Chinese also refer to Orion and Pleiades:

> The Divine Tortoise Shen-kwai is said to be the embodiment of the star "Yao Kwong" in Ursa Major. ... T'ienhwang-ta-ti, who rule the poles and regulates heaven earth and man, is said to resides in the pole star. Hsing-chu, the "Lord of the stars" resides in a star near the pole known by his name; while the spirit of the South pole has a similar celestial residence ... (Dennys, 1968. p.119)

> "The three stars appear in the sky" (A Chinese proverb meaning "A propitious time for weddings" These three stars referred to Orion's belt ... These stars appear at a time when the harvests have been gathered, and the people are at leisure. It is at these times that weddings take place – Plopper, 1935. p.40)

> In conclusion I may remark that the deity to which the above given incantation is supposed to that popular deity which is commonly called the 'seven sisters.' To some it is considered identical with the spirit of the Wega in Lyra, to others it is identified with the spirit of the Pleiades; and this latter explanation I consider to be most plausible because the Pleiades are in Chinese colloquial called 'the star of the seven ladies.'" (Denny, 1968. p.61)

Astrological lores of all ancient civilisations have the twelve signs of the Zodiac. The Chinese astrological lore is unique in the prominent places they give to the stars in the constellation of Ursa Major as the home of the Supreme God as well as the home of the several star lords, including their North Pole Star pantheon of gods, in the Dipper of Ursa Major.

Hence, the constellation of Ursa Major is of great importance in both Chinese and Hebrew astrological lores.

■ God's Throne In Northern Heavens

The Chinese emphasis of the Dipper as the place of the throne of Shang-Ti the Supreme God also matches with

Jewish traditions that God's throne is in the northern heavens:

> STARS: ... Seven of those stellar 'mansions' were allocated to each of the four quadrants of the vault of heaven. The quadrants were associated with four animals ... The Azure Dragon presides over the eastern quarter, the Vermillion Bird, i.e. the Chinese phoenix over the southern, the White Tiger over the western and the Black Warrior, i.e. the tortoise over the northern ... The morning sun is in the east, which hence corresponds to Spring; at noon it is south which suggests Summer. By similar parallelism the west corresponds to Autumn and the north to Winter ... The Great Bear occupies a prominent position in the Taoist heavens as the aerial throne of their supreme deity, Shang Ti, around whom all the other star-gods circulate in homage. The Northern Dipper, a group of stars in Ursa Major ... together with the Southern Dipper in the southern heavens. They are also styled Shou Hsing and Lu Hsing respectively, and represent the Gods of Longevity and Wealth ... The "Mother of the Measure" or the Queen of Heaven the Buddhist Goddess Maritchi ... who dwells among the stars that form the Dipper in the Constellation of the Great Bear is also worshipped ... (William, 1931. pp.336-340)

Although Confucius (Lau, 1979) had not advocated worship of gods and spirits, he indicated approval for the Shang-Ti worship and associated features like the Grand Temple of Heaven, the sacred mountain of Mount T'ai and the North Pole Star (see previous chapter on Shang-Ti). This indicates that not only Confucius accepted worship of Shang-Ti as correct but also that he associated the North Pole Star with Shang-Ti.

There are a number of scriptural references to the location of God's habitat and throne in the northern heavens:

God ... saith to the snow, Be thou on the earth ... Out of the south cometh the whirlwind: and cold out of the north. By the breath of God frost is given ... (Job 37:5-10)

Fair weather cometh out of the north: with God is terrible majesty ... (Job 37:22)

... the city of our God in the mountain of his holiness ... mount Zion on the sides of the north ... (Psalms 48:1-2)

For promotion cometh neither from the east, nor from the west, nor from the south. But God is the judge. (Psalms 75:6-7 – i.e. God is in the north)

For thou hast said in thine heart I will ascend into heaven, I will exalt my throne above the stars of God: I will sit also upon the mount of the congregation, in the sides of the north. (Isaiah 14:13)

... a whirlwind came out of the north ... out of the midst therefore came the likeness of four living creatures ... every one had four faces ... And above the firmament that was over their heads was the likeness of a throne ... and upon the likeness of the throne was the likeness as the appearance of a man above upon it ... (Ezekial 1:4-6,26)

■ Circumpolar Nature Of Chinese And Jewish Astrology And Their Old Babylonian Origin

Needham (1959, pp.172-173) notes that "the Chinese astronomy is essentially polar and equatorial, depending largely on circumpolar stars, while Greek and medieval European astronomy had been essentially elliptic, depending largely on helical risings and settings of zodiacal constellations and their paranatellons." (Figure 16.1) Needham (1959, pp.232-231) also notes that "Many European scholars have found it almost impossible to believe that a fully equatorial system of astronomy could have grown up without passing through an elliptical (zodiacal) phase, yet that undoubtedly happened ... It happened in Babylonia first ... So fixed in the Western mind was the zodiacal framework that when the Babylonian planispheres of c. 1200 were first discussed ... it was assumed that the ecliptic was represented on them ... the minor part played by the elliptic in the Chinese system was very shocking."

He discusses several aspects of the Chinese astronomy which have parallels in the Old Babylonian and also Jewish astronomy:

- According to the Kai Thien theory originated by Fu-Hsi postulated a double-vaulted heaven theory of the world. This theory was also found in Old Babylonia and ancient Israel (Needham, 1959. pp.212-213)
- Another circumstance worth noting is that the Altar of Heaven and the temple of Heaven at Peking both retains to this day three circular terraces as is to symbolise the Three Roads of Ea-Anu-Enlil of Babylonia (Needham, 1959. p.257)
- The colour symbolism, for example, in Ezekial, Zekariah and Revelation ... can be clearly related to the colours associated with the sky palaces and cardinal points in Chinese and Babylonian correlative thinking (Needham, 1959. p.257)
- Opposition of Pleides and Antares can (also) be clearly seen on the planispheres constructed by Jeremias for Babylonia c. 3200 (Needham, 1959. p.248).
- Also, inversion between Vega and Altair about c. 3600 which the Babylonian may have noted (Needham, 1959. p.251).

The possibility remains open that the text is indeed the remnant of a very ancient observational tradition not Chinese at all but Babylonian (Needham, 1959. p.246). There are some minor assimilations from Indian-Greek astronomy and it is recognised that this "system therefore goes back to the period when the new Babylonian zodiacal astronomy was being transmitted to the Greeks but when the old Babylonian equatorial astronomy still retained importance" (4th to 2nd centuries) (Needham, 1959. p.267).

One might fairly surmise therefore that the equatorial moon-stations of East Asia originated from Old Babylonian astronomy before the middle of the 1st millennium and probably a long time before (Needham, 1959. p.256). Such too was the mature conclusion of Bezold who pointed out that it does not exclude that transmission of a body of Babylonian astrological lore to China before the 6th century (Needham, 1959. p.273).

The evidence indicate that the Old Babylonian astronomy, especially the computation of solar, lunar and planetary ephemerides, passed on to China for further development (Needham, 1959. p.205).

■ The Link Between The Sphinx And The Pakua

The famous Egyptian Sphinx has astrological meanings:

> "In this zodiac there is placed between the signs of Virgo and Leo a picture of the Sphinx. The Sphinx (with the head of a woman and the tail of a lion) confirms the starting and the finishing points for the zodiac. Many scholars think that this was in fact the main purpose of the Sphinx and thus solves its "riddle". (Flemings, 1981. p.30)

Flemings is not right about the tail which is actually that of an ox not lion and the Sphinx is therefore between Aquarius and Taurus. A better interpretation of this Sphinx symbolism is found in the Bible and the Chinese astrology:

> However the four signs Taurus, Aquarius, Scorpio and Leo, because they are fixed, do not carry any of the trigrams ... Biblical symbolism makes an interesting reference to

these in a vision seen by the prophet Ezekial (Ezekial 1:10), which first alludes to 'many wheels', which are probably the circle of the Zodiac and the several circular arrangements of the I Ching; then the vision continues with a description of four beasts as follows: 'As for the likeness of their faces, they four had the face of a man, and the face of a lion, and on the right side; and they four had the face of an ox on the left side; they four also had the face of an eagle.' The 'man' is Aquarius the Water-carrier, whose opposite sign Leo is a 'lion'; whilst 'an ox' is the bull, Taurus. Lastly, mention is made of 'an eagle', which, as astrologer know, is another name for Scorpio ... The symbols of these four Zodiac signs are also contained in the Egyptian Sphinx, which has the head of a man, the body of a lion, the wings of an eagle and the tail of an ox ... (Hook, 1975. pp.99-100)

The four signs Taurus, Aquarius, Scorpio and Leo as fixed constellations in the Pakua system of Chinese astrology are paralleled in Hebrew astrology:

The four constellations which are solidly in the middle of each season are known as the Fixed Constellations ... They are today Taurus the middle of spring; Leo, the middle of summer; Scorpio, the middle of autumn, and Aquarius, the middle of winter (Joel, 1977. p.31).

■ The Abraham Factor

There are a number of Jewish traditions which help explain why Middle East astrological knowledge have several common aspects (Seiss, 1972):

Albumazer attributes the invention of both Zodiacs to Hermes; and Hermes, according to Arab and Egyptian authorities was the patriarch Enoch. Josephus and the Jewish rabbis affirm that the "starry lore" had it origins with the antediluvian patriarchs Seth and Enoch ... p.22

CHAPTER 16 CIRCUMPOLAR STAR SYSTEM

Baleus says: "From Adam all good arts and human wisdom flowed, as from their fountain. He was the first that discovered the motions of the celestial bodies and all other creatures. From his school proceeded whatever good arts and wisdom afterward propagated by our fathers unto mankind; so that whatever astronomy, geometry and other arts contain in them he knew the whole thereof." Keckerman doubts not that "our first parents delivered over to their posterity together with other sciences, even logic also; specially seeing they are the nearest the origin of all things has an intellect so much the more excellent than ours by how much they excelled us in length of life, formitude of health and in air and food ... p.150

From Adam sprang Seth, who, according to Josephus and more ancient records, followed his father in the pursuit of wisdom, as did his own descendents. It is said in so many words that "they were the inventors of that perculiar sort of wisdom which is concerned with the heavenly bodies and their conditions and indications." Hornius says: "The first mention of letters falls upon Seth's times; who, being mindful of his father's prophecy foretelling the universal dissolution of things, the one by the Deluge and the other by fire, being not unwilling to extinguish his famous inventions concerning the stars, he thought of some monument to which he might concredit these mysteries ... p.150.

Enoch is also specifically credited with special wisdom and writing, particularly as related to astronomy and prophecy. Bochart writes: "I cannot but add what is found concerning the same Enoch in Eusebius, out of Eupolemus of the Jews. he says that Abraham when he taught astrology [astronomy] and other sciences at Heliopolis, affirmed that the Babylonians attributed the invention of the same to Enoch; and the Grecians attribute the invention to Atlas, the same with Enoch." Macinus, Abulfaragius and other Arab writers say that Enoch was called Edris the sage, the illustrious and that he was skilled in astronomy and other sciences. Baleus tells us that he was famous for his prophecy and is reported as having written books on divine matters. The Jews call him the Great Scribe and say that he wrote books on sacred wisdom, especially on astronomy. That he did record certain prophecies is attested by the Epistle of Jude which gives a quotation from him. Origen also tells us that it was asserted in the book of Enoch that in the time of that patriarch the constellations were already named and divided. Arab and Egyptian authors make him the same as the older Hermes – Hermes Trismegistus, the triply great Shepherd – through whom the wisdom of the stars and other sciences were handed down to his posterity ... pp.150-151.

Cassini refers to Philo for the assertation that "Terah, the father of Abraham, who lived more than a hundred years with Noah, had studied astronomy and taught it to Abraham," who according to Josephus and others taught it to the Egyptians during his sojourn in that country ... p.149.

The Jews hold it among their traditions that Adam wrote a book concerning the creation of the world and another on the Deity. Kissaeus, an Arabian writer, gives it as among the teachings of his people that Abraham had in his possession certain sacred writings of Adam, Seth and Enoch, in which were "laws and promises, threathenings from God and predictions of many events;" and it is affirmed of Abraham that he taught astronomy to the Egyptian priests at Heliopolis ... p.150

Joel (1977) notes that the Midrash stated Terah, Abraham's father, was an astrologer (p.158) and that both Midrash and Talmud described that "Abraham wore a large astrological tablet on his breast. Each morning the kings of the East and West would gather before him to seek his advice" (p.150). The traditions traced western astrology, first, to its primeval origins to Adam, Seth and Enoch, and, second, the influence of Terah and Abraham on Egyptian and Hebrew astrology.

A Mesopotamian origin for astrology as a whole is thus a logical conclusion. Needham (1959, p.173) notes theories that Chinese astronomy originated from Babylon and wrote "What do these facts mean? They simply illuminate one of the ways by which Babylonian mathematics and astronomy, especially the computation of solar, lunar and planetary ephemerides, passed to China for further development" (p.205).

Under Whose Influence?

The Chinese and Jewish astrological lores have many remarkable similarities and must certainly come from some common sources. As their circumpolar astrology was also that of Old Babylonia, the theory is that their astrology came from Old Babylonia – a further evidence of the migration of the Chinese from the Middle East.

Jewish astrologers indicate that astrology could influence a person life but that the astrological influence could be altered through changing a person's name and-or doing special good deeds to offset the astrological danger (Joel, 1977. pp.158-162,195). However, Joel (1977) notes that many Jewish Rabbis argued that the special favour of God on Israel was enough to set Israel free from astrological influence.

The point should be taken – when a person (e.g. as a follower of God) receives special favour from God that person's life is no longer influenced by things like the stars for God directly guide that person.

But the main finding remains. There are much common links between the Chinese and Middle East-Biblical culture items; too many to be due to chance. The closeness of the circumpolar star systems between the ancient Hebrews and Chinese emphasises further their ancient kinship.

17

PAKUA-SIGIL FORMATIONS IN NINE EMPEROR GODS

■Introduction

The spinning spiral emblem of the Pakua is the earliest Chinese worship of only Shang-Ti, the Supreme God. The Pakua has those four major angels, the Chinkangs or Heavenly Kings, which, however, were often recognised for what they were – angels or spirits and not canonised human beings.

That central fiery globe of the Pakua is Shang-Ti's throne in the northern heavens, among the North Pole stars.

Early during the Chinese religious culture, there were the legends which surrounded the canonisation of various human beings into gods. There is the female Eve being worshipped as Tou Mu (Mother Goddess) or Hsi Wang Mu (Western Queen Mother Goddess), both of whom had nine sons and came from the west and both being deities before or around 2953-2838BC (Werner, 1922). This Goddess is really the canonised Eve, the mother of mankind. In the attempts to associate her with Shang-Ti, Tou Mu's home was also placed onto the Great Bear North Pole stars, the original throne location of Shang-Ti the Supreme God.

Hence, came another group of gods to be associated with the North Pole stars. These are the nine sons of Tou Mu and their worship gives rise to the spectacular often highly magical and mystical worship of the Nine Emperor Gods (Lai, 1984; Cheu 1988). Besides the famous Nine Emperor Gods worship, other aspects of these nine gods also form other popular common elements of worship among the Chinese. It may even be said that although it may not be realised the most popular form of Chinese worship today is really a modification of the Nine Emperor Gods.

Despite the apparently highly idolatrous nature of the Nine Emperor Gods, these nine personalities are actually famous highly revered Biblical figures! Just as the Mother Goddess was actually Eve, so, who were the Nine Emperor Gods?

Eve's nine sons? The answers are actually quite close!

We should remember how Fu-Hsi, Shen-Nung, Huang-Ti, Shao-hao and Chuen-Hio became the Five Emperor Gods of the Pakua. This principle is also how the nine sons of Tou Mu became the Nine Emperor Gods who are also associated with the nine points of the Pakua.

■ The Nine Emperor Gods

Although the North Pole stars are associated with the throne of Shang-Ti, the Supreme God, and His four major angels the Chinkangs, these North Pole stars also came to represent the homes of the Mother Goddess Tou Mu and her sons the Nine Emperor Gods:

> **STARS**: ... Seven of those stellar 'mansions' were allocated to each of the four quadrants of the vault of heaven. The quadrants are associated with four animals ... The Azure Dragon presides over the eastern quarter, the Vermillion Bird, i.e. the Chinese phoenix over the southern, the White Tiger over the western and the Black Warrior, i.e. the tortoise over the northern ... The morning sun is in the east, which hence corresponds to Spring; at noon it is south which suggests Summer. By similar parallelism the west corresponds to Autumn and the north to Winter ... The Great Bear occupies a prominent position in the Taoist heavens as the aerial throne of their supreme deity, Shang

Ti, around whom all the other star-gods circulate in homage. The Northern Dipper, a group of stars in Ursa Major ... together with the Southern Dipper in the southern heavens. They are also styled Shou Hsing and Lu Hsing respectively, and represent the Gods of Longevity and Wealth ... The "Mother of the Measure" or the Queen of Heaven the Buddhist Goddess Maritchi ... who dwells among the stars that form the Dipper in the Constellation of the Great Bear is also worshipped ... (William, 1931. pp.336-340)

The Nine Emperor Gods are the seven stars of the Big Dipper (Ursa Major). Four of the stars form the dipper's bowl (kui) and three its handle (shou). The two additional gods are residing each on one of the two invisible stars nearby ... (Cheu, 1988. p.v-vii)

There is various degrees of syncretic interchangeability between the worships of Tou Mu the Mother Goddess and her sons the Nine Emperor Gods:

The Nine Emperor Gods however are the sons of Doumu. The fact that the Nine Emperor Gods are manifestations of Doumu and that Doumu is a manifestation of the Nine Emperor Gods is clearly represented by the single altar dedicated to them in practically every temple. In this representation the Nine Emperor Gods are in fact manifestations of Jiuhuang Dadi and Jiuhuang Dadi is a collective representation of the Nine Emperor Gods. Thus, a Jiuhuang may manifest himself as Nandou (Southern Bushel*) controlling life or Beidou (Northern Bushel) controlling death ... In some temple, Doumu is addressed as Wudou Tianzun (Heaven-honoured of the Five Bushels) (Cheu, 1988 pp.18-19)

In the earliest myths the Nine Emperor Gods are believed to be the Nine Human Sovereigns; Tian Ying, Tian Ren, Tian Zhu, Tian Xin, Tian Qin, Tian Fu, Tian Chong,

Tian Rui and Tian Peng, the nine sons of Doumu (Bushel Mother). They could be variously grouped:

Zhongdou (Central Bushel), Central Bushel represented by the great chief (Doulao) controlling the general wellbeing of the universe. surrounded by

Dongdou (Eastern Bushel), Eastern Bushel represented by six male spirits controlling the sun;

Nandou (Southern Bushel) Southern Bushel represented by six stars controlling life; [*harmonises with Southern Bushel as Shou-Hsing, God of Longevity]

Xidou (Western Bushel) Western Bushel represented by six female spirits controlling the moon; and

Beidou (Northern Bushel) Northern Bushel represented by the nine star lords controlling death;

■ Planetary Equivalent Of Nine Emperors Gods

Cheu (1988, pp.26-27) also associates these nine stellar deities as a representation of the nine planets of the solar system and he showed that they have their correlates in Hinduism. In the cult of Nava Kiraganggal they are called the nine star lords or bagawan:

1. Surya (Sun, Ri),
2. Santhira (moon, Yue),
3. Savai (Mars, Houxing)
4. Buthan (Mercury, Shuixing),
5. Guru (Jupiter, Muxing),
6. Sukra (Venus, Jinxing)
7. Sani (Saturn, Tuxing),
8. Raghu/Iraghu (human head, naga body) and
9. Keth (naga head and human body)

Table 17.1
ASSOCIATION OF NINE EMPEROR GODS STARS WITH THE PLANETS

Name of Star	Meaning	Element	Planet
The seven stars of the Dipper			
1. T'an Lang	Greedy and Savage	Wood	Jupiter
2. Chu-men**	Great Gate or Door	Wood	Jupiter
3. Lu-ts'un (God of Wealth)*	Rank, Salary Preserved	Earth	Saturn
4. Wen-ch'u	Civil or Literary Windings (activities)	Water	Mercury
5. Lien-chien	Honesty, Purity and Uprighteousness	Fire	Mars
6. Wu-ch'u	Military Windings (activities)	Metal	Venus
7. P'o-chun	Breaker of the Phalanx Broken Army (breaker of luck)	Metal	Venus
Remaining stars of the Nine			
8. Tao-fu	Left assistant of the Celestial Emperor	Earth	Saturn
9. Yu-pi	Right assistant of the Celestial Emperor	Water	Mercury

The Chinese characters for "Lu" is the same as that for the "Lu" in the God of Wealth (Lu-Hsing)
**In "The Nine Emperor Godsø (Cheu 1988 page 15-17), this second star is believed to presides over life and may be the God of Longevity (Shou-Hsing)*

In the Hindu almanac Surya occupies the central position, Santhira the SE, Savai the S, Buthan the NE. Guru the N, Sukra the E, Sani the W, Raghu the SW and Kethu the NW ... (Cheu, 1988. pp.26-27)

In Chinese Feng-Shui, the Nine Emperor Gods are symbolised in the Nine Moving Stars. Seven of the Nine Moving Stars are identified with the seven stars of the Great Bear or Dipper constellation which annually rotates around the north polar star. They therefor correlate with the seasons of the year. The 'tail' of the constellation at nightfall points to the quarter attributed to the current season, i.e. in spring to the east, or in autumn to the west. These first seven stars are used by the Feng-Shui hsien-sheng to indicate influence on a person (Skinner, 1982. p.40) These Nine Moving Stars are associated with the planets as shown in Table 17.1. (after Skinner, 1982. Table 4, pp.41-42)

■ The Three Stars-Emperor Gods

The worship of the Nine Emperor Gods is faithfully kept regularly only by a few who could keep to its strict high level of purity (Cheu, 1988). Otherwise, the common people worship the Nine Emperor Gods once a year during the ninth month of the Chinese calendar (Cheu 1988; Lai, 1984). Yet despite the restriction of the common worship to the ninth month, the Nine Emperor Gods are more popular than thought!

Why so? Some of the Nine Emperor Gods are more universally worshipped than thought! The clue is found in the nature of some of the nine gods:

> Each day is governed by a constellation, but of them all, those most worshipped are the Northern and Southern Dipper. The Northern Dipper is supposed to control death, and the Southern Dipper is suppposed to control life ... The Spirits of the Northern Dipper record men's actions ...

246 THE CHINESE PAKUA

> Those most worshipped of this constellation are the "Three Stars"[The Three Stars shining together, i.e. May you have happiness, emoluments, and longevity]. Of these the Star of Longevity is the most important [The Hsou Hsing Lao] ... [There are the Spirits of the Three Stars and of the Northern Dipper [The fourth, fifth and sixth Stars of the Northern Dipper are called the Three Tai. The fourth Star governs long life, the fifth Star governs the happy mean, and the sixth Star governs man's income] (Plopper, 1935. pp.40-41)

That is, the very common popular household Fu-Lu-Shou, the Three Gods of Luck (Happiness), Wealth and Longevity, are actually three of the nine Emperor Gods! The associations between the popular Three Star-Gods with the different Nine Emperor Gods should have been noticed before:

> The Northern Dipper, a group of stars in Ursa Major ... together with the Southern Dipper in the southern heavens. They are also styled Shou Hsing and Lu Hsing respectively, and represent the Gods of Longevity and Wealth (William, 1931. pp.336-340)

> Nandou (Southern Bushel) Southern Bushel represented by six stars controlling life; [*harmonises with Southern Bushel as Shou-Hsing, God of Longevity] (Cheu, 1988 pp.18-19)

> In Singapore one devotee explains this by saying that the 'Nine Emperor Gods' are like nine brothers. The first brother takes care of death, the second brother takes care of life, and so on ... the Nine Emperor Gods are believed to be the manifestations of their mother ... (Cheu, 1988. pp.15-17)

Skinner, 1982:

2. Chü-men** Great Gate or Door Wood Jupiter

3*. Lu-ts'un Rank, Salary Preserved Earth Saturn (God of Wealth)*

*The Chinese characters for "Lu" is the same as that for the "Lu" in the God of Wealth (Lu-Hsing)

**In "The Nine Emperor Gods" (Cheu, 1988. pp.15-17), this second star is believed to preside over life and may be the God of Longevity (Shou-Hsing)

So, the Nine Emperor Gods and its various modifications, must be one of the most widely worshipped group of deities in the Chinese households!

■ Pakua-Sigil Formations In The Nine Emperor Gods

Although the Pakua traditionally is thought of as a eight sided symbol, the nine beings of the Nine Emperor Gods are nevertheless represented within the Lo-shu (Figure 17.1, after Cheu, 1988. pp.170-171, Figure 5).

Figure 17.1 demonstrates the conception of the Nine Star Gods in terms of Lo-shu. This is based on the ancient conception of the nine provinces of China in which Yu the Great used the Nine Ritual Steps known as Yubu or Magic Square to control the floods. The symbolic representation of the Nine Star Gods and their attributes are given in the Table below:

Star	Direction	Numeral	Element	Trigram
Tian Ying	S	9	Fire	Qian
Tian Ren	NE	8	Earth	Zhen
Tian Zhu	W	7	Metal	Kan
Tian Xin	NW	6	Metal	Ken
Tian Qin	C	5	Earth	Kun
Tian Fu	SE	4	Wood	Dui
Tian Chong	E	3	Wood	Li
Tian Rui	SW	2	Earth	Xuan
Tian Peng	N	1	Water	Kun

248 THE CHINESE PAKUA

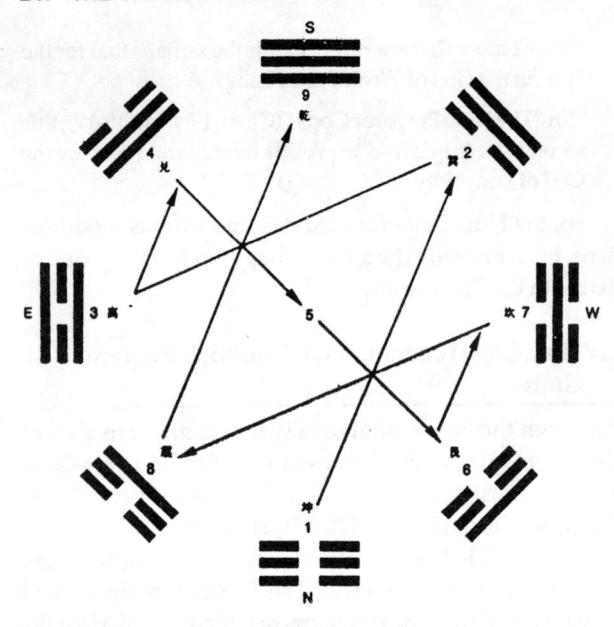

A. The Nine Emperor Gods as represented in the Eight diagrams

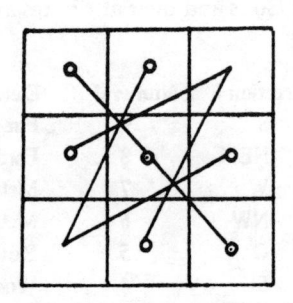

B. Sigil of Saturn (more details in Figure 2.2)

Figure 17.1 Nine Emperor Gods in Eight Diagrams and similarities to Sigil of Saturn

By drawing a single line through the nine points in their order, we get the very same design as the Hebrew Sigil Of Saturn! The representation by the Nine Emperor Gods nine points gives a closer likeness to the Sigil than the traditional eight points of the Pakua. In the original Great Tortoise shell's or Lo-shu magic square there was nine numbers. All these numbers are utilised in the Nine Emperor God's symbolisation of the Pakua while the traditional Pakua utilised eight points with the ninth implied in the centre.

The closeness of the Nine Emperor Gods and Pakua symbolisations to the Hebrew Sigil Of Saturn indicates close affinities of the Chinese ancient religious culture to that of the ancient Hebrew. Hence, the Nine Emperor Gods must have equivalent in Hebrew memory!

■ Origins Of The Nine Emperor Gods

Besides the legends that the Nine Emperor Gods are the nine sons of Tou Mu the Mother Goddess (or Hsi Wang Mu the Western Queen Mother), these nine personalities are also believed to be nine legendary human sovereigns of very ancient times:

> According to legend, the ancient ruler Yu the Great used steps in the pattern of the Great Dipper to stop the floods ... Yu later divided China into nine provinces and nine ding (cauldrons) were cast as symbols of power and prestige to represent each of the nine provinces ... The earliest recorded myths say the Nine Emperor Gods were the Nine Human Sovereigns who reigned a total of 45,600 years ... The mother of the Nine Emperor Gods is Doumu. She was born at Mo-li-che in the Western Realm, Tian Zhu Guo i.e. India ... (Cheu, 1988. pp.v-vii).

In the earliest myths the Nine Emperor Gods are believed to be the Nine Human Sovereigns; Tian Ying, Tian Ren, Tian Zhu, Tian Xin, Tian Qin, Tian Fu, Tian Chong, Tian

250 THE CHINESE PAKUA

Rui and Tian Peng, the nine sons of Doumu (Bushel Mother). Together with Doumu they are said to have ascended to heaven to be in control of the nine north pole stars ... In Taoist texts, the nine divinities are believed to be the Nine Celestial Breaths of the Supreme One, the Lord Emperor Taiyi in control of the Nine Palaces of the Brain on one level and the Nine Original Heavens on another ... Some say the cult refers to a single divinity embodying the spirits of the Nine Divine Brothers, or nine Buddhas, while others insist it refers only to the eldest of the Divine Nine ... In Singapore one devotee explains this by saying that the 'Nine Emperor Gods' are like nine brothers. The first brother takes care of death, the second brother takes care of life, and so on ... the Nine Emperor Gods are believed to be the manifestations of their mother ... (Cheu, 1988. pp.15-17)

Next following Pan Ku the so-called t'ien-huangs "Heavenly Emperors "a succession of thirteen brothers ... Each ... with a reign of eighteen thousand years ... The Heavenly Emperors were followed by the ti-huang, "Terrestial emperors, "eleven brothers. credited with having first distinguished sun, moon and constellations ... The next generation saw the jon-huang, "Human emperors nine brothers who divided the world known to them into nine countries ... These fabulous creatures form the so-called epoch of the Three (or Nine) emperors ... (Hirth, 1908. p.5)

The legends therefore indicate the Nine Emperor Gods were formerly nine human kings related in some way to Tou Mu or Hsi Wang Mu. Before them were non-human rulers who must be angelic. The legends indicate these nine kings lived long before the time of Emperor Yu (ca 2207-2157BC). As Tou Mu and Hsi Wang Mu became deities around the time of 2943-2828BC, the nine kings must have ruled around these very ancient times. The legendary long durations of their combined rules (about 24,000 years) must have indicated their long life – a phenomenon the Bible associate with antediluvian times before the Great Flood.

If the Bible mentions these legendary kings it must be of the period before the Great Flood. Who thus are these Nine Emperor Gods?

The only famous antediluvian figures who could correspond to these Nine Emperor Gods were the nine patriarchs from Adam to Lamech! Yes, there were nine patriarchs! Noah was the tenth patriarch! The Chinese remember! The Chinese remember these famous nine patriarchs as the Nine Emperor Gods. The allusion to Tou Mu as their mother is a recognition of Eve as the mother of mankind.

Nine Emperor Gods are the Nine Biblical Patri-archs from Adam to Lamech!

So, despite their greatness in the memory of the ancient Chinese, the Nine Emperor Gods are only human beings. It is not they who should be worshipped, but that God, Shang-Ti, to whom they were but the Priest-Kings.

■ Tabernacle System Of The Temple Of Nine Emperor Gods

The Nine Emperor Gods Temple is quite different from other Chinese temple designs. Figure 17.2 illustrates the relationships of other deities in the temple of the Nine Emperor Gods (after Cheu, 1988. p.29, Figure 3).

The Nine Emperor Gods and their Mother Goddess in the Inner Altar are regarded as the highest deities, superior to other Chinese deities arranged in the Central Altar. As such Tou Mu and her nine sons are the representation of Shang-Ti whose throne is in the very center of this North Pole echelon of stargods. The Taoists evidently regard them as the highest beings and the Buddhists call them the "Nine Buddhas."

252 THE CHINESE PAKUA

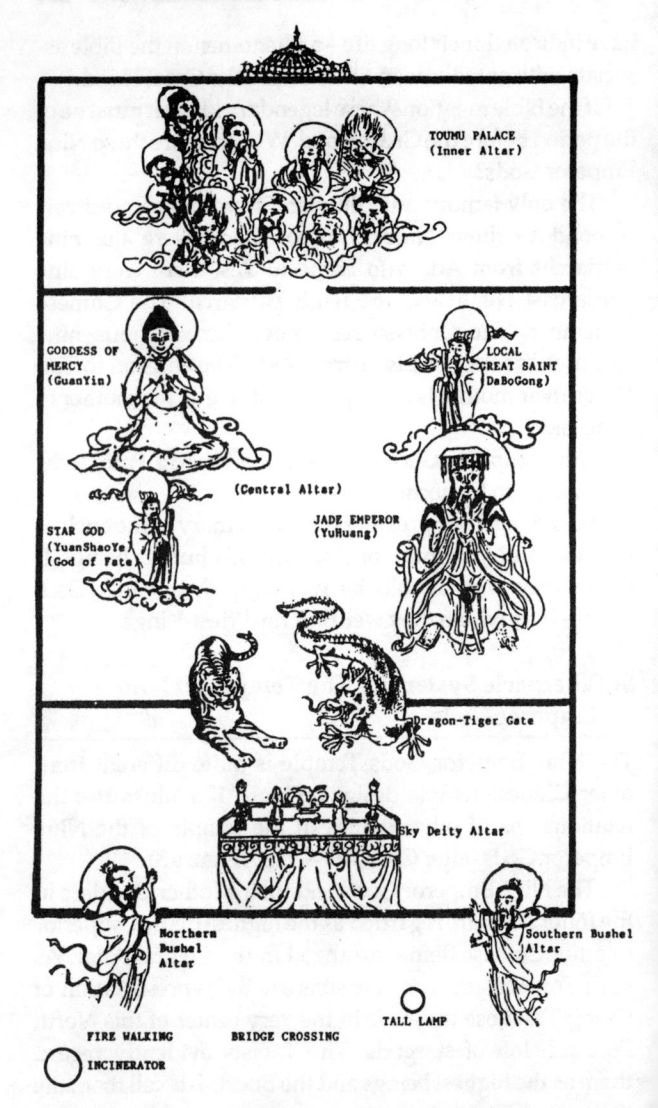

Figure 17.2 Temple Design of Nine Emperor Gods

CHAPTER 17 PAKUA-SIGIL FORMATIONS 253

A most significant aspect of the Nine Emperor Gods worship is that No one is allowed to enter into the inner altar except the censer master! This rule is not found in traditional Buddhist and Taoist temples which have no forbidden area. It should be remember that this ceremony takes place during the ninth month. What is the significance of this?:

This is the same practice as the Jewish worship of God during the Feast of Atonement! This Feast of Atonement also fall within the same period as the Nine Emperor Gods worship of the Chinese ninth month. And in both cases, only one person was allowed to enter into the holiest inner section – the censer master in the Nine Emperor Gods and the high priest in the Mosaic Temple!

The Nine Emperor Gods temple system is very similar to the Hebrew tabernacle of the One True God.

Already we know that the ancient Chinese worship of Shang-Ti is a preservation of the true worship of the One True God. The worship of the Nine Emperor Gods is also a preservation of some ancient worship of the One True God where it was recognised that once a year only one person could enter into Inner Altar – Holiest of Holy to sacrifice to the Supreme God.

The Priest Role Of The King

Remember how Fu-Hsi, Shen-Nung, Huang-Ti, Shao-Hao and Chuan-Hio were canonised as the Five Emperor Gods?:

In The Five Elements according to the Former Heaven Sequence, the five elements of wood, fire, earth, metal, water correspond respectively to east, south, centre, west and north. They are also connected respectively to the five animals azure dragon, red phoenix, yellow dragon, white tiger and black snake-tortoise and the five emperors Fu-

Hsi, Shen-Nung, Huang-ti, Shao-hao and Chuan-hsu. (Skinner, 1982. Table 5, pp.58-59)

These emperors were the ones who could offer the sacrifices to Shang-Ti. The Emperor served as the high priest or priest-king of Shang-Ti. Alike to what the Biblical Melchisedec was!

The Chinese word for king ("Wang") is often found on the Shang oracle bones (Kung and Ching, 1928. p.24). The character is supposed to be a fire in the earth or an axe and appears to indicate that "Wang "has connection with the sacrificial rite. The chief priest was also the ruler and hence the character "Wang "which originally designated the chief priest also designated the king. The term "Wang-jo-yue" appears several times in the Shu King, the Book of History and may really means the "king seized by the spirit(jo) "and indicative of the role of the king in the sacrificial ceremony where the king would be in a trance. The Chinese character "Wang "really denotes "priest-king" – which was what Melchisedec was!

Likewise, the Nine Emperor Gods, in their turns, were the priest-kings to Shang-Ti the Supreme God. They are the Nine Biblical Patriarchs before Noah, as they must have acted as the Melchisedec priest-kings in their times.

The Chinese worshipped the One True God through the Nine Emperor Gods. Parallel to that the Chinese also worshipped the One True God through the Five Emperor Gods. From then the Chinese people continue to worship the One True God through their Chinese emperors.. All were directed to the worship of the One True God whom the Chinese know as Shang-Ti.

The Pakua, through the Four Heraldic Animals aspect, is the ancient memory of the worship of the One True God, Shang-Ti, surrounded by His four major angels. In the Five Emperors form the Pakua is the reminder of the close of the Middle East era when the human races had to migrate to new horizions. So, likewise, the Pakua, in the Nine Emperor Gods form, is the reminder of those nine great sovereigns before the Flood worshipping Shang-Ti the Supreme God.

Basically, one should not anymore worship the Nine Emperor Gods but rather Shang-Ti, the Supreme God, whom they represented. The Nine Emperor Gods should be remembered in memorials for their roles as the former Priest-Kings of God.

Every way the Pakua is turned, its message is the same. The worship of the One True God, Shang-Ti, the Supreme God.

18

CHINESE "LUNG" AT THE EAST

■ Chinese "Lung" Is The Symbol Of China

A fabulous serpentine creature with its bearded horned head and fish-tail and its four limbs with eagle claws threading the clouds and riding the foams of the seas – that is the striking image of the Chinese "Lung." (Figure 18.1) The fabulous Chinese mythological creature the "Lung" is misleadingly called the 'dragon' by westerners.

The "Lung" is the symbol of ancient China. The Chinese Emperor is symbolically the "Azure Lung", seating on the "Lung" throne and wearing the "Lung" robes of gold. In Chinese philosophy, the "Lung" is the symbol of the Great Man. In Chinese Feng-Shui the energy forces affecting human destiny are called "dragon lines." The "Lung" occupies important central meanings in the ancient Chinese religious culture. Thus, in the east the "Lung" is a venerated creature and harbinger of blessings. The Chinese saying goes:

"Good fortune in the Dragon-Phoënix"

In the west the 'dragon' seems to be deemed as an evil creature and the very incarnation of Satan:

> One of the most famous mythological creations in the history of human thought is the horrid serpentine monster called the dragon. Together with the serpent and other things of the same repulsive and dangerous class, this is the universal symbol of evil – of some living power inimical to God and all good and the just, terror of all men. The Serpent stands for that form of the Evil One in which cunning, artifice, deceit and malignant subtlety are the characteristics.

CHAPTER 18 CHINESE "LUNG" AT THE EAST 257

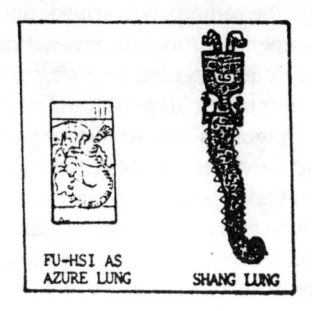

Figure 18.1 The Fabulour Lung The serpentine Lung is known only from the Han Dynasty onward. Previous to the Han Dynasty, Lung is a half-man, half-fish being (as in insert, the Shang Lung and Fu-Hsi, the first Lung).

> The Dragon represents the same power armed, defiant, and putting forth in imperial forms and devastating by force. The Serpent is the sly and creeping deceiver, smoothly gliding in to betray, insinuating his poison and destroying by stealth. The Dragon is the terrific oppressor, assailing with teeth and claws, armed all over with spikes, lifting speary wings and tail, spouting fire and fury, and rushing upon its prey with every vehemence or malignant energy. The Serpent and the Dragon are one and the same, only in different modes of manifestation. Hence the Devil is called "the Dragon, that old Serpent." Whenever the power of evil is clothed in political sovereignty, persecuting, tyrannising, and oppressing, it is always the Dragon, or some rampant figure of destruction answering to it. (Seiss, 1972. p.58)

With the 'Dragon' regarded as such an evil symbol, Christians may wonder why the Chinese consider themselves the children of the "Lung" As the so-called symbol of Satan, the Chinese "Lung" symbol would be considered out of place in the Christian life and home.

But why the remarkable difference between western and eastern regards for the 'dragon'?

The truth may surprise many people! The surprisingly simple truth is that the Chinese "Lung" is not the same as the "Biblical dragon"! The Holy Scriptures reveal there are several angelic creatures and actually show that, unlike the "Biblical dragon", the Chinese "Lung" is among the holy creatures of God! There is also a good reason why the Chinese "Lung" is the symbol animal of China!

■ The Chinese "Lung" Symbol

In the arrangements of these four symbolical animals according to the four directions or cardinal points of the Pakua (Figure 18.2) "Lung" is the East Animal.

CHAPTER 18 **CHINESE "LUNG" AT THE EAST** 259

Chinese Taoist Four Heavenly Kings (or Buddhist Chinkangs) (Williams, 1931): **Guardian of the East.** Land Bearer. White face, ferocious appearance, copper beard, carries a jade ring, a spear, magic sword

These Four Beings are also associated in the worship of the Nine Emperor Gods, the East, West, South, North and Centre are guarded by the Green, White, Red, Black and Yellow Dragons or Generals (Cheu, 1988).

STARS: ... Seven of those stellar 'mansions' were allocated to each of the four quadrants of the vault of heaven. The quadrants are associated with four animals ... The Azure Dragon presides over the eastern quarter, the Vermilion Bird, i.e. the Chinese phoenix over the southern, the White Tiger over the western and the Black Warrior, i.e. the tortoise over the northern ... The morning sun is in the east, which hence corresponds to Spring; at noon it is south which suggests Summer. By similar parallelism the west corresponds to Autumn and the north to Winter ... (William, 1931. pp.336-340)

In The Five Elements according to the Former Heaven Sequence, the five elements of wood, fire, earth, metal, water correspond respectively to east, south, centre, west and north. They are also connected respectively to the five animals azure dragon, red phoenix, yellow dragon, white tiger and black snake-tortoise and the five emperors Fu-Hsi, Shen-Nung, Huang-Ti, Shao-hao and Chuan-hsu. (Skinner, 1982. Table 5, pp.58-59)

The Chinese associate the blue-green "Azure Lung" as the creature of the East symbolising Fu-Hsi. The "Golden Lung" is the animal of the centre and of Emperor Huang-Ti. Through two ways, the eastern "Azure Lung" – and the central "Golden Lung" the Chinese "Lung" has auspicious and good symbolism in the ancient China culture.

260 THE CHINESE PAKUA

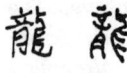

A. LUNG, "DRAGON"

Vapour and clouds personified, giving rise to rains when it flies in heaven and causes drought when it hides in wells. The ancient word is pictorial. The modern word: "Fei" on right, contracted wings; "Li" on right, top, believed to be contraction of "Tung" for heavy and used as phonetic with "Ju" on right, bottom for body.

B. SHE, "SNAKE"

Composes of "Hui" and "To", see below. It particularly refers to the Serpent or Cobra.

HUI refers to crawling creatures such as snakes, worms.

T'O the snake standing on its tails with the tongue darting out.

Figure 18.2   FUNDAMENTAL SUBCHARACTERS OF "LUNG" AND "SHE"

■ What Is Really The Biblical Dragon?

In order to unravel the truth about the Chinese "Lung" we need to look at what the Bible really says about the 'dragon':

> And the great dragon [1404] was cast out, that old serpent [3789], called the Devil and Satan which deceiveth the whole world: he was cast out into the earth and his angels were cast out with him (Revelation 12:10)

> And he laid hold on the dragon [1404] that old serpent [3789] which is the Devil and Satan and bound him a thousand years (Revelation 20:2)

> But I fear lest by any means as the serpent [3789] beguiled Eve through his subtility ... (2 Corinthians 11:3)

> Now the serpent [5175] was more subtil than any beast of the field which the Lord God had made (Genesis 3:1)

The Lord Jesus Christ called Satan's followers:

> Ye serpents [3789], ye generation of vipers, how can ye escape the damnation of hell? (Matthew 23:33 – also 3:7, 12:34 and Luke 3:7)

There is no doubt that the Holy Scriptures associate the "Serpent" with aspects of evil. Even as the Chinese do associate snakes as symbols of evil! How about the "Biblical dragon"? It appears also associated with the "serpent" and the Devil in Revelations 12:10 and 20:2 as quoted above. But the truth will surprise!

The Bible mentions the "Biblical dragon" in other places:

> In that day the Lord with his sore and great and strong sword shall punish leviathan the piercing serpent [5175] even leviathan the crooked serpent [5175]; and he shall slay the dragon [8577] that is in the sea (Isaiah 27:1)

And I will make Jerusalem heaps and a den of dragons [8577] and I will make the cities of Judah desolate without an inhabitant (Jeremiah 9:11)

Behold the noise of the bruit is come and a great commotion out of the north country to make the cities of Judah desolate and a den of dragons [8577] (Jeremiah 10:22)

The passages of Jeremiah indicate that the "Biblical dragon" is not a mythological creature but an animal commonly seen in the Middle East! The Biblical 'dragon' here was actually a natural living animal commonly seen by people in the Middle East! Really what is the "Biblical dragon"?

Note the numbers attached to the words "serpent or dragon" – these numbers indicate the original Hebrew and Greek words as follows:

Serpent:

5175 nachash a snake from its hiss, a serpent. From root word nachash [5172] which also mean divine or enchantment

3789 ophis a snake, malicious sly person, Satan – serpent

Biblical Dragon:

8577 tanniym a marine or land monster, i.e. sea-serpent or jackal – dragon, sea-monster, serpent, whale

1404 drakon a fabulous kind of serpent – dragon

(Thayer 1977 also defines "drakon" as a "great serpent, a fabulous animal")

These scriptural usages of dragon indicate that the "Biblical dragon" is an animal very much like the "serpent"! Although in Jeremiah the "dragons" inhabiting the ruins of the cities could be "jackals" it is likely snakes are meant.

The primary symbolisation of the "Biblical Dragon" is the limbless snake! After all, did not the Book of Revelation defines the "dragon" as the "serpent"?:

> And he laid hold on the dragon [1404] that old serpent [3789] which is the Devil and Satan and bound him a thousand years (Revelation 20:2)

"Drakon", being actually a snake, is rightly the term for the "Old Serpent." So John was right to called the Devil "the dragon that old serpent." But "Drakon" as we will now see is not the right term for the Chinese "Lung."

■ The Character For Chinese "Lung"

The Chinese have always regard these two classes of animals, "Snakes" and "Lung", as different. Look at forms of the Chinese character for "Lung" (Figure 18.2). Weiger (1965, p.309, Lesson 140) wrote:

> Lung. The dragon When it ascend to heaven and flies, it rains; when it hides in the wells, there is a drought. Vapours and clouds personified. The ancient form is a representation sufficiently recognisable. The modern form is explained thus: on the right, "Fei" (to fly) contracted, the wings; on the left, at the bottom "Ju" or "Jou" (pieces of dry meat) the body; on the top, "li" is thought to be "Tung" contracted used as a phonetic...

Vaccari and Vaccari (1950, p.58) wrote:

> ... dragon – The last symbol on the right is a fanciful sketch of the fabulous animal. As to the middle symbol which is near in shape to the modern one, its right component is supposed to be a contraction of "Fei" to fly (in this case symbolising the dragon's wings), the lower part ("Jou") of the left component represents the body and its upper part ("Li") is thought to be a contraction of "Tung" heavy ...

264 THE CHINESE PAKUA

Both Weiger (1965) and Vaccari and Vaccari (1950) recognise the winged nature of the Chinese "Lung." Figure 18.2 besides showing the 'wings' also shows that the pictorial form of Chinese "Lung" has:

1. four protrusions on the top of the head – likely representing the horns
2. four limbs

Figure 18.2 shows the Chinese character forms for "She" the "serpent" (Weiger, 1965. p.259, lesson 108 and p.261, lesson 110A). "She" for "serpent" is formed from "Hui" for crawling" and "To" for "snake." The pictorial representation for "To" shows the typical hissing tongue of the snake while "Hui" shows its crawling form. There are no limbs, wings and horns to the "She" "serpent." The Chinese "She" "serpent" is definitely not the Chinese "Lung"!

The Chinese characters show that the Chinese "Lung" is limbed, winged and horned – unlike the limbless "she"-serpent!

Although Chinese illustrations often do not show wings on the "Lung", the Chinese "Lung" is by implication a winged creature: "There are several varieties; some are horned and others hornless, some are scaleless, and one kind has no wings ... Celestial Dragon ... Spiritual Dragon ... Winged Dragon ... Horned Dragon ... Coiling Dragon ... Yellow Dragon... " (Williams, 1931. pp.110-111). The Chinese Winged "Dragon" is the highest of the order of "Dragons."

Therefore, the Chinese "Lung" is a creature with wings and limbs unlike the Chinese "She" which is the limbless serpent. So, why should the Chinese limbed "Lung" be considered the same as the limbless "dragon"? The "Biblical dragon" is only a natural wild serpent in the Middle East and could not be the same creature as the mythological "Lung" of China!

But if the Chinese "Lung" is not the same as the "Biblical dragon" then what is the Chinese "Lung"? The Bible does describe the Chinese "Lung" not as "dragon" but call it by a different term!

■ Original Western Version Of "Dragon"

It may come as a surprise to some to discover that the original western dragon is not an evil creature:

> As the beneficent life-giving element of water, the dragon is the national symbol of imperial China and the emblem of the Japanese Emperor. The Romans adopt it as their standard (along with the eagle) and it also appeared as the emblem of English-Welsh kings like Henry VII, Henry VIII, James I. The dragon was also the emblem of the West Saxons. The dragon is further represented as a guardian of treasure. The golden apples of Hesperides Garden were guarded by Ladon, the hundred-headed dragon. It appears that it was only in the Bible that the dragon was associated with the evil serpent (Whittick, 1960. S.177-178)

Of course! In the Greek legends about heroes fighting "dragon" these "dragons" were supposed to guard the scared treasures. The so-called Greek "heroes" were nothing more than thieves! There is an ironical twist of story. The good "dragon" trying to protect the sacred treasures is made into an evil fearsome animal, while the thieves become "good men"!

The more remarkable thing is that the type of evil "dragon" St George fought against is not the type of "dragon" the Greek had as guarding the sacred treasures:

> Our popular story of St George and the Dragon has numerous parallels in Western folklore. The stories of the laird who slew the "worme of Linton", of the knight who killed the Lambton worm, of the Chamion Conyers who

delivered Sockburn in Durham from a "worm, dragon or fiery flying serpent" ... (Dennys, 1968. p.110)

The "evil dragon" of St George is nothing more than a "large worm" – that is, a limbless snake!

■ "Lung" Different From "She" Serpent In The Four Major Angelic Beasts

It has been shown in Chapter 4 that the Chinese "Lung" and the other Heraldic Animals are the Middle East-Biblical four major cherubims or the angelic creatures of heaven (Figure 4.3):

Biblical Four Angelic Beasts

And before the throne ... were four beasts full of eyes before and behind. And the first beast was like a lion and the second beast like a calf, and the third beast had a face as a man and the fourth beast was like a flying eagle. And the four beasts had each of them six wings about him and they were full of eyes within and they rest not day and night saying Holy, holy, holy, Lord God Almighty which was, and is, and is to come (Revelation 4:6-8)

Now the cherubims stood on the right side of the house when the man went in and the cloud filled the inner court ... And when I looked behold the four wheels by the cherubims, one wheel by one cherub and another wheel by another cherub: and the appearance of the wheels was as the colour of a beryl stone ... And every one had four faces: the first face was the face of a cherub, and the second face was the face of a man, and the third the face of a lion and the fourth the face of an eagle ... And the cherubims ... stood at the door of the east gate of the Lord's house ... (Ezekial 10:3,9,14,19 – verse 9 indicates there were four cherubims)

Kabalic Four Kerubs of Tenth Key of Tarot (Levi, 1825-1875):

CHAPTER 18 CHINESE "LUNG" AT THE EAST

i.	Top, South	Woman headed Sphinx. Woman front, lion forebody and claws, eagle wings and ox backbody and tail. (Chinese parallel = phoenix)
ii.	Left, East	Kerub – Bull-Horned Bearded Man headed Sphinx. Bull-Horned Bearded Man front, backbody-tail of fish (Chinese parallel – "Lung")
iii.	Bottom, North	Typhon. The double serpents. (Chinese parallel = snake)
iv.	Right, West	Dog-headed Sphinx. Dog head, man's body. (Chinese parallel – tiger. Feng-Shui domestic equivalent of tiger is Dog)

The connection between the Chinese "Black Snake of the North" with the Jewish Kabalic "Typhon-double snakes" is quite clear.

However, the Chinese "Lung" is the Kabalic "Kerub" a bull-horned bearded man with limbed forefront and a fish backbody and tail. It is the bull-headed sphinx featured in Assyrian, Egyptian and Indian hieroglyphs (Levi. 1835. p.137) and also the angel placed to prevent Adam and Eve from reentering the Garden of Eden. The Bible indicates that this gate of the Garden was at the East – the Chinese "Lung" is at the East; different from the Serpent at the North.

In the Kabala system this "Kerub", a bearded horned fish-tailed being, is a different angelic creature from the limbless Typhon snakes. It is obvious that the Chinese "Lung" which is the bearded horned fish-tailed being,

268 THE CHINESE PAKUA

should not be associated with the "Biblical or Kabalic dragon-snake".

■ "Lung" As A Biblical Seraphim

Besides the above, the Holy Scriptures also refer to those unique creatures called "Seraphims":

> Above it stood the seraphims [8314]: each one has six wings; with twain he covered his face and with twain he covered his feet and with twain he did fly. And one cried unto another and said, Holy, holy, holy is the Lord of hosts; the whole earth is full of his glory ... (Isaiah 6:2-3)

> Then flew one of the seraphims [8314] unto me, having a live coal in his hand which he had taken with the tongs from the altar ... (Isaiah 6:6)

The "seraphims" are a special class of cherubims. While the "seraphims" may also embrace a range of angelic animals, note this Isaiah's "seraphim" has "hands" to enable it to handle a tong to collect the coal. Note too that the Isaiah's "seraphims" have some similarities (though may or may not be the same) as the four beasts of Revelation 4 in:

- having six wings
- having limbs
- praising God "Holy, holy holy" all the time.

The "seraphims" are said to be "an order of celestial beings ... act as the medium of communication between heaven and earth" (Peloubet, 1947. "seraphims"). The "seraphims" are therefore of the world of God's angelic beasts and they are a special class of cherubs or cherubims. The "seraphims" may denote holy angelic beasts of God.

The word "seraphim" is from the Hebrew "saraph" which is from another "saraph" (coded 8314) which is in turn is from another "saraph" (coded 8313 – primary root meaning being to "set on fire", to burn or kindle). Hence, "saraph" came to denote the fiery nature of a creature – the angelic seraphims of Isaiah 6:2-3,6 and also the fiery serpent [8314] of Numbers 21:8 which Moses placed on a pole to counter the bites of serpents [5175]:

> And the Lord sent fiery [8314] serpents [5175] among the people and they bit the people and much people died ... And the Lord said unto Moses, Make thee a fiery [8314] serpent [also 8314] and set it upon a pole and it shall come to pass that every one that is bitten when he looketh upon it he lived. And Moses made a serpent [5175] of brass and put it on a pole and it came to pass that if a serpent [5175] had bitten any man when he beheld the serpent [5175] of brass he lived ... (Numbers 21:6-9)

There appear some associations between the "nachash" serpent and the "saraph" seraphims. But this strange creature the Isaiah's "seraphim" is a fiery creature and possesses wings and "hands." It seems associated with a serpentine body form like the limbless serpent but is different in that the Isaiah's "seraphim" has wings and hands.

The Isaiah's seraphim is the sort of serpentine animal with wings and hands like the Chinese "Lung"!

The Chinese "Lung" is the holy "seraphim" of God mentioned in the Holy Scriptures! It is not the same as the "nachash" serpent which is the symbol of Satan. The "nachash" serpent of the Bible is an animal associated with evil – and the Chinese while associating its Chinese "Lung" with good auspicious things, do indeed associate similarly the snake with evil.

The "Biblical Dragon-Serpent" is one of the cherubims while the Chinese "Lung" is another different type of cherubims! While the "Biblical Dragon-Serpent" is a fallen angel (namely Satan), the Chinese "Lung" remains a faithful cherubim of God. The Bible call the "seraphim" holy of God – the Chinese do the same thing for its "Lung". All

270 THE CHINESE PAKUA

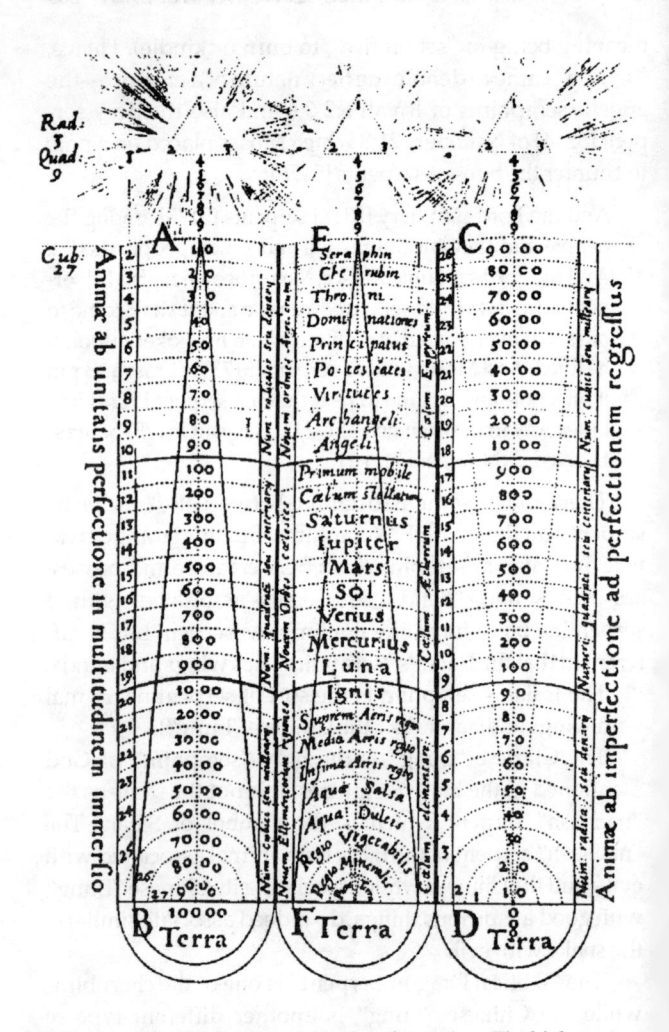

Figure 18.3 The Kabalic Hierarchy of Angels— The highest angels are the Seraphims, which the Bible described as a serpentine winged-limbed creature alike to the Chinese Dragon.

these times, the Chinese are correct to maintain their "Lung" as the symbol of the Godly. Repeat: The Chinese Lung is the Holy Seraphim of God!

Another thing is this: the Jewish Kabalic system regards "seraphims" as the highest of the angels (Figure 18.3) So, the Chinese "Lung" is among the highest angelic beings!

■ Association Of Dragons With Chinese Emperors

Why do the Chinese regard the "Lung" as the symbol of their emperors?

The Chinese Emperor is associated with a Nine Dragon motif. Needham (1959, p.253) notes the symbolism of the "Lung" and the moon as a portion of the Nine Dragons Screen wall in the Imperial Palace at Peking. Why nine? Why nine "Lung" alias 'dragon's and not ten or five, etc?

Nine is also the number of several auspicious things of ancient China. Is this number ever associated with the emperor? Yes – in the Nine Emperor Gods! The Nine Emperor Gods are believed to be the long-life nine human sovereigns who lived in antediluvian times and came after non-human rulers (Cheu, 1988; Hirth, 1908). These Nine Emperor Gods are really the nine patriarchs of the Bible from Adam to Lamech the father of Noah, all of whom were very long-life.

Nine Dragons are the symbol of the Nine Emperor Gods or Biblical patriarchs!

The "Lung" represents the Emperor who was the priest-king of ancient China. Of the humans closest to God during those times, the "Lung" denotes the highest human being – the priest-king! Hence, the Chinese Emperor appropriated the "Lung" as his Imperial symbol.

Remember again, this Chinese "Lung" is not the "nachash-draco" limbless serpent of Satan but the "saraph" winged-with-hands seraphim – 'dragon' of God.

The "nachash-draco" snake being is recognised as a wise animal:

> But I fear lest by any means as the serpent [3789] beguiled Eve through his subtility ... (2 Corinthians 11:3)

> Now the serpent [5175] was more subtil than any beast of the field which the Lord God had made (Genesis 3:1)

But the "seraphims" while obviously embodifying the same wisdom as the "nachash-draco" serpent also have another function:

> Above it stood the seraphims [8314]: each one has six wings; with twain he covered his face and with twain he covered his feet and with twain he did fly. And one cried unto another and said, Holy, holy, holy is the Lord of hosts; the whole earth is full of his glory ... (Isaiah 6:2-3)

> Then flew one of the seraphims [8314] unto me, having a live coal in his hand which he had taken with the tongs from the altar ... Lo, this hath touched thy lips and thine iniquity is taken away and thy sin purged (Isaiah 6:6-7)

"Seraphims" are creatures associated with the process of purging sins. The "seraphims" are priestlike creatures! "Seraphims" are associated with priest-functions!

That is, the "seraphim-Lung" symbol of the Chinese Emperor denotes his role as a priest-king who dealt and took away the sins of his people through the Imperial worship of Shang-Ti the Supreme God. When Huang-Ti is called the Yellow Emperor he is also associated with the central Yellow Dragon. Fu Hsi (the Biblical Adam) is called the Azure Dragon of the East. The Chinese Emperors were always the priest-kings of their nation.

"Lung" is the symbol of the Emperor as God's priest-king.

The Pakua is the symbol of the original monotheistic worship of Shang-Ti the One Supreme God. The Chinese Emperor is intimately linked to this sacred Shang-Ti worship as the priest-king of Shang-Ti. This is why both the Pakua and "Lung" are the very symbols of Chinese culture.

So, a misapplication of terminology has occurred. For, the Chinese "Lung" is not the "Biblical dragon-serpent" but the Biblical seraphim! The Chinese ancient culture did not mistakenly adopt the evil symbol of the Devil but rightly utilise the holy "Lung-seraphim" as an auspicious symbol. The ancient Chinese knew better.

⊙ PART D ⊙
A SYNTHESIS

This final section presents a synthesis, mainly devoted to explaining why the original sacred monotheistic worship of Shang-Ti the One Supreme God lapsed into a polytheistic religion where Shang-Ti becomes a forgotten God.

The deviation is reflected in the ancient Taoist Pakua Thunder Magic legend of the "Third World Human Emperor Huang-Ti Slaying of the Serpent" to release water for the people. This event, which is commemorated in the 5th Day of the 5th Moon Dragon Boat Festival, is more universally known as the Indian Ramayana, the Greek Clashes of the Titans, the Nordic Twilight of the Gods, the Middle East Battles of the Storm God ... and the Biblical Nimrod and Tower of Babel.

The section summarises the mystic features of the Pakua.

19 Pakua Link To Tower Of Babel
20 Pakua As Essence Of Ancient Chinese Culture

19

THE PAKUA LINK TO TOWER OF BABEL

■ Attempt To Destory Secrets Of God At Babel

The ancient Chinese testimony of the Pakua is that originally the religion of ancient nations was monothesitic involving the worship of only the One True God.

China kept to this monotheistic worship of the One True God, Shang-Ti the Supreme God, before the idolatrous deviation caused by political motivations during the Eastern Chou era around 550BC (Bilsky, 1975; Wu, 1982). Even then, the Chinese emperors clung to the worship of Shang-Ti at Tien-An-Mien until the fall of the Manchu dynasty. Emperor Yuan Shi-Kai, of the short-lived Yuan dynasty, was the last emperor to carry out the Imperial Shang-Ti worship.

The Chinese received their knowledge of the One True God while they, along with other nations like the Hebrew people, were in Mesopotamia before the period of 2000 to 1900BC They, along with other nations, were the descendants of Noah's family who survived the Flood of 2348BC.

But this worship was eventually corrupted. What happened?

An event which could account for this is the ancient Middle East-Biblical legend of Nimrod and his building of the Tower of Babel. So, it may be necessary to look at what Biblical scholars speculate about the Tower of Babel event.

Adam (first world Emperor Fu-Hsi alias "Azure Lung") wrote the secrets of God into the pictorial characters of the human language and the astrological configurations in the stars. Mankind would see the way of God testified in the drama of the pictorial language and stars.

Naturally, a simple way to obliterate the image of God from people's minds would be to destroy these pictorial representations of God's truths. This attempt is recorded in the ancient legend of the Tower of Babel.

■ Tower Of Babel Was A Perverted Astronomical Tower

According to Biblical traditions, something evil happened at the Tower of Babel and the people were scattered and their language and 'speech' confounded:

> Go to let us go down and there confound their language that they may not understand one another's speech (or purposes). So the Lord scattered them abroad from thence upon the face of all the earth; and they left to build the city. Therefore is the name of it called Babel, because the Lord did there confuse the language of all the earth; and from thence did the Lord scatter them abroad upon the face of all the earth (Genesis 11:7-9)

This scattering was misleadingly thought to occur during the time of the birth of Peleg ("Peleg" means "division"):

> And unto Eber were born two sons; the name of one was Peleg (a cleft or division) because in his days was the earth divided (niphl'gah – divided by cleavage) (Genesis 10:25)

The Flood occurred around 2348BC Peleg was borned around 2247BC and died 2008BC If the birth of Peleg was connected to the Tower of Babel incident, then the Tower of Babel occurred about 100 to 300 years after the Flood. But according to traditions (Hislop, 1916, quoting Eusebius) Nimrod who built Babel reigned during the time of Abraham. Abraham was born in 1996BC at least a few years

CHAPTER 19 PAKUA LINK TO TOWER OF BABEL

after the death of Peleg. Therefore, it is unlikely that the Peleg incident was the same time as the Tower of Babel.

The Peleg incident of world division is recorded in the Chinese legend of the "Five Emperors", where the third world Emperor Huang-Ti separated the nations. The Tower of Babel came soon later.

Tower Of Babel As An Astronomical Device

What was going on in Babel which aroused the "displeasure of God"? It has something to do with the city and particularly the tower:

"And the Lord came down to see the city and the tower which the children of men builded " (Genesis 11:5).

Adam (1937) says that there was something inherent very evil with the city and tower that led to God's displeasure. He says that Genesis 11:4 should have been translated:

And they said Go to, let us build us a city and a tower "and his top with the heavens" (not "whose top may reach the heavens") and let us make us a name lest we be scattered abroad upon the face of the whole earth

Adam (1937, p.67) notes that Josephus asserted that astronomy originated in the family of Seth; and he said that the children of Seth and especially Adam, Seth and Enoch, that their revelation as to the two coming judgements of Water and Fire might not be lost made two pillars (one of brick and the other of stone) describing the whole of the predictions of the stars upon them. Hence, he postulated that the Tower of Babel was built to contain certain predictions.

He quoted Lieutenant-General Chesney's discoveries among the ruins of Babylon: About five miles S.W. of Hillah, the most remarkable of all ruins, the Birs Nimroud of the Arabs, rises to a height of 153 feet above the plain from a base covering a square of 400 feet, or almost four acres. It was constructed of kiln-dried bricks in seven stages to correspond with the planets to which they were dedicated: the lowestmost black, the colour of Saturn; the next orange, for Jupiter; the third red for Mars; and so on. These stages were surmounted by a lofty tower, on the summit of which ... were the signs of the Zodiac and other astronomical figures; thus having (as it should have been translated) a representation of the heavens, instead of "a top which reached unto heavens." (p.68).

The Tower of Babel is a kind of astronomical tower with instruments and facilities to measure the stars of a zodiac or astrological system.

A Deviation From God's Purposes

What is so bad about this Tower?

The Biblical tradition is that there was a time when the whole race of mankind had only one language:

> And the whole world was of one language and of one speech (Genesis 11:1)

Adam (1937) asks: Why one language and one speech? The phrase "one speech" in the sentence seems unnecessary repetition. Marginal renderings in the King James Version give "lip" for "language" and "words" for "speech" which still do not clear up the apparent repetition. The Hebrew word for "one" is "chadim" which could be translated as "same."

He notes that the Hebrew word for "speech or words" which is "d'bharim" could be translated as: word, thing, matter, reason, business, message, purpose, request, etc. This word was translated differently as "purpose" in Nehemiah:

And Ezra the scribe stood on a pulpit of wood which they made for the purpose ... (Nehemiah 8:4 – "d'bharim" as 'purpose' not 'speech')

Hence, Genesis 11:1 could be re-translated as:

And the whole earth had the same language and the same purposes ("d'bharim" not as speech but 'purposes')

Originally, the world was one language and one "original purpose." But at Babel "a different purpose" arose which God wanted to confound:

Go to let us go down and there confound their language that they may not understand one another's purpose (not 'speech'). So the Lord scattered them abroad from thence upon the face of all the earth; and they left to build the city. Therefore is the name of it called Babel, because the Lord did there confuse the language of all the earth; and from thence did the Lord scatter them abroad upon the face of all the earth (Genesis 11:7-9)

Apparently, Nimrod had set to accomplish some serious deviations from the "original purpose of God." As the Tower of Babel was an astronomical tower, it appears this "original purpose" has to do with astrology. Nimrod was trying to change the astrological system. There was something evil in his purpose to change the astrological system. According to the Biblical legend, God also saw that this evil was so powerful He decided to frustrate Nimrod's plans.

The Biblical text indicates that the building of the city was stopped by scattering of the people! Christians got the impression that the Tower of Babel was left unfinished by the confusion of languages. But the Bible say it was the city that they did not complete – the Tower of Babel was completed.

The mixing up the language and the confounding of Nimrod 'purpose' came through the scattering of the people. It was not confusing the language first and then next scattering. But the other way round – scatter them first so that their language(s) would be mixed up. What were the people scattered by? By wars.

■ New Testament Testify Of Evil At Tower Of Babel

This legend of the Tower of Babel was known in the New Testament times and was described by the apostle Paul in his epistle Romans in the Bible. Adam (1937) that this Tower of Babel incident was meant and described in the very first chapter of the book of Romans:

> Because that which may be known of God is manifested in them; for God hath shewed it unto them. For the invisible things of him from the creation of the world are clearly seen, being understood by the things that are made, even his eternal power and Godhead; so that they are without excuse: Because that, when they knew God, they glorified him not as God, neither were thankful; but became vain in their imaginations and their foolish heart was darkened. Professing themselves to be wise they became fools, and changed the Glory of the uncorruptible God into an image made like to corruptible man and to birds and fourfooted beasts and creeping things ... Who changeth the truth of God into a lie and worshipped and served the creature more than the Creator ... and even as they did not like to retain God in their knowledge, God gave them over to a reprobate mind to do those things which are not convenient ... (Romans 1:18-32)

This passage reveals a number of things which happened at the Tower of Babel!:

1. First, there were things in ancient times whereby mankind could easily see the things of God. Things like the pictorial language of the Chinese (Kang and Nelson, 1988) and Sumerians-Egpytians which preserved the truths of God. Things like the ancient astrology in the stars (Seiss, 1972; Bullinger, 1964) which preserve the drama of God's plans and ways.
2. Second, people at that time worshipped only God.
3. Thirdly, the people did not want to be reminded of God's truths. They could only do so by destroying the meanings of the pictorial language and corrupting the meanings of astrology. These things they tried to do at the Tower of Babel.
4. Fourthly, around that evil time, man began to worship the created rather than the Creator. There was a deviation from the worship of the One True God and a corruption to worship of created beings.

■ Attack On God's Language Structure

According to Buttrick (1954, p.220, Volume 1) the oldest Semitic languages was the Akkadian cuneiform script which was syllabic and ideographic. It was later that a consonantal-alphabetic script appeared, called the Ugarite cuneiform from Ras Shamra on the Syrian seacoast. Others (like Peloubet, 1947) also attribute the invention of the alphabets to the Phoenicians.

Throughout this time until modern times the Chinese language has remained fundamentally ideographic with many added phonetic words based on the fundamental ideograms.

The Akkadian dynasty of Mesopotamia was a civilisation existing between 2334-2154 BC (Farmer et al, 1977) which was after the Great Flood. Pictorial languages were thus the original forms of language(s) just after the Great

Flood. In our discussions on the similarities between the 22-symbols of the Chinese Ganzhi system and the Hebrew Sfirot 22-alphabets (Chapter 3) there are evidence that an astrological set of symbols was used to form the alphabets.

As the alphabetic writings were invented soon after the Akkadian dynasty then its period of invention would fall into the era of Nimrod and the Tower of Babel. Through the invention of the alphabetic script, Nimrod would have attempted the irruption of the original writing forms.

But the Chinese had resisted this change and maintained the pictorial language preservation of the original God's truths.

■ Attack On God's Astrology Structure

Another clever trick is to treat astrology as an idolatrous pagan science, so as to prevent them from having any belief in an original astrology. Many Christian writers are aware that the ancient forms of astrology preserve God's truths (Seiss, 1972; Flemings, 1978; Bullinger, 1964). What had happened was an irruption of the ancient astrology.

We have noted earlier that in Babylon there had been excavated the Bars Nimroud, a tower whose top was marked with astrological signs, especially of the Zodiac:

> These stages were surmounted by a lofty tower, on the summit of which, we were told, were the signs of the Zodiac and other astronomical figures; thus having (as it should have been translated) a representation of the heavens, instead of "a top which reached unto heavens." (Adam, 1937. p.68)

As the legend states that God went down to see the city and tower and hated them, the Tower of Babel must have misrepresented the truths of the Zodiac signs and other aspects of the ancient astrology! The revelations of God in the stars were falsified. The Tower of Babel was a great abomination to God! This Tower of Babel was connected to the birth of idolatrous worship:

> Professing themselves to be wise they became fools, and changed the glory of the uncorruptible God into an image made like to corruptible man and to birds and fourfooted beasts and creeping things ... Who Changeth the truth of God into a lie and worshipped and served the creature more than the Creator ... and even as they did not like to retain God in their knowledge, God gave them over to a reprobate mind to do those things which are not convenient ... (Romans 1:18-32)

The Nimrod change of the astrological system is not without evidence. Needham (1959) provided evidence that there was a Old Babylonian astrological system going back as far as 3000BC based on the circumpolar stars like the Chinese and Hebrew astrology. But a New Babylonian astrology arose which was based on the elliptical stars and which form the basis of modern Western astrology. It is very likely that the New Babylonian astrology was the invention of Nimrod's people and a corruption of the original Divinely-inspired astrology.

The damages to the ancient astrological secrets were worse than the language changes, for, hardly any current astrological system remained faithful to the ancient forms.

■ Tower Of Babel Alias The Dragon Boat Festival Was A Major Ancient Middle East War

Many nations, including ancient China, remembered the famous Middle East-Biblical legend of the Tower of Babel ... as a time of great wars. These wars of the Tower of Babel are the Ramayana of the Hindus; the Titans clashes with the Gods of the Greek; the Twilight of the Gods of the Teutonic Europeans; the battles of the Storm God against the Dragon-Serpent in the Middle East.

THE CHINESE PAKUA

There is a theory of Nephilism that before the Flood the angels tried to have sexual relationships with men to have hybrid progenies (Genesis 6:1-4 – qv Bullinger, 1964; Adam, 1937). According to these Christian writers (Bullinger, 1964; Adam, 1937) Nephilism reared up again during Nimrod's times, giving further reasons for God to act against Babel.

The Tower of Babel incident came shortly after the Peleg division of the world. In Chinese traditions, the Peleg division is the period marked by the legend of the "Five Emperors" where third world Emperor Huang-Ti separated the races to the Four Cardinal Directions of the Pakua.

Soon after, is the legend of Emperor Huang-Ti's wars against Chih You, the leader of the giants. Chih You, who was bare-chested and wore a two-horns headdress, defeated Huang-Ti a number of times until Huang-Ti was assisted by a young hero and the "Dark Lady." Huang-Ti had to call in forces from all over the world to defeat and capture Chih You, who then was executed. Huang-Ti's wars against Chih You are actually the wars of the Tower of Babel.

In the Middle East nations, these wars were the Hittite "Storm God" Teshub (also "provider of rains") fights against Kumarbi and his offspring Ullikummi. This legend tells how Teshub fought to overcome the "illuyanka" Serpent in order to secure the much-needed rain for the land (Kramer, 1961. pp.158-175). Teshub was at first defeated by the Dragon-Serpent but was assisted by the Goddess Inara and a mortal man who became Inara's love. Inara is the Assyrian Isara a whirlpool serpent goddess and beloved of Tammuz (MacKenzie, 1926. pp.73-74). Kramer (1961, p.139) identifies Inara as the daughter of the "Storm God." Note well:

- This Hittite story of the Storm God's battles against the Serpent is very much the same story as Huang-Ti's battles against Chih You.
- The Hittite Storm God's defeat of the Dragon-Serpent to secure water for the land is also the same legend of the Chinese Dragon Boat Festival to secure rains for the land. What happened at the Tower of Babel is remembered by the Chinese in the legend of the Dragon Boat Festival of the 5th Day of the 5th Moon. This date, the summer solstice, is traditionally the most evil and dangerous of the days.

The killing of the Serpent by the Hittite Storm God is the actual basis of the use of the Pakua "Thunder Magic" by the "Human Sovereign" "Lao Chun" against the Six Demons:

> This ancient battle has to do with a battle against forces represent by the Serpent as a legend said: "All Thunder Magic sects attribute the founding of the method to Hsu Hsun, a legendary Taoist said to have died in A.D. ... his name appears in the dynastic histories, but the legend about Thunder Magic and the slaying of a great serpent do not occur in Taoist writings until the mid-Sung about 1100" (Saso, 1978. p.235)

"Human Sovereign" "Lao Chun" slaying the "great serpent" is the Human Sovereign Huang-Ti, third world Emperor alias "Golden Lung," and is thus the Hittite Storm God slaying the ancient Serpent. The westerners remember this as the legend of St. George killing the "large worm-dragon."

The ancient Middle East reeled with a series of mighty wars related with the need to secure water or rains. There seem to be a Middle East food crisis which must be linked to shortages of water for crops. The ancient nations went to wars against each other to secure their food supplies, including water supplies for food crops. The Tower of Babel with their astronomical and measuring equipments was likely a device to predict the climate and manipulate the water supplies. But not everyone agreed with the Tower of Babel and the outcome was the series of wars.

"Golden Lung" Huang-Ti was forced to act to kill the "Serpent" Nimrod to release water for the people and bring peace to the world.

The legend of the Tower of Babel is the basis of the Taoist powerful Pakua Thunder Magic and the real significance of the 5th Day of the 5th Moon when the 5-Poisons version of the Pakua is used against evil. The legend of the Tower of Babel is also the source of the Dragon Boat Festival on the same 5th Day of the 5th Moon, when "Golden Lung" Huang-Ti slew the Dragon-Serpent to release the water.

As the Tower of Babel is the time of starting of the deviation from the monotheistic worship of God, the 5th Day of the 5th moon is traditionally the most evil day of the year.

20

PAKUA AS ESSENCE OF ANCIENT CHINESE CULTURE

And further, by these, my son, be admonished: of making many books there is no end; and much study is weariness of the flesh. Let us hear the conclusion of the whole matter: Fear God and keep his commandment; for this is the whole duty of man (Ecclesiastes 12:12-13)

■ Pakua, The Device Of Time And Direction

The Pakua stands out as the permeating symbol of ancient China. Through the ages, the Pakua has been a fascinating challenge to thinkers trying to unravel its secrets.

First of all, the Pakua, as part of the Ganzhi system, is primarily a device to record the cyclic interactions of time and direction. Most of its prominent manifold auspiciousness and mysticism in the ancient Chinese culture derive from this overall principle. Through the same principle, the Pakua is also intimately involved with the development and origin, not only of the ancient Chinese history, but also of the Chinese writings and religion.

From shrewd observations through centuries, the original creators of the Pakua have formed the Ganzhi system to divide time and direction into cyclic categories and to characterise the environmental features of the categories, viz:

1. The Pakua and Ganzhi system actually itemises the major characteristics of each period of time in the 60-years sexagenary cycle of the Ganzhi. Hence, the ancient Chinese

could know 60 years in advance the likely cyclic changes in the environment.

The principle is not unlike the western "four seasons." Or, as western climatologists speculate, cyclic weather changes could be detected which are linked to the Herman sunspot cycle of 11.5 years, which is close to the Jupiter 12 years which form the Twelve Terrestrial Branches of the Ganzhi system.

2. The Ganzhi system also characterises major features of the directions. For example, the North is associated with winter cold and cold winds. The South is the place from where the sun and warmth shines in. Typhoons come from the East and are associated with "Lung" of the East Direction.

This ability of the Ganzhi system to track the environmental characteristics of each period of the 60-years cycle is the basis of Chinese astrology, which should not be seen as a superstitious art but a scientific device to categorise the cyclic behaviour of time. The Ganzhi system treats both time and direction as inseparable and this is the basis of the Tong-Shu and the mystic Feng-Shui and its device the Lo-Pan.

■ Major Historical Epochs Symbolised By The Pakua

However, the ancient Chinese do not stop with using the Pakua to track the passage of time and its cyclic categorial characteristics. Being a device of time, the Pakua is also a device to record major historical events!

Many Pakua variants are actually memorials of major events in the history of ancient China.

It is for this reason that many Chinese ideograms incorporate the Pakua Gammadion character because these ideograms are meant to preserve certain historical episodes. Hence, the layers of significance of the Pakua contain several memories of the ancient Chinese past. This record goes back to the primordial origins of mankind and then covers major epochs in the ancient Chinese civilisation.

Like other ancient civilisations, the early historical and documentary records of Chinese civilisation were closely associated with religious cultural practices. Although ancient Chinese historical chronology went back, as claimed, to 2943BC, archaeological evidence indicates Chinese civilisation started in China with the Shang dynasty in 1400BC Many aspects of Chinese records for the periods before 1400BC occurred outside China.

1. The Gammadion Four Directions design of the Pakua is a symbol of the legend of the origin of Man from Garden of Eden with its four rivers. The Four Heraldic Animals arrangement of the Pakua is also a testimony that the original ancient religion concerns the worship of only Shang-Ti the Supreme God who is surrounded by His four major angels.

2. The Nine Emperors Gods Pakua is the memorial of the time of the nine antediluvian (pre-Flood) kings.

3. The eight-members family of the Pakua together with the changes from the Early Heaven to Later Heaven Array are a memorial of the legend of the Flood.

4. Then, the Pakua, through the "Five Emperors" symbol, is a Chinese device to mark the close of an era when the major races were still in the Middle East. The "Five Emperors" era came to an end due to dwindling food supplies in the Middle East. Emperor Huang-Ti, through his understanding and wisdom, sent out the races to the Four Directions, to richer "pastures", in order to save the common people.

292 THE CHINESE PAKUA

The Chinese were sent East. As the East is the symbolic position of that "Lung" Emperor Fu-Hsi alias Adam, the Chinese race have called themselves the descendents of "Lung." The Pakua, through its identification of "Lung" at the East, is also an historical evidence that Adam went to China.

5. 5-Poisons Pakua. The use of the Pakua on the 5th day of the 5th Moon (the Dragon Boat Festival) is an ancient memory of the Middle East legend of the Tower of Babel. The legend depicts a series of wars fought to destroy Nimrod the Serpent and release water for the land.

■ Major Pakua Culture Links Between China And Middle East

The analysis and discussions on the Pakua reveal several striking similarities and close kinship between the ancient Chinese and Middle East cultures, including the Hebrew-Biblical worship of the One True God. Both the ancient Chinese and Middle East religious cultures come from common source(s).

The evidence gives an overwhelming sense of the universalism of the Pakua symbolism.

The Pakua is a testimony that the Chinese sages and ancient historians are not naive and childlike minds prone to personification, euhemerisation and even fabrication of ancient history. The Pakua shows that many so-called legendary events and figures are of the Middle East. These Chinese are rather truthful in their historical recordings, even though these may risk being mistakened as "legendary".

It is very clear that the Gammadion-Pakua principles diffused from common sources in the Middle East to reach ancient China around 1400BC The Gammadion-Pakua

CHAPTER 20 AS ESSENCE OF CHINESE CULTURE 293

principles were brought into ancient China by the ancient Chinese migrating from the ancient Middle East.

Our analysis here is by no means exhaustive and other striking similarities may be found through further research. Some pertinent points are:

1. Shang (1400-1122BC) archaeological relics and early Western Chou (1122-771BC) documents show that the only deity worshipped was Shang-Ti, the Supreme God (or Tien, Heaven).

   There were ancestral worship at these early times. The Li Chi, Book of Rites, compiled by Confucius and the indictment of Emperor Kang-Hsi (1662-1722) indicate these are essentially ancestral memorials than worships in the common sense. The sages in those times knew that these ancestors were no longer living – the concept that ancestral spirits lived after death came later.

   The ancient primordial worship of Shang-Ti the Supreme God, surrounded by his four major angels, is a primordial significance of the Pakua arrangement of the Four Heraldic Animals. As this Gammadion symbol is also universal in many other ancient cultures, this worship of the One True God must also be the original style of worship of the human races.

2. It was during and after the Eastern Chou period (771-256BC) that other deities were established to be worshipped. These deities were in all cases former human beings with legendary exploits. These human beings were often linked to ruling houses, a number of them being venerated in earlier ancestral memorial worships. Their rises from ancestral memorials to deities were politically motivated.

   A major state involved in the deviation from the original true worship of the One True God Shang-Ti was the Chin state. The Chin Emperor Shih Huang-Ti attempted to close criticism of his actions by massacring the Confucian philosophers who knew his religious practices were idolatrous. The wayward emperor also ordered the Great Burning of Books which destroyed irrevocably many ancient records which would have told the true story.

3. The Chinese pictorial language contains amazing descriptions of Middle East-Biblical legends of Creation and the Great Flood periods and the Tower of Babel.

   A number of Chinese characters indicate that the Chinese knew they came from the West. For example, the Chinese word for "migration" contains the character for "west" indicating the ancient Chinese knew they came from the West (hence indicate their Mesopotamian origin).

4. The Magic Square symbol of the Chinese Pakua or Eight Diagrams has startling similarities to the Hebrew Kabalic talisman of the Sigil Of Saturn. The symbol of the Chinese Nine Emperor Gods is also similar to the Hebrew Sigil Of Saturn.

   The Chinese Ganzhi system of twenty-two symbols, intimately linked within the Eight-Diagrams-Pakua, is really the precursor of the twenty-two Hebrew Sfirot alphabets and the earliest alphabetic script.

   The twenty-two symbols of the Ganzhi could be the source from which alphabetic languages originated.

5. The astrological lores of both Chinese and Hebrew are circumpolar, which is basically different from the elliptical astrology of the Western world. In both Chinese and Hebrew systems prominence was given to essential the same groups of stars viz the Dipper or Great Bear (Ursa Major), Orion and the Pleiades.

   Both Chinese and Hebrew astrological lores also placed the northern heavens as the location of God's throne and have similar four animals of the four cardinal points.

   There are historical evidence that the Chinese-Hebrew circumpolar astrological system originated from the Old

Babylonian system. The Old Babylonian system was apparently corrupted by the New Babylonian system which is the basis of Western astrology today.

6. The Chinese remembered the Biblical Adam as the world first emperor Fu-Hsi. Fu-Hsi and his younger sister Nu-Kua who was also his wife were the first two human beings in the world – obviously the same as the Biblical first two human beings Adam and Eve! Emperor Fu-Hsi was credited with inventions of several fundamental social practices including marriage, hunting-fishing, cooking, cloth making and writing as well as the study of animals, the last being reflective of Adam's role in naming animals.

    Noah was remembered as the second world emperor Shen-Nung by the Chinese. The Chinese preserved legends that around this time of Shen-Nung there were drastic changes in climate and earth conditions after the Flood.

7. The Chinese also remembered the Biblical first nine patriarchs from Adam to Lamech as the Nine Emperor Gods, who according to Chinese traditions were the Nine Human Sovereigns in antediluvian times. (Noah was the tenth patriarch).

    These Nine Emperor Gods were actually priest-kings alike to the Biblical Melchisedec. The priest-king was the actual role played by each Chinese emperor in the customary Imperial worship of Shang-Ti in the temple of Tien-An-Mien.

    The Chinese also remembered the Biblical Eve as Nu-Kua, the sister of Emperor Fu-Hsi. Nu-Kua was also known as the Chinese Tou Mu (Mother Goddess) and Hsi Wang Mu (Western Queen Mother) the so-called "mother" of the Nine Emperor Gods.

8. The Chinese "Lung" is not the limbless "Biblical serpent-dragon" but the limbed-winged holy seraphim of God!

In fact, "Golden Lung" is the very enemy of the Serpent. The Dragon Boat Festival is actually a memory of "Golden Lung's" feat in destroying the Serpent who tried to withold the rains for the land.

9. The "Five Emperors" arrangement of the Pakua marks the end of an era when the Chinese were still mixing with all other races in the Middle East. Dwindling food supplies, aggravated by adverse climatic conditions, in the Middle East were causing hardships and there were wars.

Emperor Huang-Ti, the third world Emperor, acted to save the people. He put an end to the wars. To resolve the primary cause of the ancient battles sent the races to the Four Directions in order to allow the people to tap other "richer pastures."

The ancient Chinese culture, locking the secrets within the Pakua-Eight Diagrams system, was full of remembrance of famous Middle East-Biblical legends, events and figures of the times of Creation, Great Flood and the Tower of Babel. It is not strange for the Chinese to remember the ancient Biblical figures, who, after all, were ancestors of the Chinese people.

The many striking similarities between ancient Chinese and Middle East cultures all point to diffusion of culture symbols from common source(s).

These evidence support theories that the Chinese people migrated from Akkadia in Mesopotamia through Khotan in Central Asia into China (Werner, 1922) and that the Chinese language was originally from Mesopotamia (Creel, 1938). The Chinese must have left Mesopotamia and arrived into China between around 1950 to 1400BC

Chinese Preserved Worship Of The One True God

Finally, the Pakua has its esoteric magical aspects such as the Pakua Thunder Magic, talismans and the divinatory use of the I Ching. This Pakua magic is the most difficult to explain to the materialistic mind. Suffice to say here – in the last analysis, as meant by the original creators, the Pakua is a device to reach into the spiritual or supernatural realms.

There are yet not fully understood links between the ability of the Pakua to record time and direction and its legendary mystic powers to manipulate time and direction. But because there are such links, the Pakua-Eight Diagrams have become so much the symbol of the ancient Chinese culture.

The esoteric spiritual secret of the Pakua could be linked to its testimony of the ancient Chinese preservation of the worship of Shang-Ti the One True God! The ancient Chinese, like the ancient Hebrews, had a monotheistic religion worshipping Shang-Ti the Supreme God until political events around 500BC introduced deviant polytheism and corruptions of original ancestor memorials into ancestor worships.

The Middle East legends indicate that mankind went through a great dispersion of races from the time of the Tower of Babel under the Nimrod (ca 1990BC). From during the Nimrod-Tower of Babel incident the original Chinese leaders, like Abraham, took their people away from idolatrous Mesopotamia. The Chinese leaders were able to preserve many original truths of God in the Chinese pictorial language, astrology, the Imperial Shang-Ti worship, and the Pakua.

Deviations from the Shang-Ti worship began in the eastern Chou era (771 to 256BC). The great Chinese sages like Confucius and Lao-tzu were aware of the deviations from the worship of the One True God and tried to encourage the Chinese people to keep to this ancient monotheistic worship of the One True God. It is not coincidence that the teachings of Confucius and Lao-Tzu are very similar to Biblical truths. During the rising deviations from the Shang-Ti worship in the Eastern Chou era (771-256BC) there were protests against the worship of human beings and other spirits as deities besides Shang-Ti.

The Chin Emperor Shih Huang-Ti (ca 220BC), a type of Nimrod, had reacted against the Confucian protests by massacring the Confucian scholars and burning their books. Fortunately, enough documents survive to preserve enough of the truths for us to piece together the original true Chinese worship of the One True God.

The Gammadion-Pakua, so universal in many other ancient cultures, symbolises this worship of the One True God which is also the original style of worship of the human races.

The most important message of the Pakua is that all people should return to this ancient sole worship of Shang-Ti, the One True God. The worship of the other deities should be abandoned and remembered as they originally were meant to be – memorials to great human figures of the past.

REFERENCES

Adam, Ben 1937. Astrology – the Ancient Conspiracy. Dimension Books. Minneapolis, Minnesota.

Bilsky, Lewster James 1975. The Ancient State Religion of Ancient China I. Asian Folklore and Social Life Monograph. Lou Tsu-k'uang, Editor. Volume 70. The Orient Cultural Service. 422 Fulin Road, Shihlin, Taipei, Taiwan, China.

Bullinger Publication Trust 1964. The Companion Bible. Zondervan Bible Publishers. Grand Rapids, Michigan

Bullinger, E.W. 1967. Number in Scripture. Kregel Publications, Grand Rapids, Michigan.

Burkhardt, V.R. 1982 Chinese Creeds and Customs. A SCMP Publication. Hongkong.

Buttrick, George Arthur Commentary Editor. 1954. The Interpreter's Bible. A Commentary in Twelve Volumes. Abingdon Press. Nashville, New York.

Chang, K.C. 1983 Art, Myth and Ritual, the path to political authority in ancient China. Harvard University Press. Cambridge, Massachusetts and London.

Cheu Hock Tong 1988. The Nine Emperor Gods, A study of Chinese Spirit-Medium cults. Times Book International. Singapore, Kuala Lumpur

Chiang Ker Chiu undated. A Practical English-Mandarin Dictionary. Chin Fen Book Store. Singapore.

Creel, Herrlee Glessner 1938. Studies in Early Chinese Culture. The American Council of Learned Societies. Wakefield, Massachusetts.

Creel, Herrlee Glessner 1958. The Birth of China, A Study of the Formative Period of Chinese Civilisation. Peter Owen Limited. London.

Denny, Nicholas, B. 1968. The Folklore of China and its affinity with the Aryan and Semitic races. Oriental Press. Amsterdam.

Earle, Ralph 1967. Adam Clarke's Commentary on the Bible. Baker Book House, Grand Rapids, Michigan.

Eberhard, Wolfram 1972. Chinese Festivals. Asian Folklore and Social Life Monograph. Lou Tsu-k'uang, Editor. Volume 38. The Orient Cultural Service. 422 Fulin Road, Shihlin, Taipei, Taiwan, China.

Farmer, Edward L., Hambly, Gavin R.G., Kopf, David, Marshall, Bryon K and Taylor, Romeyn 1977. Comparative History of Civilisations in Asia. Addison-Wesley Publishing Company. Reading, Massachusetts, Menlo Park, California, London, Amsterdam, Don Mills, Ontario, Sydney

Fleming, Kenneth C. 1981. God's Voice in the Stars. Loizeaux Brothers, Neptune, New Jersey.

de Francis, John 1984. The Chinese Language, Facts and Fantasy. University of Hawaii Press. Honolulu.

Goh, Kgir Hee, Soo, Kong Sing and Yim, Tuck Fatt 1983. Ren Yi Dao De, The Greatest Love Story. Persatuan Good Samaritan. Kuala Lumpur, Malaysia.

Goddard, D. 1938. Tao-Teh-King. In "A Buddhist Bible." p. 407-436. E.P. Dutton and Company. Inc. New York.

Gorn, Walter 1904. The Shu King or the Chinese Historical Classic. The Theosophical Publishing Society, London and Benares, John Lane, New York.

Green, Jay P. 1976. The Interlinear Bible, Hebrew-Greek-English. Baker Book House, Grand Rapids, Michigan.

Hirth, Friedrich 1908. The Ancient History of China to the end of the Chou Dynasty. The Columbia University Press, New York.

Hislop, Rev Alexander 1916. The Two Babylons or The Papal Worship. Loizeaux Brothers. Neptune, New Jersey.

Ho, Ping-Ti 1975 The Cradle of the East. The University of Chicago Press, Chicago.

Hook, Dianna Farington 1975. The I Ching and Mankind. Routledge & Kegan Paul. London and Boston.

Hsu, Chin-Hsiung and Ward, Alfred H.C. 1984. Ancient Chinese Society. An Epigraphic and Archaeological Interpretation. Yee Wen Publishing Company, Inc. South San Francisco, California 94080, USA.

Jettmar, Karl 1983. The Origins of Chinese Civilisation: Soviet Views. In "The Origins of Chinese Civilisation." Keightley (1983) p. 217-236

Joel, C. Dobin, Rabbi 1977. The Astrological Secrets of the Hebrew Sages. Inner Traditions International, Ltd. New York.

Kang, C.H. and Nelson, Ethel S. 1979. The Discovery of Genesis. Concordia Publishing House, St Louis, Montana

Keightley, David N. (editor) 1983. The Origins of Chinese Civilisation. University of California Press, Berkeley and Los Angeles, California. A Berkeley Conference on Studies on China 1.

Keller, Werner 1956. The Bible as History – Archaeology confirms the Book of Books. Hodder and Stoughton. London.

de Kermadec, Jean-Michel Huon 1983. The Way to Chinese Astrology, the Four Pillars of Destiny. Unwin Paperbacks, London. translated by N. Derek Poulsen

King, Francis 1975. MAGIC The Western Tradition. Thames and Hudson. London.

KJV, King James Version. The Holy Bible Collins' Clear-Type Press. Glaslow, Toronto, Sydney and Auckland

Kramer, Samuel Noah 1961. Mythologies of the Ancient World. Anchor Books. Doubleday and Company, Inc. Garden City, New York.

Kung, Hans and Ching, Julia 1928. Christianity and Chinese Religions. Doubleday. New York, London, Toronto, Sydney, Auckland.

Lagerway, John 1967. Taoist Ritual in Chinese Society and History. MacMillian Publishing Company. New York.

Lai Kuan Fook 1984. The Hennessy Book of Chinese Festivals. Heinemann Educational Books (Asia) Ltd. Petaling Jaya, Malaysia.

Lau, D.C. 1979. The Analects of Confucius. Penguin Books Ltd. Middlesex, England.

Lee Siow-Mong 1986. Spectrum of Chinese Culture. Pelanduk Publications. Petaling Jaya, Malaysia.

Legge, James 1967. Li Chi, Book of Rites. University Books, New York Park, New York.

Levi, Eliphas 1825. The Key of the Mysteries. Translated from French by Aleister Crowley, 1959. Rider, London, Melbourne, Auckland and Johannesburg.

Li, Ung Bing 1914. Outlines of Chinese History. The Commercial Press Ltd. Shanghai, China.

Low, C.C. and associates (editors and translators) 1989. Canonisation of Deities. Canfonian Pte Ltd. Singapore.

MacKenzie, Donald A. 1926. The Migration of Symbols and their Relations to Beliefs and Customs. AMS Press. New York.

Martin, E. 1977a. The Modern Jewish Calendar. Exposition 137. Foundation for Biblical Research, Pasedena, California.

Martin, E. 1977b. The Religion of Angels. Commentator Vol.4, No.4. Foundation for Biblical Research, Pasedena, California.

Maspero, Henry 1945. Taoism and Chinese Religion. Translated by Frank A Kierman Jr. 1981. The University of Massachusetts Press. Amherst.

Needham, Joseph 1959. Astronomy. In Volume 3 of Science and Civilisation in China. At the University Press, Cambridge. Britain.

Peloubet, Rev F. N. 1947. Peloubet Bible Dictionary. The John C. Winston Company. Great Britain.

Plopper, Clifford H. 1935. Chinese Religion seen through the Proverbs. Shanghai Modern Publishing House, Shanghai, China.

Ponder, Catherine 1967. The Healing Secret of the Ages. Parker Publishing Company, Inc. West Nyack, New York.

Ronan, Conan A. 1978 The Shorter Science and Civilisation in China. An Abridgement of Joseph Needham's Original Text. Volume 1 (Volumes I and II of the Major Series. Cambridge University Press. Cambridge. London, New York, New Rochelle, Melbourne, Sydney.

Rule, Paul, A. 1986. Kung-tzu or Confucius? The Jesuit Interpretation of Confucianism. Allen & Unwin, Australia.

Saso, Michael 1978. The Teaching of Taoist Master Chuang. Yale University Press, New Haven and London.

Sauries, Jean-Claude and Stephen, Charles. 1979. The Illustrated Horse. Harmony Book. New York.

Seiss, Jospeh A. 1972. The Gospel in the Stars. Kregel Publications, Grand Rapids, Michigan

Shumaker, Wayne 1972. The Occult Sciences in the Rennaissance. A Study in Intellectual Patterns. University of California Press, Berkeley, Los Angeles, London.

Sharf, A. 1976. The Universe of Shabbetai Donnolo. Aris and Philips Ltd. Warminster. England.

Skinner, Stephen 1982. The Living Earth Manual of Feng-Shui. Graham Brash (Pte) Ltd. Singapore

Strong, James 1890. Strong's Exhaustative Concordance of the Bible. Abingdon Press. Nashville, New York.

Vaccari, O. and E.E. Vaccari 1950. Pictorial Chinese-Japanese Characters. A New and Fascinating Method to learn Ideograms. Vaccari's Language Institute, Tokyo.

Walls, Jan and Walls, Yvonne 1984. Myths of Ancient China. Asiapac Books & Educational Aids (S) Pte Ltd. Singapore.

Walters, Derek 1983. The Alternate I Ching. The Aquarian Press. Wellingbrorough, Northamptonshire.

Wang, Shiow-Nan 1981. The Genealogy of Wang's Clan. Singapore Hokkien Ong Clansmen General Association. 32 Chin Chew Road, Singapore.

Waterbury, F. 1952. Bird Deities in China. Artibus Asiae Publishers. Ascona, Switzerland.

Weiger, L.S.J. 1950. Chinese Characters. Their Origin, Etymology, History, Classification and Significance, A Torough Study from Chinese Documents. Dover Publications Inc., New York.

Werner, E.T.C. 1922. Myths and Legends of China. George G. Harrap & Co. Ltd. London Toronto, Wellington Sydney. 1958 edition.

Whittick, Arnold 1960. Symbols, signs and their meanings. Leonard Hill Books Ltd. Nine Eden Street, N.W.1, London.

Wilhelm, Richard 1951. The I Ching or Book of Changes. rendered into English by Cary F. Baynes. 1980. Routledge & Kegan Paul. London and Henley.

Williams, C.A.S. 1931. Outlines of Chinese Symbolism. Customs College Press, Peiping, China.

Wing, R.L. 1982. The Illustrated I Ching. Doubleday Dolphin Book, San Francisco

Wu, Kuo Cheng 1982. The Chinese Heritage. Crown Publishers, Inc. New York.

Xing, Qi 1988. Folk Customs at Traditional Chinese Festivities. Foreign Language Press. Beijing.

Other books on Chinese Studies by Pelanduk Publications:–

- *Ancient Chinese I-Ching*
- *Chinese Dragon Tales and Legends*
- *Chinese Names*
- *Chinese Gods*
- *Chinese Hand Analysis*
- *Chinese Temples in Malaysia*
- *Spectrum of Chinese Culture*
- *The Origins of the Chinese People*
- *The Chinese Art of Studying the Head, Face & Hands*
- *The Baba of Melaka*
- *Wit and Humour from Old China*
- *Chinese Food for Longevity*
- *Chinese System of Food Cures*
- *The Chinese Art of Exercise to a Healthy and Long Life*
- *The Chinese System of Self-Healing*
- *The Portable Palmistry Workshop*
- *The Nyonyas*

FACE FORTUNES
The Ancient Chinese Art of Feature Reading

The Step-by-Step Illustrated Guide to Mastering your Mysterious Hidden Powers ....

Peter Shen and Joyce Wilson

Do you have a nose for money? Cheekbones for power? Can you spot your ideal husband? The perfect wife?

These are just a few of the questions face reading can answer. Now you can discover what special aptitudes, personality traits, and potential successes are hidden in your features and facial markings – and those of your friends. With step-by-step instructions and clear, practical diagrams, this fascinating guide provides all the information you need to master face and feature reading – and unlock the secrets of this ancient and mysterious art.

Assess the compatibility of a potential lover, co-worker or friend.

Pinpoint your potential for success in business and personal relationships.

Interpret what others are saying through their face and features.

Learn to immediately recognise the major features that reflect wealth, success, vitality and longevity.

LEGENDARY CHINESE HEALING HERBS

Henry C. Lu

Here is a classic collection of ancient herbal healing techniques that are as stimulating to the mind as they are healing to the body.

You'll find out how to use the medicinal properties of:
- the red-crowned crane's herb that arrests bleeding
- the thorny ginseng that strengthens bones and tendons
- the sweet apricot that relieves asthma
- the gray rhizome that sharpens vision –

plus 100 of the other fascinating herbs that are now available at health food stores and other shops.

Also included: the scientific and familiar names for each herb (with clear, closeup drawings) and the ailments they cure, as well as symptoms, treatments, and dosages.

For centuries, the Chinese have handed down traditions about the healing properties of herbs - intriguing stories of how they were discovered and of amazing cures. The stories, which were considered as important as the treatments in bringing recovery to the sick, are also featured here. These venerable tales are wonderfully entertaining - and beneficial to your health as well.